The
100% Return
Options Trading
Strategy

JON SCHILLER

Published by
Windsor Books
P.O. Box 280
Brightwaters, NY 11718

Printed in the United States

ISBN 0-930233-67-0

TABLE OF CONTENTS

FIGURES

CHAPTER 1

INTRODUCTION TO OPTION TRADING

The New York and London markets are dominated by big traders who cause big swings up and down in a short period of time during the trading day. The small trader with a modest amount of capital who is trying to build his wealth in the markets manipulated by the big traders such as mutual fund managers must use strategies that can profit in spite of the volatility those traders cause. Or, even better, profit by using that volatility. This book explains ways to use options for wealth building. A small trader can realize 100% return per year by using these methods. Two basic strategies are explained that are used during very different time periods:

1. Use of index option Covered Short Spreads (strangles) and naked Short Spreads for capital growth during an option month (4 or 5 weeks).

2. Use of my index option Delta Strategy for intraday trading in which an option position is open for only an hour or two before profiting from riding the volatility.

With these strategies you should be able to realize better capital appreciation rates than the best of the mutual fund managers who have trouble doing as well as the annual increase in the S&P 500 stock index. A capital return of 100% is a reasonable and attainable objective.

I use EXCEL workbooks to do option trading. These workbooks are described in enough detail in this book that if you are knowledgeable in the use of EXCEL, you should be able to create your own option trading workbooks.

THE BEST OPTION MARKETS TO TRADE

The two best option markets are the S&P 100 Index Options (code: OEX) traded on the Chicago Board Options Exchange (CBOE) and the FTSE-100 Index Options (American Style, code: SEI) traded on the London International Financial Futures and Options Exchange (LIFFE). These are the best two index options to trade because both the OEX and SEI have high volume and high open interest which means high liquidity. High liquidity is important because when you want to close out a position you will get a fair price if the market is liquid. If the market is not liquid, you will have a hard time finding a buyer for your position and, therefore, you might not be able to get a good price for closing a position. This extra cost of an ill-liquid market can eat into your profits or even cause a loss for a trade that should have been a profit.

Special note: In order for a US citizen to trade on the LIFFE, he or she must have a second passport and an overseas address.

S&P 100 Index Options (code: OEX) are trading instruments based on a mathematical compilation of the values of a group of 100 stocks chosen from those traded on Wall Street. When more of those 100 stocks are increasing in value than decreasing, the value of the OEX goes up, and vice versa. The S&P 500 Index Options (code: SPX) are based on a group of 500 stocks. The OEX and SPX usually move up and down together in proportion to their values and are both traded on the Chicago Board Options Exchange (CBOE). I prefer to use the OEX rather than the SPX because it has higher trading volume.

FTSE-100 Index Options (American Style, code: SEI) are based on the value of 100 stocks traded on the London Stock Exchange. The SEI Index Options are traded on the London Index and Futures and Options Exchange (LIFFE). There are also FTSE-100 Index Options which are Euro Style. The American style options can be exercised anytime during the option month; Euro style options can be exercised only during certain set periods during the option month, normally expiration day (the third Friday of the Month). "Exercised" means the stock exchange authorities can force the trade of options. This is to the individual trader's advantage. To get rid of an option position, there must be someone willing to take that position. When you want to sell or buy an American style option, even though there is no one willing to buy or sell your position, the CBOE or LIFFE can force someone to do it.

WHAT ARE OEX and SEI OPTIONS?

The OEX index option market has Call options and Put options with strike prices 5 points apart; each option representing 100 shares. The SEI index option market has Call options and Put options with strike prices 50 points apart; each option representing 10 shares. A Call option increases in value as the underlying market (S&P 100 or FTSE-100) rises; a Put option increases in value when the underlying market drops. The strike prices are at even numbers with values below and above the underlying market. For example, if the S&P 100 has a market value of 902, there will be OEX strike prices at 905, 910, 915, 920, etc. above the market and strike prices at 900, 895, 890, 885, etc. below the market. And if the FTSE-100 has a market value of 6783, there will be SEI strike prices at 6800, 6850, 6900, 6950, etc. above the market and strike prices at 6750, 6700, 6650, 6600, etc. below the market. A Call strike price above the market is said to be "out-of-the-money" and a Call strike price below the market is said to be "in-the-money." Similarly, a Put strike price above the market is said to be "in-the-money" and a Put strike price below the market is said to be "out-of-the-money." The value of an option is its "premium." For options out-of-the-money, the premium decreases as the strike price gets further out-of-the money; for options in-the-money, the premium increases as the strike price gets further in-the-money. There are options available with expirations during the current option month, during the next option month and also three months in the future. It is better to trade current option month options, since the volume is much higher and therefore the liquidity is better.

The shape of the premium versus strike price curve is a decaying exponential. If an exponential trendline is superimposed on the actual premiums points plotted on a curve, you can see that the decaying exponential is the best fit. In other words, if a Call or Put is in-the-money (meaning the Call is below the market or the Put is above the market), the farther the position gets in-the-money, the faster the premium increases. In the other direction, if a Call or Put is out-of-the-money, the farther the position gets out-of-the-money, the slower the premium decreases, following an exponential trend line. Here is a typical premium curve for OEX Call options, Figure 1.1 below:

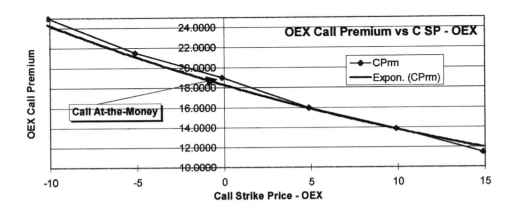

The next chart is a similar plot for SEI Call options, Figure 1.2:

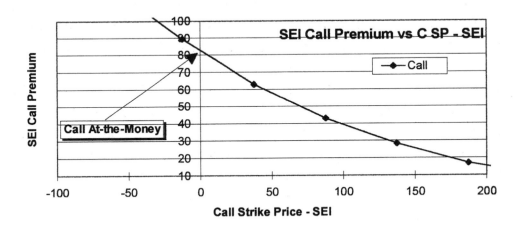

A new option month begins on the first Monday (or the first trading day) after the third Friday of each calendar month. The options month ends on the third Friday of each calendar month. When the option month ends the options are said to "expire." On expiration all out-of-the-money options become worthless and all in-the-money options have a value equal to the difference between their strike price and the underlying market at expiration. For example, if the OEX is 913.53 at expiration, a Call at strike price 915 would be worthless, but a Call at strike price 910 would be worth 3.53; a Put at strike price 915 would be worth 1.47, but a Put at strike price 910 would be worthless.

An option month is either 4 or 5 weeks long, depending on the number of Fridays it takes to get to the third Friday of the month in which the option expires. One notable characteristic of option premiums is that they decay with time. This decay can be measured by computing the "at-the-money" premium for the Call and Put options. The at-the-money Call premium for OEX may be 23 on the first day of a new option month; on the last Thursday before the third Friday expiration the at-the-money premium may be only 3. Therefore, an option is a "wasting asset." The principle objective of an option trader is to use strategies that make a profit even though the values of options decay with time and out-of-the-money options become worthless at expiration.

THE OPTION TRADING DAY for OEX and SEI

It is important to know the trading day for the options you are trading. The OEX options begin trading when the New York market opens at 09:30 New York time. The OEX options finish trading 10 minutes after the New York market closes; the New York market closes at 16:00 New York time, so the OEX options finish trading at 16:10 New York time. The option trading day for OEX is the same each day including the third Friday expiration.

The SEI options begin trading 5 minutes after the London market opens which is at 08:30 London time, so SEI options begin trading at 08:35 London time. The SEI options stop trading at 20 minutes before the London market closes which is at 16:30 London time, so the SEI options stop trading at 16:10 London time. However, on expiration day, the third Friday of each month, the SEI option market closes early: 2 hours after the London market opens. In other words, the expiration of SEI options is at 10:30 London time on expiration day. The expiration price for in-the-money options is based on the average of the FTSE-100 value between 10:10 to 10:30 London time. For a Call option in-the-money, the expiration settlement price would be the difference between the strike price for the Call and the expiration price. For a Put option in-the-money, the expiration settlement price would be the Put strike price minus the FTSE expiration price. All other Calls and Puts (out-of-the-money) expire worthless.

OPTION TRADING STRATEGIES

There are two time periods for option trading that require two different strategy types: (1) non-directional strategies for profiting during the option month that take advantage of the wasting nature of out-of-the-money options and (2) directional strategies that make a profit from the volatility of option prices during a trading day.

The first type of strategy generates a credit when the option position is opened; this credit goes into your option trading account. If at expiration the option values that generated this credit become worthless, then you get to keep the initial credit and it becomes your profit. There are two basic strategies that fit the first category: covered short spreads (strangles) for both Calls and Puts and naked short spreads (strangles) for Calls and Puts. If you have a limited amount of capital to use for trading (less than $50,000) then you can only use the covered spread strategy. The minimum margin requirement for naked short spreads is $50,000 for OEX, which means if you don't have more than $50,000 in your trading account the CBOE rules prohibit you from using naked short spreads.

The second type of strategy uses the volatility of the market to generate a profit during a trading day. This type of trading is called "intraday trading," meaning you open a position and close it during the same day. In the New York market there is a type of trader called the "program trader." Program traders are usually mutual fund managers who have a large sum of cash to use to buy a block of stocks or have a large block of stocks they want to sell. A "buy program" occurs when one of these program traders decides to buy a block of stocks: a "sell program" is when one of these program traders decides to sell a block of stocks. Most of the program traders use the same computer program that "signals" a buy or sell. That's the reason these program traders have such a big effect on the market changes during the trading day.   The buy programs cause the market to rise, so if you can detect when a buy program is starting, then you would buy Calls. The sell programs cause the market to drop, so if you detect when a sell program is starting, then you would buy Puts. During a given trading day in New York there may be up to a dozen buy programs and sell programs; many times a buy program will be followed immediately by a sell program. As a result of this intraday volatility caused by these buy and sell programs and the decaying value of options, it is not wise to hold a long Call position or a long Put position for a long time hoping for a big profit. It is better to make small profits by buying Calls when a buy program makes the market jump and to make small profits with Puts when a sell program makes the market drop. In other words, ride the coattails of the program traders to make a profit. This strategy of buying Calls or Puts during a trading day will be described as the Delta Trading Strategy.

COVERED SHORT SPREAD (STRANGLE) STRATEGY
CONDOR

The two-sided covered short spread (strangle) strategy example follows: for OEX sell 10 Calls at a safe strike price above the market and buy 10 Calls at a strike price 5 more than the Calls you sell; ALSO, sell 10 Puts at a safe strike price below the market and buy 10 Puts at a strike price 5 below the Puts you sell. Since the Calls you sell are at a lower strike price than the Calls you buy, the Calls you sell will be worth more than the Calls you buy, thus yielding a net credit. Similarly, since the Puts you sell are at a higher strike price than the Puts you buy, the Puts you sell will be worth more than the Puts you buy, thus yielding a net profit.

How much higher than the market should the Calls you sell be to be safe? How much lower than the market should the Puts you sell be to be safe? The answer to these questions depends on the statistics of the market. The Call you sell (referred to as the "short Call") should be 2 standard deviations (2 sigma) above the market and the Put you sell (the "short Put") should be 2 standard deviations (2 sigma) below the market. Using this 2 sigma measurement over the last 13 option months means the probability that the market will get above your short Call or below your short Put is only 5%. This means that the Call and Put options will expire worthless 95% of the time and you will get to keep your initial credit as profit. (See Chapters 5 and 10 for details about computing standard deviations.)

How much profit can you make using the Covered Short Spread Strategy? Typically for the OEX the premium difference between the short Call (the one you sold) and the long Call (the one you bought) will be one, and similarly the premium difference between the short Put and long

Put will be one. Since each OEX option is considered 100 shares, then for 10 Call options at a premium difference of 1, the initial credit would be 10 x 100 = $1000 x the premium difference = $1,000 less commission. The initial credit for the 10 Puts would be the same: $1,000 less commission. My broker charges a commission of $7.50 per option. Since there are 10 of each kind of option (10 long Calls, 10 short Calls, 10 short Puts and 10 long Puts) the commission would be 10 times $7.50 = $75.00 times 4 (for the number of different kinds of options you have), and that makes $300. So the total initial credit would be $2,000 - $300 = $1,700.

How much margin (collateral) is required for 10 OEX Call and Put Covered Spreads? The CBOE sets the margin requirements for covered short spreads. For each side the margin for 10 covered short spreads would be: $2,000 + 10 x 100 x (5 - Premium difference). So for the premium difference of 1, the margin for each side would be $6,000 or $12,000 for both the Call side and the Put side. I advise never using more than half your capital as margin for an option position, so in this case for 10 OEX two-sided short spreads you should have a capital of at least $24,000. What if you have only $15,000? Then open fewer short spreads. For example, if you opened only 4 short spreads rather than 10, your initial credit would be $400 x 2- commission = $800 less commission or = $680. The margin required would be $4,000 + $3,200 = $7,200 which is less than 50% of your capital. (These formulas will be developed fully in Chapter 5 and Chapter 10).

How much return can you expect on your capital using the 2 sigma Covered Short Spread Strategy? In each example above of the 2 sigma covered short spreads on both the Call and Put side the return on investment is quite attractive, if the initial credit becomes profit at expiration. In the 10 option example above, using only 50% of your capital as margin, the return is 7.08% or an annual return of 85%. The 4 option example, using less than half of your capital as margin, generates a return of 4.53% or an annual return of 54.4%. By using proper statistically safe strike prices for your covered short spreads you can earn considerably better return on your capital than a mutual fund would pay. Also in addition to the covered short spread strategy with its inherent margin requirement, you can augment your monthly income from option trading through intraday trading of Long Calls and Long Puts.

NAKED 2 SIGMA SHORT SPREAD STRATEGY

STRANGLE

The naked 2 sigma short spread strategy involves selling Calls 2 sigma above the market and selling Puts 2 sigma below the market. If the short Call has a premium of 4 and the short Put has a premium of 5, then the initial credit for 4 OEX short spreads would be 4 x 100 x (4 + 5) less commission = $3,600 - 7.5 x 4 x 2 = $3,540. If the OEX stays below the Call strike price and above the Put strike price during the option month until expiration, then this initial credit becomes your profit for the month. The CBOE requires a minimum account value of $50,000 before you are allowed to open a naked short spread. The margin (collateral) required is 15% for an out-of-the-money spread. So for 4 OEX short spreads with the OEX at 902, the margin = 902 x 4 x 100 x 0.15 = $54,120, or $4,120 more than the minimum required in your account. The return on capital = 3540/ 54120 = 6.54% or 78.49% annualized.

In the event either the Call or Put side of your short spread gets in-to-the-money, then the margin requirement jumps to 20%; so the margin for 4 OEX short spreads with the OEX at 902 would be 4 x 100 x 902 x 0.2 = $72,160. In the event the market moves above the short Call strike price or below the short Put strike price, unless you have $72,160 in your account you will receive a margin call. This means you must put up the extra cash within one day or your position will be closed out by the broker with a subsequent loss. To avoid such a margin Call, you should trade 2 or 3 options, instead of 4. One advantage of covered short spreads for people with limited capital is that there is no change in margin requirements if one side or the other gets into the money, so no margin call would occur.

LONG CALL AND PUT DELTA STRATEGY

The long Call and Put Delta Strategy consists of buying Calls or Puts near the beginning of a program trade and them selling those Calls or Puts during or after the program trade finishes. This type of trading requires no margin, so you can do the long Call and Put strategy at the same time as the Covered Short Spread Strategy. The Delta Strategy takes advantage of the volatility caused by the program traders. The strategy works as follows: when you detect a buy program is starting, buy 3 Calls in-the-money at market value to open a long Call position and, in the same order to your broker, place a sell order at a delta (difference or change) more than you paid to close out the long Call position with a profit of delta points. For example, if delta is 1, then the profit for the round trip trade of buying and selling the 3 OEX Calls would be 3 x 100 x 1 less commission = $300 less commission = $255 for a typical commission of $45 round trip. Typically the long Call would be open for an hour or less, just long enough for the premium to increase by 1 due to the buy program that was causing the market to jump up.

Similarly when you detect a sell program starting, buy 3 OEX Puts in-the-money at market value with a delta of 1. The round trip profit would be the same as for the Call or $255. The sell programs tend to happen more rapidly than the buy programs so it is more difficult to get in on the beginning of a sell program. Also, usually the market value of Calls (as compared to the market value of Puts) goes up faster for a given change in the level of the market, so it is easier to reach your delta profit objective by using Calls.

To do this type of intraday trading using the delta strategy, you need a reliable source of real time quotations for the OEX or SEI. One such source of real time quotes is the TV channel CNBC for OEX and the satellite channel SkyNews for FTSE-100 (the underlying index for SEI). Another source of OEX real time quotes is InterQuote, a pay service on the Internet. An Internet service ESI is offering real time quotes for SEI on the Internet as a pay service, and also have free delayed quotes.

How much profit can you earn using the Delta Strategy for long Calls and Puts? Assuming you make 4 trades per week on the average, and that you are careful so that each trade is profitable, then for a 4 week option month for the delta strategy asking for a delta of 1 point and buying 3 OEX options, the profit = 4 x 4 x 255 = $4,080. It is reasonable to expect that you will make at least 2 mistakes using the delta strategy and that you would lose 2 points each time. This would mean a loss of 2 x 2 x 3 x 100 + commissions = -$1,290 which would reduce your monthly profit to $2,790. This is a reasonable profit objective per month using 3 OEX options for the Delta Strategy.

How much do 3 OEX Long Calls or Long Puts cost (i.e. the investment)? During the early part of the option month an in-the-money Call or Put will have a premium of about 20, during the last week of the option month the premium will be about 8. So early in the month the cost of 3 OEX options would be = 20 x 3 x 100 + commission = $6,025; the profit of $255 is a return on investment of 4.25%. This is a nice return considering you are in the market for about an hour from the time you buy the Call or Put until you sell it at a premium 1 point higher. At the end of the month the return is even higher when the in-the-money Call or Put will have lower premiums due to the time decay of premiums during the option month.

The combined monthly income for both the 2 sigma covered short spread strategy and the delta strategy could be: Covered Short Spread = $1,700 + Delta Strategy = $2,790 for a total monthly income of $4,490 with a capital of $24,000. This would be a monthly return of 18.7%. I must warn you that some months will have a net loss, rather than a profit because there is risk in both strategies described above. If you trade carefully, it is reasonable to expect a doubling of your capital per year.

SEI TRADING EXAMPLES

When opening 10 SEI covered short spreads, the premium difference between the short and the long positions is typically 7.5 points on the Call side and 14 points on Put side. Choose the short Call and short Put 2 sigma above and below the market respectively. An SEI option represents only 10 shares rather than the 100 shares for an OEX option. The initial credit in pounds sterling (£) would be 10 x 10 x (7.5+14) less commission = £2,150 - £200 = £1,950 net initial credit. Assuming the $/£ exchange rate is 1.66, then the initial credit in dollars = 1.66 x 1950 = $3,237. The margin (see Chapter 5 for a more detailed discussion of SEI CvSS margin) required in pounds to open the 10 covered short spreads = number of options x (500 - premium difference) x 2 = 10 x (500-7.5-14) x 2 = £9,570; or in dollars = 1.66 x 9800 = $15,886, or, following the rule of using only half your capital for margin, the capital needed = 2 x 16268 = $31,772. The return on capital at the end of the option month if the initial credit becomes the monthly profit =3237/31772 = 10.2% or an annual return of 122%

Following the delta strategy for SEI, use 5 SEI options and a delta of 5. If a buy program is detected, buy 5 SEI Call options in-the-money with an order to sell when the premium increases by 5. Typically the premium is 90, so the 5 SEI Call options cost = 5 x 10 x 90 + commission = £4,500 +£25 = £4,525. When the market rises enough to trigger the sell at 95, the net profit for the round trip trade = 5 x 10 x 5-2 x 25 = £200 = 1.66 x 200 = $332. The return on this round trip trade = 200/4525 = 4.4%.

MARKET SIGNAL CHARTS TO PREDICT DIRECTION OF MARKET MOVES

A complete book could be written describing the many market signal charts that have been developed by market analysts. I will describe the four that I have found most useful in day to day option trading. The stochastics difference chart is the most sensitive to market direction changes. For example, during a trading day the stochastics difference may change direction several times when there is a lot of market volatility with big intraday market swings. The interpretation of this chart is simple: if the stochastics difference is positive, it indicates an up market; if the stochastics difference is negative, it indicates a down market. The details of how to compute the stochastics difference and the other market signal indicators will be covered in Chapter 6. Here I will just describe how to use the market signal charts. Below is the stochastics difference chart for the SEI, Figure 1.3.

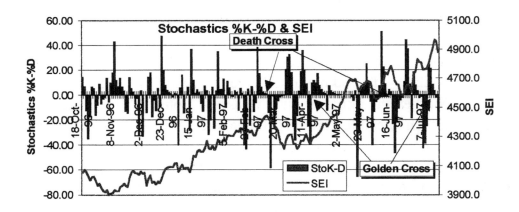

The bars show the stochastics differences, with up indicating an up market and down indicating a down market. Those points where the bars switch from negative to positive are designated "Golden Crosses" signifying a long Call will make money. Those points where the bars switch from positive to negative are designated "Death Crosses" meaning a long Put will make money. The curve for the SEI as a function of time is superimposed on the stochastics difference bars to show the correlation between a drop in the

SEI and the stochastics bars going down into the negative region. When there is a rise in the SEI the stochastics bars turn up into the positive region. The same is true for the OEX and the stochastics differences.

The 4 day exponential moving average difference (MAD4) is the next most sensitive indicator of market movements. A chart of the OEX versus MAD4 is shown below as Figure 1.4:

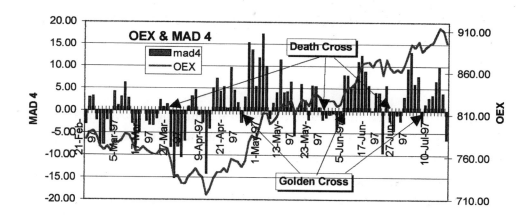

The MAD4 is shown as bars with an up bar indicating an up market and a down bar indicating a falling market. The points denoted "Death Cross" indicate a long Put would make money and the points denoted "Golden Cross" indicate a long Call is favored.

The third market indicator chart is the 9 day minus 4 day moving average difference (MAD9-4) which is useful for indicating longer term changes in market direction. It is the least sensitive to intraday market swings and is a good indicator to show when a major change in market sentiment has taken place. As with the other two charts, an up bar indicates a rising market and a down bar indicates a falling market. The OEX MAD9-4 chart is shown in the following Figure 1.5:

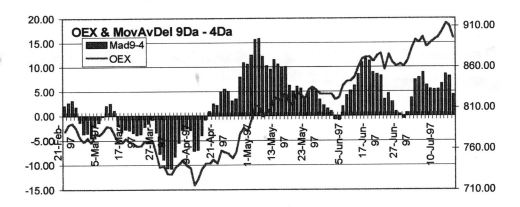

You can see by comparing the MAD9-4 with the OEX that this chart shows major changes in market direction and doesn't change from plus to minus with the smaller wriggles in the OEX curve.

The final market indicator is a different type than the first 3 indicators. It is called the Welles-Wilder Indicator (WWI), named after the developers, and is sometimes referred to as the relative strength indicator (RSI). It is most useful in showing when the market is oversold or overbought. If the short term (7 Day) WWI is greater than 80 this means the market is over-bought; if the WWI is less than 20 this shows the market is oversold. If the market is overbought, this is an indication there will be a downward correction in the market soon. If the market is oversold, this means the downward movement has gone too far and an upward recovery is imminent. The WWI for SEI is shown in Figure 1.6 below:

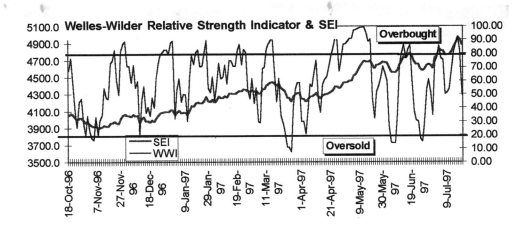

When the WWI moves into the overbought region, then a downward correction occurs; and when the WWI moves into the oversold area, then an upward movement happens soon afterward. This is a particularly useful indicator to show you when an excess in the market (either up or down) is about to end. In short, it is a good predictor of future market direction.

USE OF OPTION HEDGE STRATEGY TO AUGMENT CAPITAL GROWTH

To do option trading you need to open a trading account with a broker who specializes in option trading. The amount of capital needed to begin option trading is in the range of $5,000 to $25,000 (except for trading with naked options which requires at least $50,000). You can either leave this capital as cash which receives small interest payments of, say, 5% or less, or you may use stocks or bonds for the capital. Typically a broker will only allow about 80% of the value of securities as collateral for option trading. If you use stocks for the capital you have the added risk of a drop in the stock price that would reduce your capital and collateral for option trading. One way to reduce this risk and still benefit from the potential rise in the value of the stocks and the dividends the stocks may pay is by the use of a hedge position, similar to the strategy used by the big mutual fund managers. For example, buy shares in General Motors (GM) which has low volatility and pays good dividends, but protect yourself from a drop in GM when a market correction occurs by buying enough GM Puts to cover the GM market exposure. If GM goes down, the Puts go up and you have protection. This is called the Option Hedge Strategy.

If the market is in a long term up trend, then another way to use your trading capital with the Option Hedge Strategy is to buy S&P Deposit Receipts (SPY) traded on the AMEX exchange. The SPY is usually equal to one tenth of the SPX, so buying SPY shares is equivalent to buying S&P 500 shares (which don't exist) so you can benefit from the increase in the SPX. Use the option hedge strategy to protect yourself from a market correction. Buy enough OEX Puts to cover the exposure to SPY. Use OEX rather than SPX Puts since the OEX follows the SPX very closely, so the protection is equivalent and, as I said before, OEX has higher trading volume and is more liquid since the spread between bid and ask prices is smaller. Since hedging is used to protect securities you own rather than for wealth building, it will not be covered in detail in this book.

WHAT TOOLS ARE NEEDED
FOR OPTION TRADING?

In my opinion you would be foolish to do option trading without a Personal Computer (PC) with good software to aid in your trading and a modem for connecting to the Internet. Personal Computers are so much easier to use than they used to be that, even if you've never used one before, you can master using it in a few days with the help of the manuals that come with all modern computers and with the built in "Help" items included in the computer software plus the intuitive features of WINDOWS 95 and its successors. The PC should be a 486 or better with 16 MB of RAM or more and a hard disk with 1.2 GB of memory or more. You should have Microsoft (MS) Windows 3.1 or better; preferably Windows 95. The Microsoft Office 95 program, which includes both EXCEL and WINWORD is a necessary tool for keeping track of the daily market variations and generating the type of charts described above. The appendices describe a set of useful EXCEL workbooks for OEX option trading and a second set for SEI trading. Both workbooks provide copies of the work sheets with equations and charts. If you are good at using EXCEL you probably can generate your own workbook with the work sheets and charts needed for OEX option trading. However, if you want to do it the easy way, the author will be happy to furnish you the EXCEL workbook on a 3.5" diskette for a nominal price. The author can be reached at e-mail address: jonsch@vnet.es

You need to be connected to the Internet to obtain the necessary up-to-date market information for index option trading over your telephone line at the cost of a local phone call. Your PC should have a modem with 33.6 Kbaud connect speed for fast access and you will need a reliable Internet Server Service that includes high speed connection capability. Also, you need e-mail service, since there is so much information about option trading available via e-mail.

I recommend InterQuote of Wisconsin for obtaining a real time quote of your own individualized portfolio of OEX options and the Index values. A portfolio useful for OEX trading is included in the appendices. The charge for InterQuote is about \$27/mo., which I think is well worth the cost. A free quote service is provided by Lombard which makes a good back-up to InterQuote during those rare times when InterQuote may have problems sending current information on the net. Another feature of Lombard is the availability of an intraday chart showing the minute by minute fluctuations of the OEX. During the trading day you can use it to see the buy and sell programs clearly on your PC screen.

A British company called ESI provides real time quotes for the SEI for those who trade this option. The cost is modest as well. This quote service includes the complete range of SEI strike prices and the Call and Put premiums for each strike price. ESI has a delayed quote for SEI that is free. European television sets have many Teletext pages, available on request and superimposed on the TV screens, displaying international market trading information. This service is supplied by local, national and satellite TV. Perhaps it will come to the US along with High Definition or Digital TV.

CNNfn, the financial data Internet service of the CNN broadcasting company, provides a lot of interesting data during the trading day. One page provides a summary of US economic data released during the trading day as well as the value of DJIA, NASDAQ, and the 30 Year US Bond, updated frequently. CNN also has a page updated each minute or so with a free market update of major US indexes such as DJIA, SPX, OEX, NYX, AMEX and NASDAQ; these indices are updated frequently, but with a short delay. I find this daily information valuable to indicate what is happening in the market place. This quote system is a handy back-up to the pay services such as InterQuote - but without option quotes. CNN also provides an end-of-day wrap up of market information about both the US markets and the London markets that I find very helpful to give an overview of market action. This page of CNN also gives the US economic data that will be released during the next trading day. These economic reports often drive the market either up or down, so keeping track of them helps avoid taking positions that might prove dangerous.

The Wall Street Journal Interactive is also on the Internet at a cost of $5.95 per month. I find the information provided by the WSJI another important tool for option trading. The WSJI provides a daily wrap-up of the NY markets as well as the London markets. The "Money" page provides a chart of the DJIA on a minute by minute basis so at the end of the day you can examine the intraday volatility as reflected by this index. This DJIA chart can be used to estimate the moves of the OEX since ordinarily the OEX and the DJIA track each other closely. On rare occasions, when there is strange market behavior taking place, there may be a discrepancy in the movements of these two indices.

Barron's has an Internet site that provides a weekly market summary issued each Saturday. It's nominal $27 yearly charge is waived if you subscribe to its sister site, the WSJI discussed above. I find this weekly market review handy in understanding what happened during the past trading week.

Barron's gave me a week's early warning when the CBOE decided to split the OEX on November 24, 1997. It was my only regular source of information that gave me this vital news. The lower price of the OEX after the split cut the Call-At-The-Money (CATM) and Put-At-The-Money (PATM) premiums and the cost of trades, hedges and the margin for naked short spreads down to half their previous value. Traders could open more positions for the same amount of capital. It was the intention of the CBOE to raise the trading volume of the OEX which had been slipping because of the high value of the market. Now the OEX varies at about 48% of the value of the SPX instead of about 97% as it did before the split. Figure 1.7 below shows a comparison of the theoretical values of the SPX with the old OEX and the new split OEX.

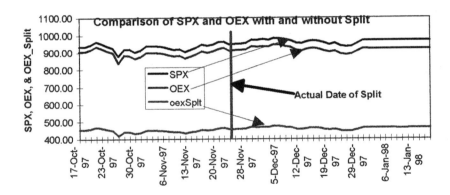

CHAPTER 2

PREDICTING OPTION MARKET MOVEMENT OVERVIEW

A successful option trader needs to be aware of the direction the market being used is headed. Watch the movement of the underlying market of the option traded. If you are trading OEX options (my recommended option for the US market), then you must determine when the OEX is on a long trend up or down. I think this long term trend is best shown on a six month (or so) chart of the daily fluctuations of the OEX.

The market trend is especially important when using the 2 sigma covered short spread (strangle) strategy in which the position is open for 3 to 5 weeks during the current option month. You want to choose your position so that market movement won't take either your short Calls or short Puts into-the-money. The value of the Call 2 sigma is an important measure of the amount the market has been moving up during the option month for the last 13 months; the value of the Put 2 sigma measures how much the market has been dropping during the option month for the last 13 months. Chapter 5 details how to compute the 2 sigma and the statistical significance of this important measure of market volatility and Chapter 10 summarizes the 2 sigma equations.

If you want to do intraday trading using the Delta Strategy for long Calls or Puts, then you must become interested in predicting short term movements of the underlying market. Often a movement lasting an hour or less is the difference between a profit and a loss. Different techniques must be used to predict these intraday ups and downs for delta strategy trading than for the 2 sigma covered short spread trading. There are several clues available to predict when a buy program is imminent that will cause a rapid rise in the market or when a sell program is starting that will cause a rapid drop in the market. There may be several buy and sell programs during a trading day that cause the market to whipsaw up and down. The objective of the intraday delta strategy is to detect a buy program and buy OEX Calls with an order to sell the Calls at a premium "delta" more than the premium paid for the Calls; or to detect a sell program and buy OEX Puts with an order to sell the Puts at a premium "delta" more than the premium paid for the Puts. You would select a delta of 1 point if you expect an ordinary move. A delta of 1 means a profit for 3 OEX options of $300 less commission or about $255. If your signal indicates a larger than ordinary move in the market, then you may want to use a higher value of delta than 1, an intermediate move could use a delta of 1.5. For 3 OEX options, a delta of 1.5 would yield a profit of $450 less commission or about $405. If the indications are for a really big move, then a delta of 2 may be used - a successful trade of 3 OEX options would have a profit of $600 less commission or about $555.

WHAT ARE SOME SIGNALS
FOR OEX INTRADAY MOVEMENTS?

The SPX (S&P 500) and the OEX (S&P 100) track each other very closely, so an indication of a movement of the SPX means a similar movement for the OEX. Normally, the level of the OEX is about 97% of the level of the SPX. The SPX futures price and cash or spot price is widely reported during the trading day; for example, on CNBC TV channel. When the futures price is greater than the cash price, this is a signal the market is going to rise - meaning a long Call may be profitable; when the futures price is less than the cash price, this signals a market drop - meaning a long Put may be profitable.

If you watch a real time quote system which updates the value of an index each minute, then a series of up-ticks in the market is a signal for a

buy program which means buy Calls; if there is a series of down-ti
is a signal a sell program is in progress, meaning buy Puts. The rap
the rise or fall is an indication of how far the market may be moving; if it is
moving slowly in one direction this would mean an ordinary move or a
delta of 1; an intermediate speed in the movement would call for a delta of
1.5; a rapid move would mean a delta of 2 could be profitable. **A warning**: buy and sell programs cause the market to jump or drop very rapidly
(for example 1%) in 10 or 15 minutes; if you are using the tick method to
detect the sell or buy program you must decide quickly and place your
order. Otherwise, you may miss the movement, find yourself getting into
the market at or near the end of the movement when you will pay a high
premium. When the market changes direction, the premium of the long
Call or Put drops, meaning you may not be able to close out your position
at the delta requested.

Another useful signal to use is the SPY, sometimes referred to as
"Spyders", which are S&P Deposit Receipts or a deposit trust made up in
the same ratios of all the stocks of the S&P 500. The SPY can be bought
and sold like a stock on the American Stock Exchange (AMEX). The SPY
is approximately a tenth of the SPX. Normally the SPY follows the SPX
very closely. For example, a SPY of 90.5 would correspond to a SPX of
905. The SPY tends to move before the SPX (and, therefore, the OEX) and
both are strongly influenced by the SPX futures price. So the SPY can give
an early warning of a movement of the SPX and OEX. If 10 times SPY is
greater than SPX by 1.5, this is a signal that a buy program is imminent
and a long Call is signaled; if 10 times SPY is less than SPX by 1.5, this is
a signal that a sell program is imminent and a long Put should be opened.
The amount that ten times SPY is greater or less than the SPX signals how
much greater or less the move could be. So a difference of 1.75 may mean
a delta of 1, a difference of 3 may signal a delta of 1.5 and a difference of
5 may mean a delta of 2.

If you are watching SPX and SPY on a real time quote system, the tick
by tick movements are a good signal for predicting a buy or sell program.
If the SPX is flat or descending and the SPY is ticking up, then this is a
signal a buy program is imminent and a long Call may be profitable. If the
SPX is flat or rising and the SPY is ticking down, this indicates a sell program is coming and a long Put using the delta strategy may be profitable.

WHAT ARE SOME SIGNALS
FOR SEI INTRADAY MOVEMENTS?

The underlying market for the SEI is the Financial Times Stock Exchange of 100 stocks traded in London (FTSE-100). The satellite TV channel SkyNews gives Europeans a minute by minute real time update of the FTSE-100 by Teletext during the trading day. So the tick method can be used to detect a rising or falling market. For a rising market buy Calls, for a falling market buy Puts; with a close out order a delta more than the premium paid for the Calls or Puts. The rate of rise or fall of the FTSE-100 can be an indication of how far the market will go up or down. For example, if the market is climbing at the rate of 2 points per minute, it is probably going to be a big rise, if the market is rising at the rate of ½ point per minute, then it may not be a very big rise. A typical delta for SEI is 5 premium points. The OEX has intraday swings much wilder than the FTSE-100 has; nevertheless this market sometimes changes direction two or three times a day. The program traders have arrived in London, but they don't cause such rapid jumps or drops as in New York.

The difference between the FTSE-100 futures price and cash price is another good indication of a rising or falling market. If the futures price is, say, 20 points greater than the cash price, this is an indication that an up move of 10 or 15 points is in the offing. Conversely, if the cash price is greater than the futures price, this signals a pending drop in the market. The FTSE-100 futures and cash prices are reported on the German satellite channel 3SAT television and they are updated about every 10 to 20 minutes during the trading day. This channel also reports the SPX futures price as well as the SPX cash price before the US market opens. If you have access to this satellite TV channel, you have a reliable indication of how the US market will move at open. For example, if at 15 minutes before the New York open, the 3SAT channel reports the SPX spot price (traded in Frankfurt) is 3 points higher than the close the night before, this almost always means that, within about 10 minutes after the New York open, the SPX will be up 3 and the OEX will be up about 2.75 and the DJIA will be up about 24. What happens after this opening move depends on the NY program traders. The DJIA has been known to move up 25 points in the first 10 minutes, then, when a sell program started, the DJIA dropped to a loss of 60 points in the next 15 minutes after open. Such is the volatility of the New York markets caused by the big fund managers and their program trading.

The ESI company in the United Kingdom provides a real time quote service for SEI options on the Internet. If you subscribe to this pay service for a nominal sum, you have the advantage of watching in real time the premiums for the long Call or long Put positions you are considering for the delta strategy. The free delayed quote system of ESI is normally adequate for SEI trading, since there is a more limited amount of intraday volatility in London than NY.

CHAOS PATTERNS FOR PREDICTING MARKET MOVEMENTS

There are certain predictable market moves that come out of the seemingly chaotic motions of the market of the underlying indexes for the options traded. The market moves are referred to as "chaos patterns." I have examined the OEX market fluctuations over the last 10 years and have identified and statistically quantified many of these chaos patterns. Some of them are summarized below. The patterns can be used to indicate whether to use Calls or Puts in your trading; if the market rises most of the time on a given date, such as the first trading day of the month or the Monday of expiration week, then a long Call is favored: If the market falls most of the time on a given date, such as the first Monday of the new option month, a long Put is favored:

- Expiration Day: market rises 64% of the time and drops 36% of the time, Call favored

- First Monday after expiration: market drops 59% of the time and rises 41%, Put favored.

- Last 2 days of 1st quarter: market drops 82% of the time and rises 18%, Put favored

- First 2 days of 2nd quarter: market rises 70% and drops 30% of the time, Call favored

- The next day after a jump of more than 10: market rises 75% and drops 25% of time, Call favored

- The next day after a drop of more than 10: market rises 55% and drops 45% of time, Call slightly favored

- The next trading day after 4ᵗʰ of July: market rises 70% and drops 30% of time, Call favored

- The last week of option month: market rises 70% and drops 30% of time, Call favored

- On Christmas eve: market rises 64% and drops 36% of time, Call favored

- The next trading day after Christmas: market rises 55% of the time and drops 35% of time, Call slightly favored

- Last day of year: market rises 40% of time and drops 60% of time, Put favored

- Next day after a drop of 2.7% or more: market rises 67% of time and drops 33% of time, Call favored

- Next day after a jump of 2.9% or more: market rises 60% of time and drops 40% of time, Call favored

IMPACT OF ECONOMIC REPORTS ON MARKET MOVEMENT

The US government issues economic reports on almost a daily basis. The calendar of these economic reports can be found in the Internet version of the Wall Street Journal Interactive for the next 4 weeks, updated weekly. The CNNfn Internet page also communicates the economic reports to be issued the next day on a daily update basis. This CNNfn web page also gives the predicted value of each report and the impact it may have on the market. One of the big market drivers is the monthly non-farm jobs report that comes out on the first Friday of each month. If the number of new jobs is greater than predicted, the market will drop and a Put is favored; if the number is less than expected the market will rise and a Call is favored; it the number is about that predicted the effect on the market is neutral.

Most of these economic reports come out an hour before New York market open, so it is possible to know the results before the market opens. CNNfn and WSJI (both on the Internet) regularly disclose these numbers just a few minutes after a report is issued, so you can refer to these pages and know what is happening. Also, if you get a reading on the SPX futures (which opens an hour and 10 minutes before the New York market open) the futures number will give an early clue as to whether the market is going to drop or jump as a result of the economic report issued that day. If the SPX futures price before New York open is greater than the closing cash price of SPX the day before, then the market will probably rise; if the futures price is lower than the night before cash price at close then the market will probably fall. The German 3SAT satellite TV channel has a Teletext page (number 163) that reports the cash price of the SPX traded on the Frankfurt exchange. Another good indicator of the effect of an economic report on the market can be obtained by getting a reading of the SPX spot price about a half hour before the New York opening. If the Frankfurt SPX cash price is higher than the New York close the night before, then the New York market will rise by that amount near the opening; a long Call is signaled. If the Frankfurt SPX cash price is lower than the night before New York SPX close, then the NY market will drop at open; a long Put is favored.

The most closely watched economic report is that issued by the Federal Open Market Committee (FOMC) or Fed, for short. The Fed meets several times per year to examine the US economy and to decide whether to raise, lower, or leave unchanged the Short Term Interest Rates, the overnight rates banks charge. The market analysts watch carefully for clues in the economic reports about whether the economy is rising too fast; if the economy is overheating, this may cause inflation and the Fed may raise interest rates at their next meeting. This speculation by the market analysts about what the Fed may do has a big impact on market moves on the days leading up to one of the Fed meetings. Normally these Fed meetings cover two days and at about 2PM New York time on the second day the Fed releases its decision and the minutes of the meeting. On this second day of the Fed meeting, the US markets sit and wait, with very little movement up or down. When the Fed meeting report is issued, then the market either jumps or drops depending on the report. If the interest rates are left unchanged (or the rare case of lowering) the market normally jumps; a Call is favored. If the interest rates are increased, the market usually drops; a Put is favored.

THE LONG BOND:
A SIGNAL FOR MARKET DIRECTION

The spread between the interest rate of US Treasury 2 Year Notes and the overnight interest rate charged between banks (the rate set by the Fed) is a good indicator of which way the New York stock market is going to move. A spread of 50 basis points (0.5%) is neutral. Above 50 means a down market (Put favored); below 50 means an up market (Call favored). In March 1997 the spread increased to 100 points and there was an almost 10% downward correction in the New York market indices. On the third of July 1997 the spread was down to 41.5 and there was a jump of over 12 points (1.4% rise) in the OEX on that day. This is a spread well worth tracking as a predictor of market movement.

HOW FAR IN-THE-MONEY FOR
A LONG CALL OR PUT POSITION?

When using the delta strategy for intraday trading, an important decision is: how far in-the-money should the Call or Put be? The further in-the-money the more the Call or Put costs, but the higher the slope is and the smaller the market move required to reach your delta and close out your position with a profit. It is tempting to buy a Call or Put at-the-money or slightly out-of-the-money to reduce the amount spent to open the position. However, this is penny-wise and pound-foolish. The slope (the change in premium per change in market) increases rapidly as you move further in-the-money. If you open a position well into the money (5 to 10 points), the increase in premium is almost equal to the increase in market. In other words, if the OEX rises 1 point, a Call well in the money would rise about 1 point, and a delta of 1 would be closed out with a profit. If you are near the at-the-money point, the increase in premium is about half the increase in market; in this case the OEX would have to rise by 2 to get your delta of 1. A similar case is true for Puts: well in-the-money, a 1 point rise in the market results in nearly a 1 point increase in Put premium; near at-the-market, a 1 point rise in the market results in a half point rise in the Put premium.

The OEX Call slope versus the Call Strike Price minus OEX (or distance in-the-money) is shown below in Figure 2.1.

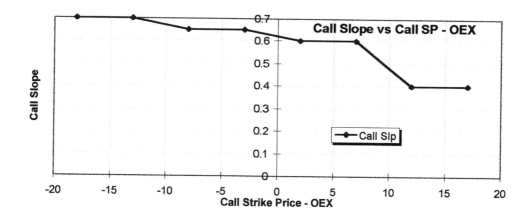

For the OEX, the strike prices are 5 points apart so the chart above shows that the OEX Call just in-the-money had a slope of 0.65 on the day I made this chart. Go up on the line labeled minus 5 (-5) until it crosses the Call slope line. This means that for each increase of 1 point in the OEX, the Call premium would increase by 0.65 point. If the OEX increased by 3, then the Call premium would increase by 1.95.

Below is the chart for the OEX Call premium as a function of the distance from at-the-money or Call Strike Price minus OEX, Figure 2.2:

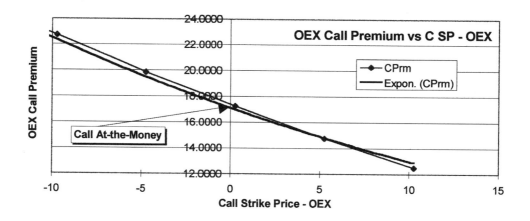

The first Call strike price in-the-money has a premium of 16.5 and the next in-the-money has a premium of 19.75 for a difference of 3.25; this yields a slope = 3.25/5 = 0.65, the same as shown on the chart, Figure 2.1.

Positions on the London market follow the same pattern. The SEI Call slope versus the Call Strike Price minus SEI (or distance in-the-money) is shown below in Figure 2.3.

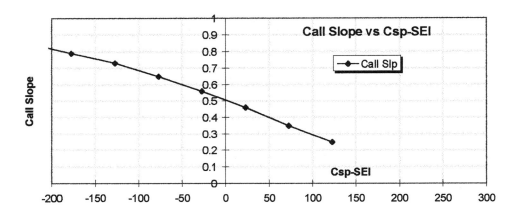

The difference between strike prices for the SEI is 50, so the curve above shows that for a strike price 25 in-the-money (go up on the line half way between 0 and -50) the slope is 0.55; in other words for each point rise in the SEI the Call premium increases by 0.55.

Figure 2.4 directly below shows the SEI Call Premium versus Call Strike Price minus SEI chart for the same day as the slope chart above.

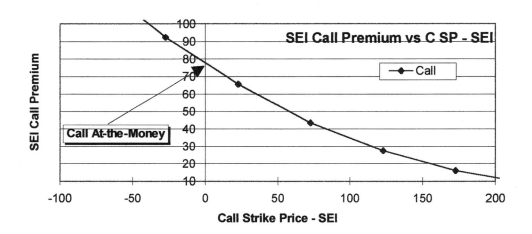

The premium for the closest SEI Call in-the-money is 92 and the next Call 50 points lower is 68, or a difference of 24, giving a slope = 24/50 =

0.48. This is very close to the at-the-money slope of 0.5 shown on the curve of Figure 2.3 which was generated using data reported by LIFFE.

SOME EXAMPLES OF OEX TRADES USING MARKET DIRECTION SIGNALS

On the first trading day after the fourth of July, the German Sat3 channel teletext page 163 reported at one hour before New York open that the SPX was up 4.1 points above the last close. This was a signal that the New York market would open up and we could expect the OEX to rise by about 4 points in the first few minutes after the New York open. This up signal was consistent with the Chaos Pattern that 70% of the time the market rises on the day after the 4th. I decided to open 3 long Calls at a strike price in-the-money. I gave the following order to my broker 14 minutes after New York open when the DJIA was up 20 points and the OEX was up 3.55 points: Buy 3 OEX Call 890 at market and sell at a premium 1.5 more than received. I soon received confirmation that the 3 OEX C890 were bought at 17¾. Since I had said to sell at 1.5 more than received, a sell order was automatically in place for 19¼. My real time quote service at 42 minutes after NY open showed the OEX C890 had traded at 19¼; a few minutes later I received confirmation from my broker that the 3 OEX C890 sold at 19¼ as ordered. The profit for this trade = 3 x 100 x (19.25-17.75) - round trip commission = $450 - 45 = $405.

The same day, at 4 hours after market open (13:30 New York time), I noted a sell program was starting by watching a tick by tick quote of the DJIA on the teletext display of the SkyNews satellite channel. I decided that since the OEX was off its high of the day, a strong downward move was coming. I placed the following order: buy 3 OEX 895 Puts at market and sell at a premium of 2 more than received. A few minutes later I received confirmation the 3 OEX P895 were bought at 10¾. I continued watching the real time quotes and the OEX continued slowly dropping. Then it made a slight rise about 15 minutes after my buy order was placed. At such times I always wonder if I took the right side. But at about 14:00 a strong sell program started and the OEX dropped like a rock. Now I knew for sure I'd get my sell executed at 12¾. A little more than an hour after the 3 OEX P895 were bought, I received a notice from my broker that they had sold for 13; it's always a nice surprise when I get more than I expected. The profit for the 3 long Put 895 = 3 x 100 x (13-10.75) - round trip commission = $675 - $45 = $630. The profit for the 2 day trades = 630 + 405 = $1,035. This is how the delta strategy works when all goes well.

The market on that first trading day after the 4th of July was a roller coaster; first it went up and then it went down, with a total daily swing of some 13.5 points or 1.5%. On this day the market ended down after having been up strongly earlier in the day. Variations like these have become common in the New York market in the late 1990's. This kind of volatility can be used to profit using the delta strategy for day trading.

What predictions could be made for the rest of the option month, since there were only 9 more trading days? Let's look at two charts to decide, first the Stochastics %K-%D chart, Figure 2.5 below: Since this chart was generated on Monday, July 7, all the items to the left of that date are based on actual data and those beyond that date are mathematical predictions.

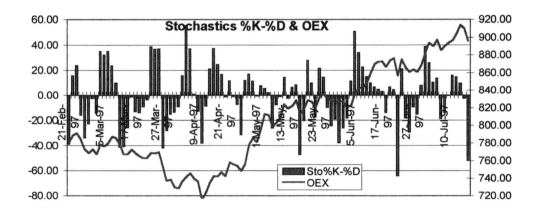

The trend to the end of the option month is shown to be up, even with the drop on July 7. The Stochastics %K minus %D chart signals an up market and the 50 day extrapolated trend of the chart also shows an up market, with the rising above 900 for the OEX.

Let's look at the Welles-Wilder Indicator (WWI) chart to see if the market is overbought or oversold, see Figure 2.6 below:

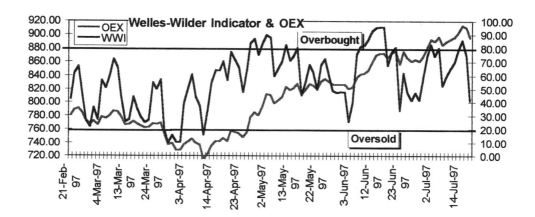

The WWI chart shows that with the slight downward correction on July 7 the market is just above the overbought level, and it also shows the continuing upward trend for the OEX. So the two charts of Figure 2.5 and 2.6 both show that the market will probably continue up until option expiration. So far during this month I had not opened a covered short spread position but with this optimistic information, I decided to try it.

Could we make some profit using the 2 sigma Covered Short Spread Strategy? The market had been on a strong uptrend all this option month, and as a result there were no 2 sigma Call positions available. So how about opening 15 Put 2 sigma covered short spreads? I gave my broker the following order near the end of the July 7 trading day: sell 15 July Puts 885 and buy 15 July Puts 880 at market close today to open a new Put covered short spread. I received the confirmation from my broker that the short Puts at 885 sold for 9.75 and the long Puts at 880 were bought for 8.25. The initial credit for the 15 Put covered short spreads = 15 x 100 x (9.75-8.25) - Commission = $2,250 - 7.5 x 15 x 2 = $2,025. (The 7.5 is the commission per option required by my broker.) If the OEX stayed above 885 at expiration, then I would get to keep the initial credit of $2,025. On July 9, I worried a little when the OEX hit 879.65 intraday but it finished at 885.33. The next day the intraday low was 880.85. However the OEX finished at 890.22 and the rest of the month was clear sailing. The OEX expired at 895.86 so I got to keep the $2,025 as profit which had been in my account since the position was opened.

The margin required by my broker for these 15 Put covered short spreads = 2000 + 15 x 100 x (5-1.5) = $,2000 + $5,250 = $7,250. (The term in the formula (5-1.5) shows there were 5 points between the two positions and the 1.5 is the difference between the premium paid for the long Put and that received for the short Put.) Using the rule that you should have a capital twice the margin in your trading account, then you should have a minimum of $14,500 in your account to make this trade.

SOME EXAMPLES OF SEI TRADES
USING MARKET DIRECTION SIGNALS

I was watching the satellite channel SkyNews which gives a minute by minute real time quote of the FTSE-100. An hour after the London Market opened, a surprise increase in inflation was announced. An immediate sell program started with the FTSE-100 at 4797.9, down 12.8 from the previous close, which I could see by the down ticks on the real time quote on the SkyNews teletext screen. I immediately placed a FAX order to buy 5 SEI Puts 4800 at market and sell at 10 points more than paid. I received confirmation that I paid 63 for the Puts. The FTSE-100 continued to fall during the day. Four and a half hours after market open, when the FTSE-100 was down 42.9, I received confirmation that the five long Puts at 4800 had been sold at 73 or a profit of 10 points. Profit for the trade = 5 x 10 x 10 - Comm = £500 - £50 = £450. Since the exchange rate was 1.6930 $/£, the profit in dollars = 450 x 1.6930 = $762. The position was open for 3½ hours. At close that day the FTSE-100 finished down 52.2 at 4758.5.

I examined the FTSE-100 charts in anticipation of taking another position at strike price 4750 the next day, July 9. On the day the FTSE-100 dropped 52 points (above), the New York market had finished strongly up, with the DJIA up 103 points to a new all time record. On this day the two-day meeting of the Bank of England Money Policy Commission began, so there was a lot of nervousness in the London market, since the next day at mid-day London time the MPC would announce their decision about raising the interest rate. Often the London market moves in sympathy with the New York market, but with the weight of a possible interest rate rise hanging over the London market, I wanted to know as much as possible about the market sentiment before I decided to open any positions. I looked at the SEI (the underlying index for the FTSE-100) Stochastics %K minus %D chart shown in the following Figure 2.7 and observed that the stochastic bar for July 9 was down (negative), thus signaling a Put position even though the extrapolated trend was up:

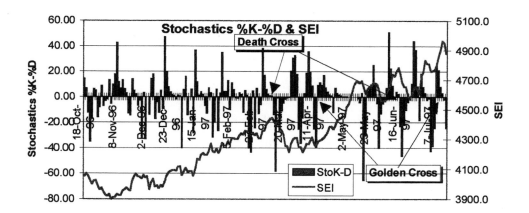

I also examined the WWI chart to see if the SEI was overbought or oversold. This chart is shown as Figure 2.8 below. On this date, July 9, the curve for the WWI or Relative Strength Indicator (RSI) was squarely in the middle at 50, meaning the market was neither oversold nor overbought.

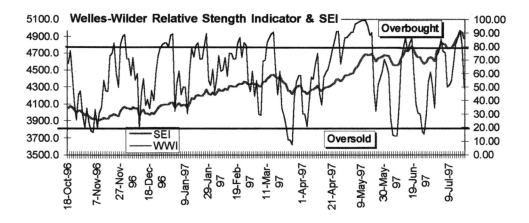

I watched the FTSE-100 real time quotes on SkyNews and the FTSE-100 opened up 7.9, but about 8 minutes after market open, a sell program started and the market began dropping. When the market went negative and was down 10 and dropping fast, I decided to use the delta strategy. I rushed my FAX order to buy 5 SEI Puts at 4750 at market and to sell at 4 more than received. Six minutes later I received confirmation that I paid 74 for the P4750 and had already sold at 83. In 6 short minutes I had a profit of 9 points when I had only asked for 4. This happens occasionally when the market is moving very fast in the direction of your position. In this case the market was dropping like a rock at more than 4½ points per minute. **What was my 6 minute profit in $'s?** Profit = 9 points x 5 Puts x 10 - 2 x 25 = £400; the exchange rate at this time was 1.6872 $/£ so the profit in dollars = 1.6872 x 400 =$675 or more than $100 per minute! **What was the return on capital at risk?** The cost of the 5 SEI Puts at 4750 = 5 x 10 x 74 +25 (comm.) = £3725 = 1.6872 x 3725 = $6,285. Return = 675/6285 = 10.7%.

I hope these examples show you the power of the delta strategy for long Calls and long Puts. But I must warn you, as Bruce Cameron, a friend I met on the Wall Street Journal Interactive discussion group said, "if your trigger finger is rusty or you don't have computer aided trading, don't try it!" It was Mr. Cameron who explained to me in the discussion group how to ride on the coat tails of the program traders and profit. My experience has shown it really works.

CHAPTER 3

WHAT OPTIONS TO USE FOR TRADING

OPTIONS and MARKETS

The Chicago Board Options Exchange (CBOE) which uses New York stock indexes and stocks and the London International Financial Futures and Options Exchange (LIFFE) are the two best markets in the world to do option trading. The CBOE trades a wide variety of options (both American and European style) including Index Options, Equity (or stock) Options, Currency Options, Treasury Options, Long Term Treasury Options, and LEAPS (Long Term Equity AnticiPation Securities). I recommend trading only OEX, the American Style S&P 100 Options, if you trade on the CBOE.

The LIFFE has an even broader array of options including Index Options (both American and European style), Commodity Options, Equity (Stock) Options, Interest Rate Options, and Bond Options. I recommend trading only SEI, the American Style FTSE-100 Options, if you trade on the LIFFE. If you have a broker in London, you can trade both the OEX and SEI from the same trading account. **Special note: a US citizen can not trade on the LIFFE unless he or she has a second passport and an overseas address.**

The New York Stock Exchange (NYSE), which trades the stocks underlying the CBOE index and stock options, is dominated by program traders who push a button and buy or sell hundreds of millions of dollars worth of a basket of stocks. This causes a sharp jump in prices if it is a buy program or an equally sharp drop if it is a sell program. The magnitude of the rise or fall in the index depends on the size of the buy or sell program or the dollar value traded. Such buy and sell programs completely swamp the tiny volumes of the small options traders. So the small trader must use strategies that profit from the big moves caused by the program traders. To give you a feeling for the number of program trades on a typical trading day, I will give two examples:

1. One day when the OEX had a total swing of 13 points, but finished up 4.85 points, there were 18 buy programs and 11 sell programs; the biggest buy program caused the OEX to jump 5 points in 5 or 10 minutes, the biggest sell program caused the OEX to drop 3.8 points in 3 minutes.

2. The day before the first example the OEX had a total swing of 20 points and finished down 11.91 points or 1.3% down, there were 12 buy programs and 12 sell programs; the biggest jump was 4.6 points that took place in less than 5 minutes and the biggest drop was 7 points which took place in about 3 minutes.

I hope these two examples show you the futility of trying to buy OEX Calls or Puts and hold them for a few days hoping to make a profit. The extreme volatility of the New York market coupled with the time decay of option premiums make such strategies almost unworkable. This same volatility makes the delta strategy for long Calls and Puts works so well. Take advantage of the program traders by anticipating their moves by a few minutes and taking a position that will make you a quick profit. The covered short spread strategy works in spite of the volatility by having Call CvSS and Put CvSS well outside the range of volatility caused by the program traders.

The London International Financial Futures and Options Exchange (LIFFE) trades American style SEI options which means you can buy and sell options at any time during the option month and options can be exercised any day during the option month. European style options only permit exercise of option positions on the last trading day of the option month or on expiration day. Therefore, it is necessary to use American style options if you want to use the delta strategy method. The underlying index for SEI options is the FTSE-100 index. The FTSE-100 has a lot of volatility like the OEX, but it has a different character. There are buy programs and sell programs as in New York, but the ones in London last longer - typically 30 minutes compared with the 5 minutes for the OEX. That means you have time to detect a buy program by a series of up ticks or a sell program by down ticks, send in your delta strategy order to buy Calls for a buy program or Puts for a call program and still benefit from the continuing buy or sell program. In New York the buy and sell programs are over extremely rapidly so unless you anticipate its beginning it's over before you can get your delta strategy order in and filled.

The SEI buy and sell programs are different from those of the OEX in another important respect: most take place in the morning during the first hour, so you can detect the first buy or sell program by watching up or down ticks for the first 8 to 10 minutes, send in your delta strategy order to buy Calls or Puts and if you ask for only 4 or 5 points you will get your close out before the sell or buy program ends. During the last hour and 40 minutes of option trading there is a lot of up and down activity in the FTSE-100 which moves up and down in sympathy with the DJIA.
Below are three examples of using the delta strategy with the SEI:

1. I detected a sell program by down ticks about 15 minutes after the London open; I placed an order to buy 5 SEI in-the-money Puts at market and to sell them at 4 more than received. The market drop accelerated. About 10 minutes after placing the order I received a FAX confirmation that the 5 had been bought at 74 and sold at 83 for a total of 9, or 5 more than I had asked, for a profit = 5 x 10 x (83-74)-5 x 5 (comm.) = £400 = 400 x 1.6872 ($/£ exchange rate) = $675.

2. Two trading days later I detected a buy program that started at open and continued. I entered a delta strategy order to buy 5 in-the-money Calls at market and sell at 5 more than received. A fax from the broker informed me I paid 77 for the 5 Calls, 9 minutes later I received confirmation that I sold the 5 Calls at 82 for a profit = 5 x 10 x (82-77)-25 = £200 = $338.

3. The next trading day I detected a sell program even though the FTSE-100 opened up 13 points and rose to 14.4 before turning around 9 minutes after open. I sent an order to buy 5 in-the-money Puts at market and sell at 5 more than received. Again I had a quick buy and sell: I bought at 68 and 6 minutes later sold at 73 for a profit of £200 = $376. Half an hour after my position was closed, the British Government released a report that the consumer price index (CPI) had dropped by 0.1%. This news caused an immediate buy program. If I had immediately sent in a FAX order for a Call position with a delta at 5 points I would have received a quick close out, but I hesitated for 20 minutes and didn't place an order. In 20 minutes the market rose 20 points that would have given me another sure 5 point profit ($376) within those 20 minutes. Then the market stalled. So when you detect a buy or sell program you must take action. If you wait too long you lose the opportunity. But my advice is don't get greedy. It is a good thing I didn't ask for a delta of 10 points for the long Put that gave me the quick profit for a delta of 5 (example number 3 above), because the market turned around before the change in premium reached 10, which would have placed me in a deep loss position!

Another difference between the FTSE-100 and the OEX markets is that the FTSE-100 usually has its major moves during the first hour or so after market open. The OEX often has a major move during the first 10 minutes after open and the opening CBOE option market responds to the early move with a sudden change in the premium prices from the close the night before. The opening Call and Put premiums reflect the orders placed before market open, so it is difficult to profit from the first move of the day. If you open a position at open you are apt to receive quite a different premium than at close the night before. These opening moves of the OEX are responding to economic news released normally an hour before New York market open. The OEX also has major moves during the last hour to hour and a half of the trading day. The FTSE may have a significant move after the New York markets open (when the FTSE still has 2 hours of trading left before close, the SEI options have an hour and 40 minutes of trading left), since the FTSE often moves in sympathy with the DJIA. So if the DJIA opens up, it may pull the FTSE up or if it opens down, it may force the FTSE down.

To give you a feel for the number of program trades of the FTSE during a typical trading day I will give you two examples:

1. On one day when the FTSE-100 finished down 52.2 points (the day before the Money Policy Committee raised the interest rates 25 basis points) there was one buy program that lasted 40 minutes and had a rise of 20 points and two sell programs, one that lasted 3 hours and dropped 20 points and a second one that lasted an hour and fell 23 points.

2. On a day when the FTSE-100 finished up 31.7 there was one buy program that lasted for 30 minutes and rose 33 points starting at market open, there was one sell program that lasted for an hour and dropped 14 points.

As you may see, the buy and sell programs in London are much fewer and last much longer than those in New York. As a result, the delta strategy for SEI Calls and Puts is easy to use. You can detect the program trades by watching down ticks and up ticks. You have time to enter your delta strategy order and if you use modest values of delta like 5 to 10 points, you have a high probability of a turn-around trade within a half hour to an hour - sometimes in only 10 minutes or less such as the 3 trading examples I gave earlier in this chapter.

MICROSOFT & INTEL: STOCKS SUITABLE FOR OPTION TRADING

Options for Microsoft (MSFT) and Intel (INTC) stocks are good to use for the delta strategy. I suggest these two stocks because they have high volume and good volatility to insure wide swings in price for intraday trading using long positions.

Letter symbols are normally used to read an option premium value on an Internet quote system or to specify to a broker. If a stock symbol has more than 4 letters such as MSFT (Microsoft) or INTC (Intel), then just use the first 2 letters of the symbol + Q for the option symbol; in other words the Microsoft option symbol would be MSQ and the Intel option symbol would be INQ. The stock symbols must be followed by two letters to specify Call or Put, the month and strike price (the letter codes specified by the CBOE are detailed in Figure 7.1 of Chapter 7). A Microsoft July Call at a strike price of 125 would be MSQ GE. An Intel July Call at a strike price of 50 would be INQ GJ. An Intel July Put at 55 would be INQ SK.

As one example, see the following theoretical trade for Microsoft options on one day in July 97:

- At 13:08 when Microsoft is at 132.8125 you buy 10 MSQ GE (July Microsoft Calls at strike price 125) at a premium of 8.5 and ask for a delta of 2.5; the cost = 10 x 100 x 8.5 + comm. = $8,500 + 10 x 5.5. = $8,555

- Shortly before close at 16:00 you sell the 10 MSQ GE and receive a premium of 11.0, so your profit for the round trip = 2.5 x 10 x 100 - 2 x comm. = 2500-55 x 2 = $2,390. A good profit for less than 3 hours; a return on cost = 2390/8555 = 27.9%. Microsoft closed at 135.9375 on the day of this example. You will note that all the stocks traded on the New York Stock Exchange are now quoted in sixteenths which was a change in July 97. Some people say this change from the nearest $1/32^{nd}$ to the nearest $1/16^{th}$ added volatility to the NYSE market.

A chart showing the closing price as a bar and the volume as a line is shown below in Figure 3.1 for a group of stocks that are suitable for option trading. The stock names for many of the stock symbols in this figure are listed in Appendix C.

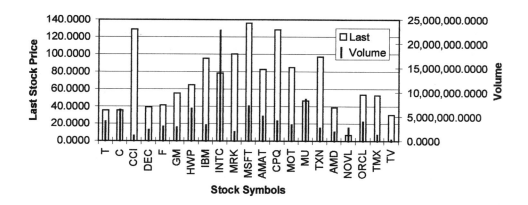

As you will note Intel (INTC) has the highest volume on this day and generally Intel has the highest volume of any stock traded on the New York Stock Exchange - this is the day that Intel split for a second time, so the prices are only half as much as the day before, plus the rise of the day. Intel must be popular because almost everyone (except the Apple owners) has an Intel chip in his/her PC. This is the same day as the Microsoft option example given above. You can see that Microsoft closed just under 135.9375 on this day, a rise of 6.1875 for the day, a day that the NASDAQ exchange reached its eighth daily record in a row, caused mainly by rises in the technology stocks such as Intel and Microsoft.

A chart showing the daily variations and the option month cumulative change for Intel is shown below in Figure 3.2. Please note the strong growth in Intel which is even greater if you consider there were two stock splits during this period from 5 January 1995 to July 1997.

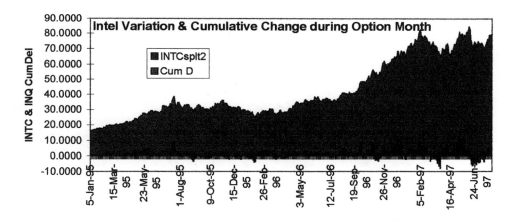

A similar chart showing the daily variations and the option month cumulative change for Microsoft is shown following in Figure 3.3. Microsoft has had one stock split during this period.

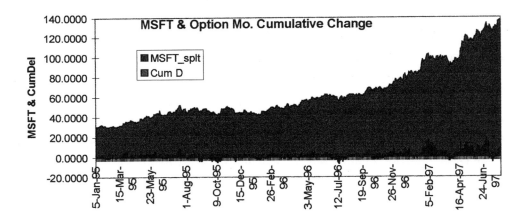

A similar chart showing the daily variations and the option month cumulative change for IBM is shown below in Figure 3.4. IBM has had one stock split during this period.

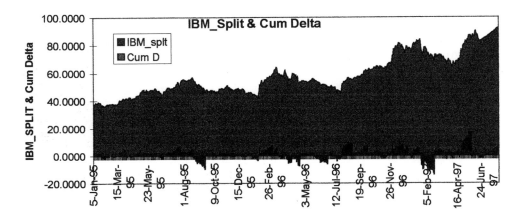

Note that IBM had a maximum cumulative delta (change) of 17 during the May option month on a split basis, but since this was before the split that took place on May 28, this was a cum delta of 34 on a pre-split basis. When the price of a stock gets too high, the company likes to split to keep the price under $100.

Normally there is not a sufficiently wide selection of strike prices for even high trading volume stocks like Intel, Microsoft and IBM to do 2 sigma covered or naked spreads (strangles), but they do make good candidates for the delta strategy as illustrated by the examples given earlier in this subsection of Chapter 3.

S&P 100 (OEX) INDEX OPTIONS

The OEX Index Options are traded on the CBOE in Chicago with the trading hours from 09:30 to 16:10 NY time. A single option contract is $100 times the index level with premiums (or value of the option) quoted in 1/16s ($6.25) for premiums below 3 and in 1/8s ($12.50) for premiums above 3. So a single OEX option with a premium of 8.25 would be valued at $825. The exercise of OEX options is American style meaning the options you hold can be exercised on any business day before the expiration date (see explanatory paragraph below). The S&P Index is a capitalization weighted index of 100 stocks from a broad range of industries, so it represents reasonably well the fluctuations in the NYSE stocks. The capitalization weightings are adjusted periodically to reflect changes in capitalization from such things as mergers.

Margin Requirements: If you sell an OEX option short (sometimes called "writing the option) the margin required is 15% of the underlying index (S&P 100) times $100 (for the option multiplier) minus the amount the option is out of the money. For example, if the OEX is at a level of 948 and you sell 3 OEX Calls at a strike price of 980, then the margin = 3 x 100 x 948 x 0.15-3 x 100 x (980-948)+comm. = $42,660 - $9,600 + $22.50 = $33,082; if you also opened 3 short Puts at 918 the margin would be essentially the same. You are required to have margin on only one side of a naked short spread. In addition there is a requirement that the seller of naked short options have a minimum in his or her trading account of $50,000.

Option Strike Price Intervals: Normally there are OEX options available at even 5 point intervals above and below the current level of the OEX. For example, if the OEX is at 948 there would be strike prices above at 950, 955, 960, 965, etc. and strike prices below at 945, 940, 935, 930, etc. However, I have found that during times of rapid market movement often a range of strike prices is missing. You might ask for a Call strike price 30 points above the market after a sudden 40 point jump and find there are just no options available, or one or more may be missing. You might query an internet quote service and get a report back saying "option strike price not found!", so you can't buy or sell the option strike price you wanted.

Option Exercise Style: You might receive an option exercise notice on any trading day for American style options (such as OEX). In such a case you must make settlement by cash on the next business day. An exercise notice is a command to do something you don't want to do: sell a long option you want to hold or buy a short option you want to hold until expiration. It usually happens when another trader wants the option position you are holding. In all the years I've been option trading I've only received one exercise notice and that was during the Gulf War when I held a Microsoft short spread and had to close it to meet the requirements of the notice when I wanted to hold it open. It has never happened when I held either an OEX or SEI option position.

Option Margin Call: You could also receive a different type of notice, a margin call. It usually happens when one side or the other of your naked short spread is in-the-money. This also requires a settlement in cash on the next business day. One way to settle a margin call is to sell one or two Puts and Calls on each side of your spread. Or you can buy back the in-the-money Puts or Calls and sell the same number again 5 or 10 points out-of-the-money. Either way, it will cost money. However, if you only use about half of your capital for any given short spread, you will not get any margin calls - assuming you don't just sit and let a naked spread position get far into-the-money. Normally you don't get margin calls for OEX covered short spreads because CBOE has a simple formula for margin requirements and the margin doesn't change, even if one side or the other is in-the-money. If you are trading SEI covered short spreads you may get a margin call because of the complicated rules LIFFE has for margin requirements for SEI.

Expiration for OEX is at 16:10 NY time on the third Friday of each month. If you are holding a short spread or a covered short spread that finishes safely, it will be worthless, so there is nothing to consider after the close on Friday. If you held an option that had value at expiration, then the value is the premium at option close on the third Friday. Actually, official expiration for the OEX is the Saturday after the third Friday.

Position limits are not something that will concern most of you readers but, to give you an idea of what the big program traders are involved in, the limit for an individual trade is 250 OEX options. To give you an idea of the amount of money involved in such a trade, to buy the limit of 250 OEX Puts at a premium of 18, a trader would have to put up cash or collateral = 250 x 100 x 18 = $450,000. Most individual investors wouldn't want to risk that much capital on an individual trade; I wouldn't ! There are exceptions to these limits if the trader is using the position as a hedge position. Sometimes a mutual fund manager uses Puts to protect the value of a basket of stocks he holds in case of a market drop: this is called a hedge.

How does the OEX vary relative to other Indexes? The following chart shows three indexes, the OEX, the SPX, and the NYX an index covering all stocks traded on the NYSE, plotted on the same scale. See in Figure 3.5 that the OEX is the middle curve with the SPX above and the NYX below:

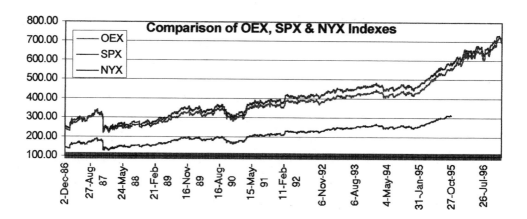

Please note that the OEX and SPX follow each other very closely, generally with the OEX about 98% of the value of the SPX. All three indexes follow the broad market patterns fairly closely. You can see the sudden one day drop of the October 87 market crash and the market droop during the Gulf war in August 90 and the market's sudden recovery after the Gulf war ended in early 1991.

How does the OEX vary over a 10+ year period? The chart below shows you variations in the OEX going back to December 1986 for over 10 years to give you a feeling for the ups and downs during those years. See the following Figure 3.6:

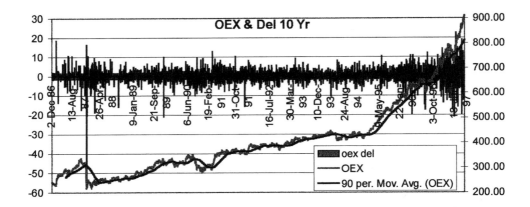

You will note in the above chart that the daily variations (OEX del = delta = change) and the 90 day moving average of the OEX are plotted on the same chart. This chart shows the first time that the OEX rose above the 900 level, almost 4 ½ times higher than the market level after the October 87 market crash. The steep market climb that started in 1995 is the steepest sustained climb the New York market has seen. Also along with the steep climb, large daily variations in the OEX with daily swings above 15 to 20 are occurring frequently. Also note that during the steep rise the OEX stayed above the 90 day moving average except for periods of correction such as that in July 96 and March-April 97. The daily high, low and close of the OEX during this period of steep rise is shown in the chart below, Figure 3.7, for the period April 97 through July 97:

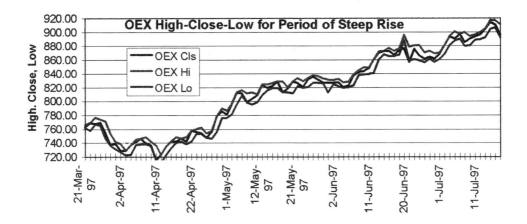

The upper line is, of course, the high and the middle line the close with the low at the bottom. The difference between the high and low is the daily swing. The average daily swing during this period was 12.44. The Figure 3.8 chart shows the daily swing for the same period, see below:

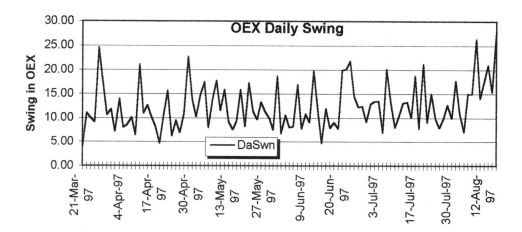

Note that during several days the daily swing was over 20 points. This daily swing is what makes the OEX delta strategy work. The amount of premium difference is related to the daily variation by the slope of the premium between strike prices. (The slope = difference in premium divided by difference in strike prices.) Since the delta strategy buys Calls or Puts in the money, this slope is about 0.6 during the beginning of the option month and the daily vacillation amounts to a premium swing = 0.6 x 12.44 = 7.46. Later in the month the in-the-money slope is about 0.8, so the vacillation amounts to a premium swing = 0.8 x 12.44 = 9.95. The delta strategy works by getting *part* of this daily premium swing. No one is clever enough to get all the fluctuation. The premiums go down as well as up during the day, so for a given day both Puts and Calls may turn a profit if you ask for a delta of say 1 to 2; remember, if you get greedy and ask for too high a delta, your plan can backfire and cause a loss if the market turns around suddenly. Buy and sell programs can cause this sudden turnaround. You may be sitting holding a long Call or Put with a small paper profit but less than your delta would give; a sudden gyration in the market can switch that paper profit to a big loss in a matter of a few minutes. That's why I recommend that you make a small amount using small deltas when you trade the delta strategy; this will reduce the probability that one of these sudden market turnarounds can cause you a big loss.

FTSE-100 (SEI) AMERICAN STYLE INDEX OPTIONS

The SEI options are traded on the London International Financial Futures and Options Exchange (LIFFE) using the FTSE-100 as the underlying index with the trading hours from 08:35 to 16:10 London time. A single option contract is £10 times the index level with premiums (or the value of the option) quoted to the nearest half point. So a single SEI option with a premium of 10 would be valued at £100. The exercise of SEI options is American style meaning the options you hold can be exercised (bought or sold) on any business day before the expiration date. The FTSE-100 Index is a index of 100 blue chip stocks from a broad range of industries on the London exchange.

Margin Requirements are set by the London Clearing House (LCH), an entity that guarantees all option transactions by brokers, that considers such factors as volatility and how deep the premiums are out-of-the-money. As an example, for 10 two-sigma covered short spreads (strangles) for SEI with initial premium: LC5100 = 17, SC5050 = 25.5, LP4700 = 51.5, SP4750 = 65, the initial margin = NOPS x (500 - SCprm + LCprm - SPprm + LPprm) = £9,500. For this short spread, the initial credit = NOPS x 10 x (SCprm - LCprm + SPprm -LPprm) - NOPS x 5 x 4(Comm) = 100 x (8.5 + 13.5) -200 = £2,000. The LIFFE applies more complex margin rules than the equation above (which is a good approximation) based on Risk Matrices which are given on the LIFFE "All Statistics" Internet page that is updated daily about 2 or 3 hours after London market close. See Chapter 5 under Margin for CvSS for a discussion of SEI margin requirements.

Option Strike Price Intervals: There are SEI options available at even 50 point intervals above and below the current level of the SEI. For example, if the SEI is at 4875 there would be strike prices above at 4900, 4950, 5000, 5050, 5100, etc. and strike prices below at 4850, 4800, 4750, 4700, etc. I have found that almost always there are strike prices available 2 sigma above and below the current market value of the SEI (FTSE-100) index.

Option Exercise Style: When using American style options you might receive an option exercise notice on any trading day for which SEI is traded. In such a case you must make a settlement by cash on the next business day. An exercise notice is a command to sell a long option or to buy back a short option you want to hold until expiration. Since there must be a seller for every buyer, exercise is a procedure that keeps the market moving.

The month end expiration is at 10:30 London time on the third Friday of each month. If you are holding a covered short spread that finishes safely (with the market between your short Call and Short Put positions), it will be worthless, so there is nothing to take into consideration after the option expiration and you get to keep the money you received when you opened the position. If you are holding long in-the-money options at expiration, their value at expiration is computed as the average premium for the last 20 minutes before market expiration (10:30 London time). The official expiration is the Saturday after the third Friday as with NY options.

How does the FTSE-100 vary relative to the Dow Jones Industrials? Figure 3.9 shows the FTSE and DJIA plotted on the same chart.

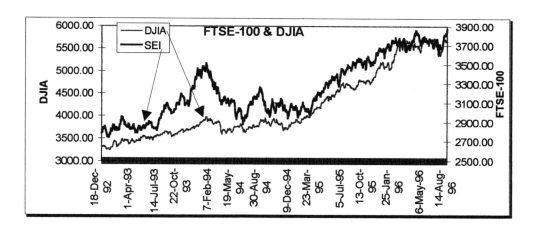

Please note that the FTSE-100 and the Dow Jones Industrial Average follow each other fairly closely, generally with the FTSE 60% to 75% of the value of the DJIA. Both indexes tend to have corrections at the same time, such as August 1986 and March 1987. During a given trading day, the FTSE-100 often moves in sympathy with the DJIA after New York opens (9:30 am New York time) which is two hours before London closes (4:30 PM London time). In other words, if the DJIA opens up, the FTSE-100 often rises also and if the DJIA goes down, the FTSE-100 often follows it.

The daily swing which makes the SEI delta strategy work is typically 30 to 60 points for the FTSE-100. The amount that the premiums of the various SEI positions change is related to the daily swing by the slope of the premium between strike prices. Since the delta strategy buys Calls or Puts in the money, this slope is greater than 0.5 during the option month when the daily swing amounts to a premium variation of 15 to 30. Remember, the delta strategy works by getting **part** of this daily premium swing. Since you need to wait a few moments to decide whether the market is heading up or down before you place your position request, you automatically lose out on a few points of the premium rise. The premiums go down as well as up during the day, so for a given day both Puts and Calls may turn a profit if you ask for a delta of no more than 4 or 5. The SEI option market is particularly risky if you get greedy and ask for too high a delta, and can cause very large losses if the market turns against your long Call or long Put position and you wait too long to close out the position. London has buy and sell programs like New York that can cause sudden turnarounds but the London buy and sell programs don't move as rapidly as those in New York. You might find yourself sitting with a long Call or Put with a small paper profit but less than your delta would give; a sudden U-turn in the London Market could switch that paper profit to a big loss in a matter of an hour or two. ***N.B.: make a small amount using the delta strategy by using small deltas to reduce the probability that a market turnaround can hit you with a big loss.***

SOME GENERAL OBSERVATIONS ABOUT OPTION PREMIUMS

An informative discussion of the prices of indexes and their premiums copied from the Internet page of the Chicago Board Options Exchange (CBOE) can be found in Appendix C under "Option Premiums."

Most traders want to sell their positions when their price is high and to buy positions when the price is low. The best way to know whether a premium is high or low is to look at the charts that show the premiums as a function of distance out-of-the-money and to study the values of the Call-at-the-money (CATM) and Put-at-the-money (PATM). If the CATM and PATM rise from one day to the next, it means the premiums are larger than usual, since the CATM and PATM decay with time and normally they decrease from one day to the next. An OEX Call premium chart is shown in the following Figure 3.10:

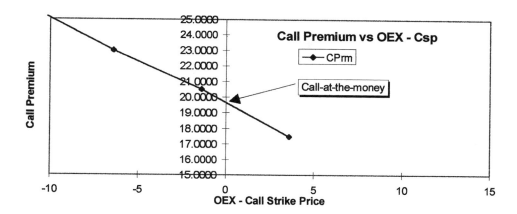

Note that the CATM from this chart is about 19.625. If this value is higher than the day before it means the premiums are greater than usual, a phenomenon which can be caused by big moves in the OEX.

CHAPTER 4

CAPITAL GROWTH USING THE DELTA TRADING STRATEGY

The delta trading strategy uses long Calls and Puts to profit from market movements during a trading day. To make a profit from a long Call or Put position you must be able to predict the direction the market is going to move. If the market is going to move up, then you buy Calls with an order to sell at a premium of **delta** more than you paid for it; if the market is going to go down, then you buy Puts with an order to sell at a premium of **delta** more than you paid for it. This is the **Delta Strategy** for option day trading. Both the OEX options traded by CBOE in Chicago and the SEI options traded by LIFFE in London are suitable for the delta strategy.

I choose long positions in-the-money, because the premium slope (increase in premium per point increase in OEX or SEI) is greater so it takes less movement in the OEX or the SEI to reach my delta. If the OEX market is at 917, the first long Call in-the-money would be 915. The premiums of the at-the-money Calls and Puts decay as the number of days til expiration (NDTE) decreases. Figure 4.1, on the following page, shows a typical decay in OEX Call at-the-money (CATM) and Put at-the-money (PATM) premiums for a month with 19 trading days.

NDTE	CATM	PATM
19	22.375	21.500
18	22.000	19.250
17	19.750	19.250
16	19.125	18.000
15	18.125	16.750
14	20.250	17.000
13	17.000	16.375
12	17.125	15.625
11	15.625	15.500
10	15.250	13.375
9	13.250	11.875
8	11.875	11.125
7	13.375	10.000
6	10.875	9.750
5	9.250	7.875
4	8.000	7.250
3	5.875	6.250
2	6.250	4.875
1	3.125	4.750
0	0.000	0.000

At the beginning of the option month the OEX CATM and PATM pre-miums are both over 20. Near the end of the option month the ATM premiums are less than 10 and they decay rapidly during expiration week. A plot of the decay of OEX Call and Put at-the-money premiums versus the number of days remaining until expiration is shown below in Figure 4.2.

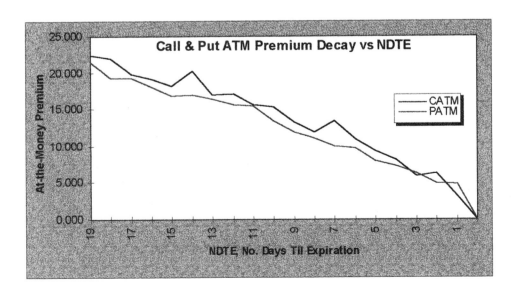

On the 13th day until expiration the C915, which is slightly in-the-money, would have a premium about 1 more than the CATM premium or about 18. The premium slope (discussed in Chapter 2 under "How Far in-the-money for a Long Call or Put Position?") is about 0.6, so if the OEX increased to 921, a 4 point increase, then the C915 premiums would increase as follows: C915 = 18 + 0.6 x 4 = 18 + 2.4. If you had made your delta less than 2.4, then your sell order would have closed. As the market goes up, the premiums on in-the-money Calls increase faster than the premiums on out-of-the-money Calls; as the market goes down, the premiums on in-the-money Puts increase faster than the premiums on out-of-the-money Puts. If you ask for a delta of 1 for an in-the-money Call or Put you will get your request with less market movement than if you choose an out-of-the-money position.

HOW LARGE A DELTA SHOULD YOU REQUEST?

The paragraphs above pointed out it takes a move of about 2 on the OEX to produce a delta of 1 in the premium of an at-the-money position. Several of the program trades that take place each day in New York make the OEX go up or down by 1½ to 2 points. For these normal program trades I think a delta of 1 is appropriate. There are often a couple of program trades that cause the OEX to go 3 to 4 points up or down. For these moderate moves, a delta of 1½ will close out your position before the market turns around. At least once per day there will usually be a buy or sell program trade that will make the OEX jump or drop 5 points. For such a big move, you can ask for a delta of 2 for the premium increase on your OEX long position and get it.

The FTSE-100 market in London also has buy and sell programs that can be used for the delta strategy using the SEI options. The number of switches back and forth in the market is fewer in London than in New York. New York may have as many as a dozen or more switches per day. London will only have one or two, which makes program trading easier in London. The best way to judge the magnitude of a move on the FTSE-100 is to watch a real time quote such as on the British satellite channel SkyNews and watch how many points per minute the FTSE is changing. Half a point per minute would indicate a normal move up or down and this would indicate you should ask for a delta of 4 or 5. A move of 1 or 1½ points per minute is a moderate move and would signal a delta of 10. A very rapid change, like more than 2 points per minute, would mean a delta of 20 could close out safely.

Market charts can help you recognize the correct market conditions for using long positions. If the 7 day WWI (Welles-Wilder Indicator) chart is above 80 (in the overbought area) this is a signal that the market is ready for a correction and a long Put is indicated. The Stochastics %K-%D chart is the most sensitive for indicating long Calls or Puts: when the Stochastics indicator is above zero this signals a Call, when it is below zero this signals a Put. The WWI and Stochastics charts are better for indicating delta strategy positions than either the MAD4 or the MAD9-5 charts. The MAD4 charts are good for signaling intermediate term market trends and the MAD9-5 charts are better for longer term market trends so these two charts are more useful when you are doing covered short spread trading. Positive for both indicate an up market, negative for both indicate a down market.

WHEN HAS THE MARKET MOVED ENOUGH TO GET YOUR DELTA?

When your broker is busy he might not notify you in a timely manner that your delta strategy position has closed with your requested delta. Say for example, you sent in an order to buy OEX long Call in-the-money options when the OEX was 934 and you asked for a delta of 1.5. You see the OEX jump to 937.5 (a rise of 3.5); at a premium slope of 0.6, the premium will increase by 2 or more, so you can expect your long Call will be closed at your delta of 1.5 or more. Sometimes the movements in the OEX caused by program trades is so rapid that your broker is able to get more for you when he sells your position than your requested delta.

HOW TO PREDICT MARKET DIRECTION

It is essential that you have tools for predicting short term option movements. A variety of techniques and strategies for trying to foretell market directions are presented below.

Before the markets open, the Futures Market can predict the direction the cash market will move at open. The SPX futures market opens an hour and 10 minutes before the New York market opens and before the CBOE OEX option market opens. If the SPX futures market is moving higher before open and is higher than the close the day before, this is a strong indication that the OEX is going to open higher and vice versa. If the futures market predicts the cash market is going to rise, then buy Calls at open with a delta of 1; if the futures market predicts the cash market is going to drop, then buy Puts at open with a delta of 1. Very often the market reverses within the first 30 minutes after market open and heads the other way. If you are trading at market open, to make a quick profit and avoid having a long position that turns from a profit to loss, make sure you ask for a *small delta - like 1*.

After market open you can detect a buy (or sell) program that makes the market rise (or fall) rapidly by watching a real time quote system. On US TV, the CNBC provides a real time ticker tape of SPX and other market indices. When you see the SPX rising rapidly, like an increase of a point per minute, that indicates a buy program. When you see the SPX dropping, that's a sell program. A drop of 5 points in 10 minutes is not unusual for a sell program and a rise of 5 points in 10 minutes is not unusual for a buy program. These rapid buy and sell programs are what make the delta strategy work. I strongly recommend subscribing to an Internet real time quote system such as Interquote, provided by Paragon Software, Inc., of Wisconsin. With such a quote system you can watch both the OEX and the Put and Call premiums for the strike prices of interest by merely clicking on the *Get Quote* button as frequently as you wish. With this tool at your fingertips, you can watch both the OEX value change as well as the option strike price premiums change when a buy or sell program is in progress.

For the delta strategy to work, rapid action is required because the New York buy and sell programs move quickly and often last less than ten minutes. The London buy and sell programs move more slowly and there are typically fewer reversals than in the New York market. To make sure you get into the market near the beginning of the buy or sell program, when you detect the program, as quickly as you can, place an order to buy at market with a simultaneous order to sell at a premium delta above what you receive for the market order. If you have selected the right direction and have asked for a reasonably small delta, then your buy and sell order is often executed in less than 15 to 30 minutes giving you a small but quick profit.

EXAMPLES OF OEX AND SEI DELTA STRATEGY TRADES

OEX Delta Strategy Trade Examples:

1. On 22 May 97 at 12:46 New York time, I bought 3 OEX June C820 at 20.5, cost = 20.5 x 3 x 100+22.5 = $6,172; at 11:59 the next day, sold 3 OEX June C820 at 22, received = 22 x 3 x 100 -22.5 = $6,577 for a profit = 6577-6172 = $405, or a return on capital at risk = 405/6172 = 6.56%. Note: in the mathematical formula used for these computations, the first number is the premium, the next number is the number of options, the third number is 100 for OEX and 10 for SEI (because each OEX option represents 100 shares and each SEI option represents 10 shares), and the fourth number is the broker's commission which is plus when you are buying a position and minus when you are selling a position.

2. On 9 June 97 at 11:50 New York time, bought 3 OEX June C820 at 26.5, cost = 26.5 x 3 x 100+22.5 = $7,972; 38 minutes later, sold 3 OEX June C820 at 28.5, received = 28.5 x 3 x 100 -22.5 = $8,527 for a profit = $555, or a return on capital at risk = 555/7972 = 6.96%.

3. On 12 June 97 at 11:50 New York time, bought 3 OEX June C820 at 28.75, cost = $8,648; 21 minutes later, sold 3 OEX June C820 at 30.25, received = $9,053 for a profit = $405, or a return on capital at risk = 405/8648 = 4.68%.

4. On 19 June 97 at 13:42 New York time, bought 3 OEX June C820 at 8.5, cost = $2,573; 48 minutes later, sold 3 OEX Jun C820 at 9.5, received = $2,828 for a profit = $256, or a return on capital at risk = 256/2573 = 9.95%.

5. On 24 June 97 at 14:33 New York time, bought 3 OEX July C875 at 20.875, cost = $6,285; 26 minutes later, sold 3 OEX June C875 at 22.375, received = $6,690 for a profit = $405, or a return on capital at risk = 405/6285 = 6.44%.

Please note that for these five example trades spanning just over one month the total profit was $2,026 for an average of $405 with all trades profitable. All except one trade were open less than an hour. The average cost per trade was $6,330 for an average return on capital at risk = 405/6330 = 6.40% for the month, or an annual return of 76.78%.

The five sample trades are representative of what you can expect trading at the level of 3 OEX options using the delta strategy. The maximum cost for the trades was $8,648 in example (3). Using the rule of using only half your capital for a trade, this means your minimum capital should have been $17,296 for this set of trades. So your return on total initial capital was 1231/17296 = 7.12% per month or 85.4% on an annual basis. With the $17,296 capital you would also have had enough capital to open five covered 2 sigma short spreads with an initial credit of about $1,175, giving you a total monthly return on capital =1175+2026 = $3,201 or an annual return = 3201/17296 = 18.51%/mo. = 222% annual return, well over 100%.

SEI Delta Strategy Trade Examples:

1. On 20 May 97 at 08:50 London time, bought 5 SEI June P4650 at 77 with delta of 5, cost = 77 x 5 x 10+25 = £3,875; 30 minutes later, sold 5 SEI June P4650 at 83, received = 83 x 5 x 10 - 25 = £4,125 for a profit = 4125-3875 = £250 = 250 x 1.6392 = $410, or a return on capital at risk = 250/3875 = 6.45%. (Note: the exchange rate from pound to dollars changes constantly.)

2. On 3 June 97 at 08:50 London time, bought 5 SEI June P4600 at 80 with delta of 5, cost = £4,025; 30 minutes later, sold 5 SEI June P4600 at 86, received = £4,275 for a profit = £250 = 250 x 1.6331 = $408, or a return on capital at risk = 250/4025 = 6.21%.

3. On 9 June 97 at 08:50 London time, bought 5 SEI June C4600 at 102 with delta of 10, cost = 102 x 5 x 10+25 = £5,125; 30 minutes later, sold 5 SEI June C4600 at 112, received = 112 x 5 x 10 -25 = £5,575 for a profit = £450 = 450 x 1.6310 = $734, or a return on capital at risk = 450/5125 = 8.78%.

4. On 13 Jun 97 at 08:50 London time, bought 5 SEI June C4700 at 99 with delta = 10, cost = 99 x 5 x 10+25 = £4,975; 30 minutes later, sold 5 SEI June C4700 at 110, received = 110 x 5 x 10 -25 = £5,475 for a profit = £500 = 500 x 1.6355 = $818, or a return on capital at risk = 500/4975 = 10.05%.

5. On 18 June 97 at 08:50 London time, bought 5 SEI June P4700 at 66 with delta of 10, cost = £3,325 with a delta of 10; an hour later the market started rising and I mistakenly saw this as a turn-around, so placed a sell order and sold 5 SEI June P4700 at 60, received = £2,975 for a loss = £250 = -250 x 1.6371 =-$573, or a return on capital at risk = -250/3325 = -7.52%. Had I been more patient and waited another hour I would have seen the premium go up to 79 and an hour later than that the premium hit a high of the day of 89. So I would have reached my delta of 10 and earned a profit of £450 instead of the loss of £250.

6. On 24 June 97 at 08:50 London time, bought 5 SEI June C4550 at 109 with delta of 10, cost = 109 x 5 x 10+25 = £5,475; 30 minutes later, sold 5 SEI June C4550 at 122, received = 122 x 5 x 10 -25 = £6,075 for a profit = £600 = 600 x 1.6689 = $1000, or a return on capital at risk = 600/5475 = 10.96%.

The total profit on these 6 SEI trades was £1,800 or an average of £300 per trade. The profit in US$ = $2,797 for an average per trade of $466 was for just one month of trading. All of these trades were closed on the same day they were opened. Most trades were closed within an hour of opening. Also several of the trades received a premium difference greater than the delta requested in the order.

For the 11 trades (5 OEX and 6 SEI) for a one month period the total profit was = 2026 + 2797 = $4,823. Note the SEI trading yielded 1.38 times as much as for OEX trading during this month. The better profitability for SEI versus OEX is because the London market has fewer ups and downs during a trading day than the New York market. The London buy and sell programs last longer than those of New York, so it is easier to detect a buy or sell program in London and to take profitable advantage of it with SEI options using the delta strategy.

DELTA STRATEGY OPPORTUNITIES DURING EXPIRATION WEEK

One particular characteristic of the option month during expiration week (the last week of the option month which always ends on the third Friday of the calendar month) is that the at-the-money premiums are small and have a rapid daily decay. The low premiums mean the cost of the in-the-money premiums are small, but the premiums decay significantly each day until at expiration all premiums are zero except the in-the-money strike prices. The chart below shows this premium decay for the at-the-money premiums during the last seven days of the option month, Figure 4.3:

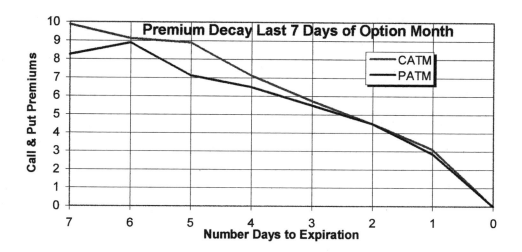

CATM means Call-at-the-money premiums and PATM means Put-at-the-money premiums. This chart starts with the Thursday before the last week (between 7 and 6 on the bottom line with line 6 showing the at-the-money premiums at market close on Thursday and using those numbers for the at-the-money premiums at market open on Friday). The Call premium decay during that day is small, and the Put premium actually rises slightly. The next day (between 6 and 5) is Friday a week before expiration, between 5 and 4 is the Monday of expiration week and finally between 1 and 0 is Friday, which is expiration day. The Call premiums at-the-money (ATM) decay at about 1.5 points per day from Open Monday (the first day of the option trading month) to close on Thursday of the final week, but on expiration Friday the ATM decay during the day is about 3 points for both the Calls and Puts expiring on that day.

Making profitable OEX Delta Strategy trades during expiration week:

1. On Monday 14 July 97, the SPX futures were up strongly (9 points higher) compared with the close the night before which signaled the

market was going to open up. The OEX had closed at 893.59 on the Friday before and thirteen minutes after market open on Monday the OEX was up 3.3, so I decided to buy 3 OEX July C890 at market and placed a delta order to buy 3 July C890 at market and sell when the premium increased by 1.5. I received notification that I paid 12.5 for the 3C890 with cost = 12.5 x 300 + comm. = 3750 + 22.5 = $3,772.50. An hour and a half later I received confirmation that the 3 C890 had sold at 14.25, a quarter of a point more than I had requested (always a nice surprise!) for which I received = 14.25 x 300 - 22.5 = $4,252.5 for a profit = $480. The OEX closed at 896.53.

2. On Tuesday 15 July 97 the SPX futures again indicated an up market for this day (up 8 points) and the Frankfurt SPX spot cash price was also up. The OEX rose to 900 a few minutes after open so I decided to wait and see what happened before opening a position. The OEX fell back to 893.08 or down 3.45 about 45 minutes after New York market open. I was still convinced this would be an up day because of my earlier SPX reports and also I would get a better premium for the Call if I entered the market while it was down. I placed a delta order at 50 minutes after New York open to buy 3 July OEX C890 at market and sell at 3 more than received. I got confirmation that I paid 9¾ for the Calls for a cost = 9.75 x 300-22.5 = $2,947.50. The premium rose to 10¾ an hour later, and I almost sent in an amended sell order to settle for a delta of 1. But I looked at my records of the SPX futures and cash price and also realized the market was near the "magic number" of 900. With the plus that the market almost always goes up during expiration week, I decided I could make more than usual today. Finally at an hour before New York close I received notice that the 3 C890 sold at 12.75 and I received = 12.75 x 300 - 22.5 = $3802.50, for a profit of $855. The OEX closed at 904.20 with the C890 closing at 15.5, so I could have made even more had I asked for a delta of 5 more instead of 3.

3. On Wednesday 16 July 97, again the SPX futures indicated an up market. The chaos patterns indicate the market rises during the last week of the option month. On this day the market jumped at open with the OEX up over 908 after less than 5 minutes. I have learned that when the market jumps at the beginning, the premiums I pay are higher than

I expect and the market often falls back after the opening leap up. This happened today, so I decided to wait until the market had been open for a while. Finally 3½ hours after market open I decided to open a long Call position, well in-the-money to get a high slope on the premiums. I placed an order to buy 3 OEX July C890 at market and sell at 2½ more than received. I received confirmation that I paid 21½ for a cost = 300 x 21 - 22.5 = $6,322.5. The market didn't do much for the next 1½ hours, as it often does in the middle of the day. Then finally about an hour before close, a buy program started that took the OEX up to over 917. I received notice well before it hit that high of the day that the 3 OEX C890 sold at 24 for a profit = 2.5 x 300 - 45 = $705. The OEX closed at 913.82, a new all time high.

Although there were still two days to go, I decided to stop OEX trading for the month and be happy with the three day profit of $2,040. One thing to learn in option trading is when you've had good success, take a rest, particularly on the last two option days which are treacherous because of all the volatility and the rapid decay in premiums. For example, on this month's expiration Friday (18 Jul 97) the OEX ended down 14.72 points closing at 898.86, far below the all time high at that time. There was an immediate drop of 10 points in the first 45 minutes of trading. To profit from a long Put, you would have had to open it immediately after open, but at that time the SPX futures was predicting an up market and you would have been inclined to open a long Call instead. So my decision not to trade on expiration Thursday and Friday turned out to be a good one!

Making profitable SEI Delta Strategy trades during expiration week:

1. On Monday 14 July 97 the FTSE-100 opened up 13.7 at 4813.2 and rose up to plus 14.2 some 8 minutes after London open, then started dropping, indicating a sell program was starting. Some 20 minutes after London open I decided to open a long Put position with a delta of 4. I placed an order to buy 5 July SEI P4850 at market and sell at a delta of 4 more than received. I received confirmation that I paid 68 for a cost = 68 x 5 x 10 - 5 x 5 = £3,425 = 1.6805 x 3425 = $5,756. Nineteen minutes later I was notified the 5 July P4850 were sold at 73 , or a delta of 5,

rather than the 4 I had requested to give a profit = (73-68) x 5 x 10 - 5 x 5 x 2 = £200 = 200 x 1.6805 = $336. Later in the day (about an hour after London open) the market turned around and started back up. The FTSE-100 finished up 57.9, so another delta strategy using long Calls at 4800 would have produced a profit. When the market started back up you could have bought a July C4800 at about 45 and made a delta of 10, since the C4800 closed that day at 63.

2. On Tuesday 15 July 97 the FTSE-100 opened on a positive tone when it rose 10 points to 4867 during the first 43 minutes after open. I placed an order to buy 5 July SEI C4800 at market and sell at 10 more than received. I got confirmation that I paid 76 for the C4800 for a cost = 5 x 10 x 76 + 5 x 5 = £3,825 = 1.6874 x 3825 = $6,454. The market stayed within a narrow range for an hour or so, then started a gradual climb and by 2 hours after London open was up 30 points. Then 3½ hours after open there was a fast upward movement with the FTSE-100 hitting 4900, up 42.6 points. At that time I received notice that the 5 C4800 were sold at 100 - what a nice surprise to get 14 more than the 10 I asked for! This trade yielded a profit of 24 points = 5 x 10 x 24 - 5 x 5 x 2 (comm.) = £1,150 = 1.6848 x 1150 = $1,937.

3. On Wed 16 July 97 the FTSE-100 opened up strongly (10 points at 4909) and continued it's rise. Five minutes after market open I placed an order to buy 5 C4850 at market and sell at 5 more than received. I received confirmation that I paid 92, when the market was up about 18. The market continued to rise and half an hour after market open it was up 26.7 at 4926 when I received notice that I had sold the 5 C4850 at 97, just what I had asked for. The profit on this trade = 5 x 10 x 5 - 2 x 5 x 5 = £200 = 200 x 1.6766 = $335.

4. On Thursday 17 July 97 the FTSE-100 opened up 6.5 at 4970 and showed a definite upward trend. Five minutes after market open I placed an order to buy 5 July SEI C4950 at market and sell at 5 more than received. I got confirmation that the C4950 cost 80. The FTSE-100 continued up and hit 4992.7 up 28.5 by 22 minutes after market open. I received notice that the 5 C4950 options were sold at 85 giving a profit of £200 = 1.6698 x 200 = $334.

I decided not to trade on expiration Friday 18 July, since the SEI options expire only an hour after market open on expiration day. My profit for the 4 SEI trades for the 4 days of the July 97 expiration week was £1,750 or at the last $ to £ exchange rate on that day = $2,922.

WHAT IF THE MARKET
SWITCHES DIRECTION AGAINST YOUR LONG?

What should you do if you open a long Call or Put delta strategy position and the market turns around and moves against your position before it closes out? I have analyzed a number of such bad trades and it is imperative that you either use a stop loss order or use a mental stop loss to prevent a large loss from occurring in such a case. In my judgment, it is better to use a mental stop loss order rather than a formal stop loss order. A reader of my first book who was a floor trader on the Copenhagen exchange told me the floor traders know where all the stop loss orders are and will manipulate the market to close out those stop loss orders. It is better for you to keep the power of deciding when to sell rather than turn that decision over to others. When using the mental stop loss method, if you see the OEX move 2 points in the wrong direction for your open long Call or Put, then place an immediate order to "sell at market" to reduce the loss to about 1 premium point. If you see the FTSE-100 move 5 points in the wrong direction for your open SEI Call or Put, then place an immediate sell at market to reduce your loss to about 2½ premium points. Yes, this action will cause a loss, but it will limit your loss to a reasonable level. For the OEX, a mental stop loss of 2 points would limit your loss to about $600 plus commission for 3 options; for the SEI, a mental stop loss of 5 points would limit your loss to about £250 plus commission for 5 options. *In long trading, it is better not to wait and hope when your trade turns bad - close it out and take a small loss - otherwise the loss can quickly grow to a very big loss!*

If the market should switch direction and start moving against your position, it is better to take a small loss and place a sell order. This is psychologically difficult - to accept you are going to have a loss and to cut it short as quickly as possible. In today's volatile market these changes in direction can happen very quickly in the New York market with the program traders causing a dozen or so reversals during a trading day. Sometimes these changes happen so fast you don't have time to respond to them. For example, assume you are holding a long Call with a delta that doesn't get reached before a strong sell program makes the market drop lower: These sell programs can cause very sudden falls, sometimes with a 1.5% drop in the OEX in just 10 minutes. Your long Call can suddenly flip from a nice profit to a huge loss without your having time to protect it.

If, for some reason, you don't get your stop loss order to your broker in time to keep your losses relatively small, there are some things you might do to try to limit your loss as you sit there with your money going down the drain. The only good thing about a losing long position is that you can only lose as much as the position cost, whereas with short positions, the loss can be unlimited. These efforts to try to rescue a losing position, of course, are very risky and require nerves of steel. The first plan is to keep watching the market for a sell or buy program going in your direction. Watch especially carefully near market open and close; both the OEX and SEI show more wild activity at those times and often reverse the direction they have gone during the middle of the trading day. Get on the Internet and read everything available about what the experts think the market will do in the next few days. Look at the prediction charts to see what they indicate the market might do soon; especially study the Welles Wilder chart to see if the market is overbought or oversold. Perhaps you will find indications your position might get better in the next few days.

How do you get out of your bad position? If you are in a hurry to get out, as when the market is going down many points a minute, the fastest way is to say, "Sell at market." There are several problems with this method. When the market is moving rapidly, the premiums increase much faster than usual, so you might have to pay more than you would expect to get out.. If the market has leveled out, the premiums sometimes recover a little. At recovery times like this, you can check the current premium prices for your position (on the Internet or by calling your broker) and put in an order "Sell at 25" or something near the quoted price. This is tricky, as you will not get out of the market if your requested premium is too high. Usually I tend toward the quick *sell at market* as the lesser of two evils

When you have an open long Call or Put you should watch the market closely using a real time quote system such as the CNBC on TV for the SPX or SkyNews for the SEI (FTSE-100) or an Internet quote system such as Interquote to make sure the market is moving in a favorable direction to your long position.

If you are holding a long Call that loses a lot of premium in a short time, perhaps you should consider holding it rather than selling at a big loss. If the market trend is up and the drop was caused by some economic report or just a big sell program, then if you wait a day or so to sell the position, you may reduce the loss considerably or even obtain a profit.

An example of hold and profit for a long Call position: I placed an order to buy 3 OEX C930 at market with a delta of 2, and paid 12.5 for it. At market close that night, the premium reached 13.5 which was not enough to trigger my sell order. The next day the OEX opened down with the C930 premium at 9.75, a big loss if I sold the Calls. I decided to wait; the premium hit a high of 12.625 (just a little more than I paid for it) before dropping down to close at 11.5. Since the market was in a good upward trend and it was not the last week of the option month expiration when rapid premium decay becomes a problem, I decided to wait another day. The next day the OEX opened up strongly and within an hour and a half after market open I received confirmation that my C930 sold at 14.5 for the 2 points I had asked for when the position was opened two days before.

An example of hold and profit for a long Put position: I placed an order to buy 3 OEX P920 at market with a delta of 2 on a day the OEX was up 9.5, expecting the sell programs to take it down so I could get the 2 points of profit for the long Puts. I paid 12.75 for the Puts. For the first time in a long time the sell programs didn't materialize that day and at market close my P920 was 11.5. The next day the market moved up during the first half hour dropping the premium on my long Puts to 10.25 which was 2.5 less than I paid for them. A half hour after market open the National Purchasing Managers' report came out indicating a rise in prices (a possible inflationary sign). This triggered an immediate sell-off in the market. Forty minutes later the OEX had dropped 11.71 points below the close the day before and the premium on the P920 jumped to 15.875. Shortly afterward I received confirmation that my 3 P920 had sold for 15.75 giving me a delayed profit = 3 x 100 x 2 -Comm. = $600 -2 x 22.5 = $555.

Waiting for a day or two to close out a losing long Call or Put can be, to say the least, *uncomfortable - my wife says nerve wracking -* when the delta strategy normally returns a profit in less than an hour. Nevertheless, it is sometimes the best strategy to avoid a big loss and return the profit you had expected when you opened the position.

WHAT CAN HAPPEN WHEN
THE SEI MARKET DIRECTION SWITCHES

Market action on Wednesday 23 July 1997, after a 154 point rise in the DJIA: The FTSE-100 opened up 55.4 and a strong buy program during the first ten minutes (from the FTSE open to 5 minutes after the options open) saw the market rise 62.4 points to 4909.2. This was in response to the DJIA's strong rise (the Greenspan rally) the day before. The FTSE-100 had dropped 158.7 points in three days from a high of 4964 before recovering 41 points on Tuesday 22 July. Since both the DJIA and the FTSE had risen on Tuesday, I decided that the FTSE would recover most of that 158 point drop. I placed a buy order for 5 SEI August C4900 and included an overly-optimistic sell order at 12 points more than received - Mistake No. 1. Twenty minutes later I received confirmation that I bought the 5 at a price of 133 and the broker was working to sell at 145. I was very surprised the premium was 133 since this was 51 points higher than where the SEI C4900 closed the day before. This high premium meant the Call slope was about 0.7. At this time the September futures were 4956 indicating there was still upward pressure on the FTSE. So I felt my sell order would be filled soon. During the next half hour the FTSE slipped back to a rise of only 66 to 4913, before another buy program set in that took it to 4931.5, up 84.8, the high of the day. I was surprised my sell order wasn't filled. Later I received the statistics for the C4900 from LIFFE on the Internet and found the high of the day for the C4900 was 135, only 2 points higher than the premium I paid for my 5 C4900 options. Later that day, half an hour after NY open with the FTSE at 4915 up 68, a sell program started that took the FTSE down to 4866.9 at options close or up only 20.2 and the C4900 closed at 82.5, down 50 points from where I bought - a paper loss of $4,405 for the day.

I complained to my broker that I felt I paid too much for the C4900, only 2 points less than the high of the day, and that when I placed the order the FTSE was up 62.5 and later hit a high of up 84.8, presumably the high for the C4900. At a Call slope of 0.53 the premium should = 81 (the C4900 close Tuesday) + 0.53 x 62.5 = 114, not the 133 I paid.

After reading my broker's answer to my query, here is what I think happened in the SEI option market on the day in question:

1. The big jump at open caused the Call premiums to be greatly inflated over their normal values : I didn't realize the premiums could increase so wildly.

2. The broker was late getting the order in and the FTSE was up 75 by the time the order was filled and the 133 I paid was the market value at that time.

3. For the next hour the market languished between 4922 and 4913; this slowing down of the market caused the inflated premiums to decay back to their normal levels. During the next half hour when the FTSE hit the daily high of 4931.5 (up 84.8) the premiums were equal to or even less than the high of the day, so I should have closed out at market here.

4. The premiums decayed to 107.5 half an hour after the New York open, with the FTSE up 65.4, making my paper loss on the trade $2,180. The DJIA jumped up 80 points a few minutes after New York open and then slid back to no change about 20 minutes before the SEI options close that day. This slide in the DJIA caused a sympathetic slide in the FTSE down to 4866.9 or up 20.2 at options close. The C4900 premium fell to 82.5 at close making the paper loss = $4,405.

What should I have done? When I got the first quote from ESI (the delayed quote of SEI premiums on the Internet) at 15 minutes after New York open and saw the C4900 premium had dropped to 112.5 (a paper loss of $1,759) immediately I should have placed a sell at market order. If the DJIA was up 70 at this time and the FTSE wasn't responding in sympathy, the game was over for this day. I should have cut my losses and run. Instead I waited and at close after the rapid FTSE slide during the last hour and 10 minutes of the SEI option market, the C4900 premium was down to 82.5 making a paper loss 2½ times worse than the early close out would have been.

What did I do to reduce the losses on this bad trade of C4900?
I knew the FTSE was going to open up on Thursday because, during the 20 minutes between SEI options close and FTSE close on Wednesday, the FTSE rose 7 points to close at 4874.5, with the September futures at 4891. The DJIA held on to a gain of 26 at close on Wednesday, giving a positive

tone to the market close. With the Call slope = 0.53, I figured if the FTSE opened up 25 or so to 4900, the SEI C4900 premium would probably reach around 100 considering the premium inflation that goes with such an extreme market opening on the up side. So I placed an order to sell the 5 SEI C4900 at 95.5 or more. Instead the FTSE started dropping. I got impatient and decided I didn't want to spend any more time worrying about this position. I changed my order to sell *at market*. I got closed out at 73 to give a loss on this bad trade of $5,051. In this particular case, had I waited and left the order to sell at 95.5 open, it would have been filled later in the day, thus reducing my loss by 5 x 10 x (95.5 - 73) x 1.6815 = $1,892 or to a total of $3,159. This would still have been a big loss, but a lot less than the $5000 I really lost. I hope this example shows what **waiting and hoping** can do in long position option trading.

YOU CAN'T MAKE BACK A LOSS

Occasionally you will suffer a big loss using the delta strategy even though you have done your best to avoid it. It is important for you to continue asking for small achievable deltas rather than requesting larger deltas to try to recoup what you lost. Never try to *make back* a loss. After the misfortune, start with a fresh outlook and don't dwell on the amount of money you lost. The delta strategy makes money if you don't get greedy. If you ask for too high a delta "trying to make back a loss" you are more likely to increase your losses rather than to enhance your earnings.

DELTA STRATEGY FOR STEADY MONTHLY INCOME AND CAPITAL GROWTH

Let's move on to something less depressing than the previous section. Here I want to present a conservative strategy to use during Bull Markets by using only long Calls for your delta strategy and always using a delta of 1. This way the Bull Market is working in your favor and usually if you wait long enough your delta of 1 will be reached.

If you use the delta strategy a few times per month, ask for a small delta of 1, and you are careful to avoid losses when the market goes against your long position, then you can generate a steady monthly income and watch your capital grow. During the Bull Market period over the 33 month period from November 94 to August 97, it was better to use a long Call position since Calls become more valuable when the market rises. Even if you ran into a set back on a day or two, if you waited holding on to your position, the records show you usually would have ended up collecting your delta of 1. I used my historical records of the period from November 94 to August 97 to set up the charts in the following sections.

How much capital growth could you expect over 33 months starting with $5,000 Capital using OEX options? In the first few months use 2 options and only try the delta strategy 3 times per option month. As your capital grows you increase to 3 options and 8 times per option month or about twice per week. Using this careful application of the delta strategy, Figure 4.4 shows your monthly income and capital growth on the same chart for the 33 month period:

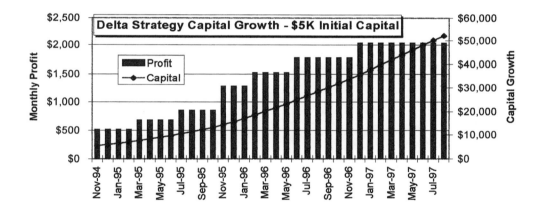

The above chart shows in the beginning the delta strategy yields a steady $500 per month. Then as the capital grows the monthly profit rises to $2,000 and after 33 months the capital has grown to $52,000.

How much capital growth could you expect over 33 months starting with $25,000 Capital using OEX options? In the first few months use 3 options and only try the delta strategy 3 times per option month. As your capital grows you increase to 10 options and 8 times per option month or about twice per week. Using this careful application of the delta strategy with 5 times the starting capital used in the chart above, the following Figure 4.5 shows the monthly income and capital growth on the same chart for the 33 month period:

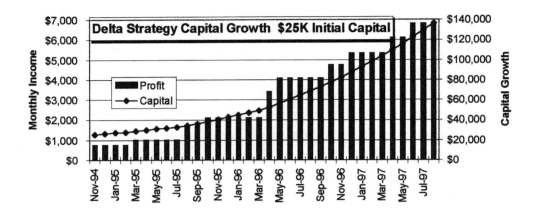

The above chart shows in the beginning the delta strategy yields a steady $800 per month. As the capital grows the monthly profit rises to $6,800 and after 33 months the capital increased to $136,000.

CHAPTER 5

COVERED SHORT SPREADS (STRANGLES)

The covered short spread (strangle) strategy is a good way to generate a steady monthly income without the daily effort of constantly watching the market which the delta strategy requires.   There are several covered short spread strategies than can be used:

1. **Open a two sided covered short spread** (CvSS) by selling Calls (short) 2 sigma above the market and Puts (short) 2 sigma below the market and buying the same number of Calls (long) 1 strike price higher than the short Calls and buying an equal number of Puts (long) 1 strike price lower than the Puts sold. The two sided CvSS can be opened either at the beginning of the new option month or by waiting a week or two into the new option month.

2. **Open a Bull Covered Short Spread** during strong up-trend markets by selling Puts 2 sigma below the market and buying an equal number of Puts 2 strike prices below the Puts sold.

3. **Open a Bear Covered Short Spread** when the market trend is down by selling Calls 2 sigma above the market and buying an equal number of Calls 2 strike prices above the Calls sold.

4. **Allow the Covered Short Spread Position** (strategy 1, 2, or 3 above) to remain open until expiration. If the underlying index (OEX or SEI) finishes between the Short Call and the Short Put, then the Calls and/or Puts expire worthless and the initial credit received opening the position becomes profit.

5. **Close out the CvSS early** if the premium difference between the short and the long becomes a small fraction of the premium difference received when opening the position. This will cost another commission and the premium difference, but it then eliminates any further risk of the market threatening the short Call or Put. This strategy provides almost as much profit and frees the margin collateral needed for the position.

OEX 2 SIDED COVERED SHORT SPREADS (STRANGLES)

Ten two sided, covered short spreads with the OEX at 930 would consist of 10 short Calls at strike price C960, 10 long Calls at strike price C965, 10 short Puts at strike price P900, and 10 long Puts at strike price P895.

How much initial credit is generated by the 2 sided CvSS? When you open a two sided covered short spread position:

The initial credit = (SC Prm - LC Prm) x 100 x NOPS + (SP Prm - LP Prm) x 100 x NOPS- Comm

where: SC Prm = Short Call Premium
LC Prm = Long Call Premium
SP Prm = Short Put Premium
LP Prm = Long Put Premium
NOPS = Number of Options bought and sold
Comm = commission = 7.5 x NOPS x 4

The first step in opening a two sided CvSS is to take the market value of the underlying index (OEX in this example) and compute the strike prices of the short Call and short Put: The short Call = market value + Call 2 sigma, rounded off to the nearest strike price, the short Put = the market value - Put 2 sigma, rounded off to the nearest strike price. Assume the computation gave 960 for the short Call and 900 for the short Put. Then the long Call = 960 +5 = 965 and the long Put = 900 -5 = 895.

To open the Call side for ten, 2 sided CvSS you would place the following order: sell 10 Calls at strike price 960 and buy 10 Calls at strike price 965. With such an order you would receive for the short Call at 960 the Bid price and for the long Call at 965 the Ask price. For example the market quotes for the Calls may be:

Strike Price	Bid	Ask
960	6.00	6.37
965	4.50	4.875

You would get the bid premium = 6.00 for your short C960 and the ask premium = 4.875 for your long C965. The premium difference = 6.00 - 4.875 = 1.125. So for your 10 options the initial credit = $1,125 - Comm = 1125 -10 x 2 x 7.5 = $975.

To open the Put side for ten, 2 sided CvSS you would place the following order: sell 10 Puts at strike price 900 and buy 10 Puts at strike price 895 for which you would receive the Bid price for the short P900 and the Ask price for the long P895. For example the Put quotes may be:

Strike Price	Bid	Ask
900	5.125	5.5
895	3.875	4.125

You would get the bid premium = 5.125 for your short P900 and the ask premium = 4.125 for your long P895. The premium difference = 5.125 - 4.125 = 1.0. So for 10 options the initial credit = $1,000 - Comm = 1000 - 10 x 2 x 7.5 = $850.

How much margin is required to open a two sided CvSS for OEX? If you are trading OEX options, the margin required by the CBOE is given by the following simple equation. Margin computations are much more complex on the London Exchange. Below is the CBOE equation:

The required Call margin = 2000 + NOPS x 100 x (LCSP - SCSP - SC Prm + LC Prm)

The required Put margin = 2000 + NOPS x 100 x (SPSP - LPSP - SP Prm + LP Prm) where: NOPS = number of options, LCSP = long Call strike price, SCSP = short Call strike price, SC Prm = short Call premium, LC Prm = long Call premium, SPSP = short Put strike price, LPSP = long Put strike price

The margin for the ten, 2 sided CvSS described above is:
the Call margin = 2000 + 10 x 100 x (5 - 6 + 4.875) = 2000 + 3875 = $5,875; the Put margin = 2000 + 10 x 100 x (5 - 5.125 + 4.125) = 2000 + 4000 = $6,000. So the total 2 sided CvSS margin = $11,875

In the example above for a two sided CvSS the initial credit = 975 + 850 = $1,825 and the margin required = 5875 + 6000 = $11,875. The return on margin = 15.37%. I recommend you use no more than 50% of your capital for margin requirements, so the return on capital would be half that or 7.68% or an annual return of 92.21%. If the market stays less than the short Call and more than the short Put until option expiration then both the Call CvSS and Put CvSS become worthless, and the initial credit received becomes profit for the option month.

The penalty if the market moves above your short Call or below your short Put is great. For the worst-case scenario, if the OEX finished above 965 for the example above, then the Call CvSS instead of being worthless at expiration (which is what you want) would be worth = 10 x 100 x (965-960) = $5,000 + Comm = $5,150 - or considerably more than the initial credit received for the whole position, both Puts and Calls, of $1,825. In this case, the loss = $5150-$1825 = $3,325; there is no additional penalty for the Put position because it would expire worthless. Obviously, there is no way both the Put and Call side of the position could be in the money at the same time.

If, for example, the OEX expired only one point above the short Call position at 960, then the CvSS would be worth 1 point and the value of the Call CvSS would be = 10 x 100(961-960) = $1,000 + Comm = $1,075. Since the long Call at 965 would have expired out-of-the-money (worthless), the commission would be due only on the short Call, so the commission = 7.5 x 10 = $75, used in the calculation above. The monthly profit for this case = $1825 - $1075 = $750.

So, if either your Call or Put CvSS is threatened by an extreme market movement, corrective action is necessary to avoid a big loss. The initial total credit for both sides of our example two sided CvSS was $1825 and in the worst-case scenario just above (when the market was above <u>both</u> the short and long Call position) the maximum loss was $3,325. Please note that for the example above the maximum loss was almost double the initial credit ($3,325 divided by $1,825 which is 1.82).

USING STANDARD DEVIATION
(2 SIGMA) TO PREDICT MARKET MOVEMENT

How much does the OEX move during an option month? Our best method for predicting how far up or how far down the market is going to move is to use standard deviation (sigma) computations based on the maximum up and down the OEX moved over the last 13 months which is shown in Figure 5.1. Standard deviation is a mathematical system where all the data points are grouped under a "bell-shaped curve" with most of the data contained in the center of the "bell" which leaves a small percentage of the data (called 2 sigma) in each of the 2 outer edges of the curve. If we choose our Call and Put positions so that they are 2 sigma away from the market level, those positions will seldom be crossed by the ups and downs of the market moves.

Figure 5.1, on the following page, shows the Max (amount up) and Min (amount down) for the OEX over 33 months, with the 13 month 2 sigma values for this period of time, using the numbers in the Max and Min columns to compute the 2 sigma values:

Op Mo	MAX	MIN	C2sig13	P2sig13
Nov-94	0	19.47	9.37	16.34
Dec-94	6.82	5.89	9.42	16.35
Jan-95	0	15.6	9.52	16.87
Feb-95	6.95	2.88	9.46	16.96
Mar-95	21.42	0.00	12.89	17.34
Apr-95	16.70	0.00	14.07	17.89
May-95	17.46	0.60	14.86	18.33
Jun-95	19.47	0.00	15.11	13.24
Jul-95	21.96	0.00	16.47	13.57
Aug-95	21.28	0.00	17.73	14.43
Sep-95	8.19	3.57	17.09	13.70
Oct-95	26.29	2.42	18.08	13.11
Nov-95	11.26	2.23	17.37	12.60
Dec-95	12.79	10.28	15.34	9.50
Jan-96	10.82	2.82	14.81	9.37
Feb-96	2.16	18.96	14.11	10.92
Mar-96	48.00	0.24	22.19	10.63
Apr-96	15.18	11.19	21.41	11.46
May-96	16.67	10.84	21.33	11.83
Jun-96	23.09	7.11	21.51	11.61
Jul-96	9.88	6.79	21.97	11.35
Aug-96	7.62	40.47	22.57	21.47
Sep-96	20.89	17.53	22.50	21.41
Oct-96	24.61	4.31	22.78	20.94
Nov-96	22.59	16.61	22.37	20.88
Dec-96	21.96	14.04	21.99	20.36
Jan-97	33.28	10.41	23.13	19.65
Feb-97	31.44	13.47	23.67	19.62
Mar-97	10.33	18.13	23.74	19.00
Apr-97	6.09	47.78	22.88	26.34
May-97	81.55	4.52	37.49	25.66
Jun-97	63.91	0.00	42.93	26.96
Jul-97	37.4	19.67	42.87	26.94
Aug-97	43.63	1.59	43.52	27.64

Figure 5.1

The accompanying chart was generated using the Excel program for handling math activities on my personal computer. Excel includes the following formulas which were used for calculating standard deviation, multiplied by 2 since we want 2 sigma. The OEX will stay within the +/- 2 sigma limits about 95% of the time - meaning our covered short spread will finish safe (worthless) 95% of the time.

Formula for choosing your Call position =2 x STDEV(W6:W18)

Formula for choosing your Put position =2 x STDEV(X6:X18)

STDEV means standard deviation. The term W6:W18 is the highest the OEX went up (the MAXIMUM level) each month from the month called out in line 6 up to and including the month called out in line 18, which is 13 months. The term X6:X18 is the lowest the OEX went down (the MINIMUM level) each month from the month called out in line 6 up to and including the month called out in line 18, which is 13 months.

I use 13 months worth of daily variation data to calculate the 2 sigma values because I want a good sized sample of how much the market went up and down. Notice in Figure 5.1 that in May 97 the market went up 81.55 and in April 97 it went down 47.78, much larger changes than shown for the other months around these dates. If I chose only 3 months for the 2 sigma computation, including these months, the 2 sigmas would be bigger than necessary.

To choose your covered spread position, look at the 2 sigma numbers in Figure 5.1 for the last option month. For instance, at the beginning of the August option month, look at the data through expiration for the July 97 option month. The Call 2 sigma is 42.87 and the Put 2 sigma is 26.94. The OEX on the last day of the July 97 option month was 895.86. For your short Call position, add the July 97 Call 2 sigma (42.87) to the most recent close for the OEX (895.86) and you get 938.73. Since OEX strike prices are given in intervals of 5, the closest strike price for your short Call is round-off (938.73) = 940. Your long Call would be 5 points higher or 945. For your short Put position, subtract the July 97 Put 2 sigma (26.94) from the most recent close for the OEX (895.86) and you get 868.92. Since OEX strike prices are given in intervals of 5, the closest strike price for your short Put is round-off (868.92) = 870. Your long Put would be 5 points lower or 865.

If you are opening your short spread during the option month, use the value of the OEX at close on the previous day. You might also reduce the

2 sigma numbers a little if you wait until later in the option month to open your position.

Please note that occasionally the market will move either up or down more than the 2 sigma, these are the months the 2 sigma CvSS strategy gets into trouble. Here are some examples of the market moving more than 2 sigma during the option month:

1. March 95 the Call 2 sigma = 12.89, but the maximum movement up was 21.42, so the Call CvSS would have lost money.

2. March 96 the Call 2 sigma = 22.19, but the maximum up was 48, so the Call CvSS would have lost money.

3. April 97 the Put 2 sigma = 26.34, but the minimum down was 47.78, so the Put CvSS would have lost money.

4. May 97 the Call 2 sigma = 37.49, but the maximum up was 81.55, so the Call CvSS would have lost money.

5. June 97 the Call 2 sigma = 42.93, but the maximum up was 63.91, so the Call CvSS would have lost money.

For the 33 months included in Figure 5.1 only 5 months would have had the maximum loss if no corrective action were taken. Since the maximum loss is equal to about 1.82 times the initial credit, these 5 months could have eliminated the profit from about 9 months.

CORRECTIVE ACTIONS

What can you do if movement in the market threatens either the Call or the Put side of your CvSS? The CvSS strategy appears to be an excellent way to make a steady monthly income as long as the market stays within the limits of 2 sigma up and 2 sigma down during the option month. But during those months in which the market moves more than 2 sigma up or down, it is difficult to avoid a loss. However, you can limit the loss by taking corrective action when either the Call or Put side is threatened. Figure 5.2 shows the Put Bid and Ask prices for strike prices above and below the OEX which was 923.26 on this sample day. Assume we have a Put CvSS with short Put at 925 and long Put at 920 and we expect a further drop in the market before expiration.

Put	Bid	Ask
890	4.7500	5.0000
895	5.5000	5.8750
900	6.0000	6.3750
905	7.5000	7.6250
910	9.0000	9.5000
915	10.5000	10.7500
920	11.7500	12.2500
925	13.5	14.2500
930	16.625	17.3750

If we estimate that the market will not drop to less than 915 we could place the following order to protect our threatened Put CvSS: buy 10 P925 and sell 10 P920 to close Put CvSS and sell 10 P915 and buy 10 P910 to open new Put CvSS. The predicted cost of this protective change is as follows, P925 ask = 14.25, P920 bid = 11.75, P915 bid = 10.5, P910 ask = 9.5:

Close out existing Put CvSS credit (negative) = 10 x 100 x (14.25 - 11.75) + Comm = -1000 x 2.5 - 7.5 x 10 x 2 = -$2500 - $150 = -$2,350

Open new Put CvSS initial credit = 10 x 100 x (10.5-9.5) - Comm = $1000 -$150 = $850

The net cost of this protective action = -2350 +850 = -$1,500.

In order to reduce the loss or get as much profit as possible from a corrective change, you need a strategy to get the least premium difference possible. The program traders cause the New York market to go up and down several times a day so this is a strategy to take advantage of that volatility to get the minimum premium difference for the position being closed and to get more for the new position being opened. First, calculate the theoretical predicted cost of your protective change as above. Look at the quoted premiums at the time you are considering the corrective action. Using the numbers in the premium table in the example above, the close out of the existing Put CvSS had a premium difference of 2.5; place an order with your broker to buy back the 10 P925 and sell the 10 P920 at a premium difference of 1.25 or less. For the new position, place an order to sell the 10 P915 and buy the 10 P910 at a premium difference of 1.75 or more (instead of 1.0 given by the premium table). Note the close out premium difference requested is 1.25 less and the new premium difference requested is 0.75 more. This makes your broker work harder to get what you requested instead of just taking the market bid and ask numbers at that moment and makes the daily volatility work for you to reduce your loss or increase your profit. Asking for these adjusted premium differences allows the close out difference to be less when there is an up jump in the market and the new difference to be more when there is a drop in the day's market movement.. By using these premium differences you would end up better off by =10 x 100 x (1.25+0.75) = $2,000, than if you just took the premiums of the moment; in other words, after the change, you end up having a gain of $500 instead of having a loss of $1,500.

The cost of a protective action is usually about equal to the initial credit of the 2 sided CvSS when opened at the beginning of the month, so for all practical purposes the profit for the CvSS is wiped out for this month. But had we not taken protective action and let the market drop below our long Put the loss would have been = 10 x 100 x (925-920) + Comm = $5,150 (the same as for the Call CvSS if the market rose above the long Call). Without protective action the month's loss would have been = $1825 - $5125 = -$3,300. In other words, the protective action eliminated a loss of $3,300. We didn't make any profit for this option month, but at least we didn't have a big loss. That is why you take protective action. Remember, out of the 33 months only 5 would have had serious problems with the two sided CvSS.

THE BULL and BEAR COVERED SHORT SPREAD STRATEGIES

What about other Covered Short Spread Strategies besides the 2 sigma double sided CvSS? We can look at June 1997 as an example: the OEX rose 63.61 points, but didn't fall at all during the option month. A strategy that takes advantage of such a month is to open a Put CvSS with the short

Put close to the market and the long Put several strike prices below the market. This strategy is called the Bull CvSS strategy. If you were convinced the market was going to rise until expiration you might want to place the following Bull CvSS order using Table 5.2:

Sell 10 P920 and buy 10 Put 895 for which you would receive the Bid premium for the P920 = 11.75 and the Ask premium for the P895 = 5.875. The initial credit = 10 x 100 x (11.75-5.875)-7.5 x 10 x 2 = $5,725. The margin required = 2000 + 10 x 100 x (920-895-11.75+5.875) = 2000 +1000 x (25-5.875) = $21,125. If the OEX stays above 920 at expiration, then the initial credit of $5,725 become profit for the trade.

If you decided the market rise had stalled and was not going up any further or was going to drop, then you might want to open a Bear covered short spread. The premiums for the day for the example Bear CvSS are given in Figure 5.3.

Call	Bid	Ask
920	17.2500	17.5000
925	13.7500	14.2500
930	11.1250	11.3750
935	9.3750	9.5000
940	7.1250	7.2500
950	4.0000	4.1250
960	2.0625	2.1250

The OEX at this time is at 923.26. To open the Bear CvSS you give the following order: Sell 10 Call 930 and buy 10 Call 950. The premiums from Table 5.3 for the C930 use the Bid Premium = 11.125 and for the C950 use the Ask Premium = 4.125 for a premium difference of 7. The initial credit = 10 x 100 x (11.125-4.125) - 10 x 7.5 x 2 = $7,000 - 150 = $6,850. The margin required for this Bear CvSS = 2000 + 10 x 100 x (950 - 930 -11.125 + 4.125) = 2000 + 1000 x (20-7) = 2000 +13000 = $15,000. If the OEX remains below 930 at expiration, then the $6,850 initial credit becomes profit for the Bear CvSS.

How about the risk of the Bull CvSS and the Bear CvSS?
These two strategies sound like a good way to make a lot of profit, but the risk is significant if you misjudge the movement of the market. If the market should plunge after you open a Bull CvSS or zoom up after you open a Bear CvSS then you could lose a considerable amount of capital. If

at expiration the market drops below the Long Put of the Bull CvSS or rises above the Long Call of the Bear CvSS, what is the loss for the two examples given above:

1. Maximum loss for the Bull CvSS example = 10 x 100 x (920 - 895) + Comm - Initial credit = $25,150 - $5,725 = $19,425.

2. Maximum loss for the Bear CvSS example = 10 x 100 x (950 - 930) + Comm - Initial credit = $20,150 - $6,850 = $13,300.

You will note that the maximum losses in these two examples are less than the CBOE required margin of $21,525 for the Bull CvSS and $15,000 for the Bear CvSS. The Bull and Bear CvSS strategies are worth considering in your bag of tricks as long as you remain aware of the risk involved if your judgment of market direction is wrong. One of the advantages of the 2 sigma CvSS is that you use the best knowledge available on how much the market can move by computing the two sigma using 13 months of historical market movement data. The probability that the market will remain less than 2 sigma up or 2 sigma down is 95% according to the gaussian bell shaped curve theory.

What about closing out a safe one sided CvSS early when the premium difference drops to a small fraction of the initial premium difference? On a Monday I opened 10 Bear CvSS with the short Call at 925 and the long Call at 935 for a premium difference of 2.75. After I opened the position, the market dropped that day, and on Tuesday and Wednesday as well so the premium difference dropped to around 0.625. On Thursday the OEX dropped over 6 during the first hour and half of trading. I placed an order to sell the 10 C935 and buy the 10 C925 at a premium difference of 0.25 or less to close the Bear CvSS. A few minutes later I got confirmation that the C925s were bought at 5/8 and the C935s were sold at 3/8 giving me the 0.25 premium difference requested. In less than 4 days my Bear CvSS gave a profit of 2.75 - 0.25 = 2.5 points = 10 x 100 x 2.5 - 10 x 4 x 7.5 = $2500 - $300 = $2,200. Now I had no CvSS to worry about and the margin was released for other trades I might want to make.

Get out of a Bull or Bear CvSS position when the premium difference decays to a small part of your original premium difference.

THE NAKED (NON COVERED) SHORT SPREAD

How much initial credit can be made using the Naked Short Spread (Strangle) Strategy? The naked short spread strategy requires a minimum capital in your trading account of $50,000 by CBOE rules. If you have that much in your account you may want to consider this strategy for generating a steady monthly income. You must take immediate corrective action when either the Call or Put side of your short spread is threatened.

To open a naked short spread, first look at the 2 sigma table. For this example the OEX = 923 and the Call 2 sigma = 37 and the Put 2 sigma = 27. Open a 2 sigma naked short spread by selling 2 C960 (923 + 37 = 960) and 2 P895 (923 - 27 = 896, round to nearest strike price) for which you would receive (using Tables 5.2 and 5.3) a C960 premium = 2.0625 and a P895 premium = 5.5. The initial credit = 2 x 100 x (5.5 + 2.0625) - Comm = $1,512.50 - 2 x 7.5 x 2 = $1,482. The margin = 923 x 2 x 100 x 0.15 = $27,690 which is roughly half the required minimum is $50,000.

Over the years I have been trading naked short spreads I found the market sometimes penetrates the Put or Call for just one day and then moves back inside the spread. If one side or the other of your short spread is in-the-money, the margin requirement jumps from 15% to 20%. In the case above, the margin would jump to 923 x 2 x 100 x .20 = $36,920. If you are holding a naked spread position using as much of your capital as possible, your broker would give you a margin call if one side or the other moved in-the-money, and you would have to put more money in your account or else buy back one or more of your spreads. Buying back a naked spread is similar to buying back covered short spreads in that you usually end up losing money that month. But if you are only using about half of your capital for margin, even with the increase from 15% to 20%, you would have enough capital to cover your position. You would have the option of waiting for the market to move back within your spread, if market conditions looked favorable.

MARGIN REQUIREMENTS FOR CvSS

The margin requirements are intended to protect the exchange (and your broker) from losses that may occur if the market moves adversely to your

CvSS. If you have a two sided CvSS there is a margin required for both the Call and Put side. The margin requirement is set by the CBOE for the OEX and is a simple formula that takes into account the number of options, the width between the short and the long portion of the CvSS, and the initial premiums received plus a fixed amount of $2,000.

The margin requirement for the OEX:

Call CvSS = 2000 + NOPS x 100 x ((Long Call SP-Short Call SP) - (SC Prm -LC Prm)

Put CvSS = 2000 + NOPS x 100 x ((Short Put SP-Long Put SP) - (SP Prm - LP Prm)

Where: 2000 is a fixed $2000 for each trade, NOPS = number of options, SP = strike price, SC Prm = short Call Premium, LC Prm = long Call Premium, SP Prm = short Put Premium, LP Prm = long Put Premium

Example OEX Margin Computations:

1. Ten two sided 2 sigma CvSS with short Call = 950, bid premium = 5.25 ; long Call = 955, ask premium = 4.00, short Put = 890, bid premium = 7.375 long Put = 885, ask premium = 6.250. **Margin** = 2000 x 2 + 10 x 100 x (5-5.25+4) + 10 x 100 x (5-7.375+6.250) = 2000 + 3750 + 3875 = **$9,625.** The initial credit = (1.25 + 1.125) x 100 x 10 - Comm = $2,075.

2. Three Bull CvSS with short Put = 890, bid premium = 7.375, long Put = 865, ask premium = 1.25. **Margin** = 2000 + 3 x 100 x ((890-865) - (7.375-1.25)) = 2000 +300 x (25- 6.125) = **$7,662**. The initial credit = (7.375-1.25) x 3 x 100 - Comm = $1,792.

3. Five Bear CvSS with short Call = 950, bid premium = 5.25, long Call =970, ask premium = 0.75. **Margin** = 2000 + 5 x 100 x ((970-950) -(5.25-0.75) = 2000 +500 x (20-4.5) = **$9,750**. The initial credit = 5 x 100 x (5.25-0.75) - Comm = $2,175.

The margin requirement for SEI is based on SPAN risk arrays collected from your broker by the London Clearing House (LCH) to cover potential losses that may arise because of adverse price movements requiring the LCH to close out a losing position. SPAN (Standard Portfolio ANalysis of risk) is a method of calculating initial margin by evaluating portfolio risk under a number of scenarios. It was originally developed by the CME (Chicago Mercantile Exchange). SPAN has no impact either on the methods of settlement of contracts or on the methods employed by brokers to cover their liabilities.

SPAN parameters for SEI

1.   Inter-month spread charge per lot £150
2.   Scanning range per lot £3750
3.   Inter-commodity spread credit 55%
4.   Delta ratio 1:1
5.   Inter-commodity charge £500

Example SEI Margin Computations:

1. Ten two sided 2 sigma CvSS with short Call = 4900, bid premium = 8.5 ; long Call = 4950, ask premium = 4.00, short Put = 4600, bid premium = 37, long Put = 4550, ask premium = 26. **Margin** = £150 + £500 + 10 x (50 x 10-8.5+4-37+26) = £650 + £4845 = **£5495**. The initial credit = (8.5-4+37-26.5) x 10 x 10 - Comm = £1,500 -10 x 5 x 4 = 1500-200 = £1,300.

2. Three Bull CvSS with short Put = 4750, bid premium = 65, long Put = 4650, ask premium = 39.5. **Margin** = £150 + £500 + 3 x (100 x 10-65+39.5) = £650 + £2923 = **£3,573**. The initial credit = (65-39.5) x 10 x 3 - Comm = 765 -3 x 5 x 2 = 765-60 = £705.

3. Five Bear CvSS with short Call = 5150, bid premium = 8.5, long Call =5250, ask premium = 2. **Margin** = £150 + £500 + 5 x (100 x 10-8+2) = £650 + £4970 = **£5,620**. The initial credit = (8-2) x 10 x 5 - Comm = 300 -5 x 5 x 2 = 765-50 = £715.

INCREASING YOUR CAPITAL
WITH COVERED SHORT SPREADS

During the last few years we have had a continuous bull market with only an occasional downward correction that didn't last long. The following Figure 5.4 shows that in such an upward trending market it is better to use Bull CvSS than two sided CvSS:

Op Mo	MAX	MIN	C2sig13	P2sig13	OEX 1ST	OEX LST	Shrt Call	Short Put	<sc	>sp
Nov-94	0.00	19.47	9.37	16.34	430.92	430.76	430	415		
Dec-94	6.82	5.89	9.42	16.35	430.76	429.53	440	415	1	1
Jan-95	0.00	15.60	9.52	16.87	429.53	431.38	440	415	1	1
Feb-95	6.95	2.88	9.46	16.96	431.38	448.62	440	415	(1)	1
Mar-95	21.42	0.00	12.89	17.34	448.62	464.85	460	430	(1)	1
Apr-95	16.70	0.00	14.07	17.89	464.85	482.31	480	450	(1)	1
May-95	17.46	0.60	14.86	18.33	482.31	493.33	495	465	1	1
Jun-95	19.47	0.00	15.11	13.24	493.33	515.29	510	475	(1)	1
Jul-95	21.96	0.00	16.47	13.57	515.29	529.52	530	500	1	1
Aug-95	21.28	0.00	17.73	14.43	529.52	527.95	545	515	1	1
Sep-95	8.19	3.57	17.09	13.70	527.95	553.73	545	515	(1)	1
Oct-95	26.29	2.42	18.08	13.11	553.73	561.2	570	540	1	1
Nov-95	11.26	2.23	17.37	12.60	561.2	573.99	580	550	1	1
Dec-95	12.79	10.28	15.34	9.50	573.99	590.51	590	560	(1)	1
Jan-96	10.82	2.82	14.81	9.37	590.51	584.31	605	580	1	1
Feb-96	2.16	18.96	14.11	10.92	584.31	620.5	600	575	(1)	1
Mar-96	48.00	0.24	22.19	10.63	620.50	620.73	635	610	1	1
Apr-96	15.18	11.19	21.41	11.46	620.73	622.36	645	610	1	1
May-96	16.67	10.84	21.33	11.83	622.36	645.45	645	610	(1)	1
Jun-96	23.09	7.11	21.51	11.61	645.45	646.17	665	635	1	1
Jul-96	9.88	6.79	21.97	11.35	646.17	616.72	670	635	1	(1)
Aug-96	7.62	40.47	22.57	21.47	616.72	644.50	640	605	(1)	1
Sep-96	20.89	17.53	22.50	21.41	644.50	665.39	665	625	(1)	1
Oct-96	24.61	4.31	22.78	20.94	665.39	690.00	690	645	(1)	1
Nov-96	22.59	16.61	22.37	20.88	690.00	712.59	715	670	1	1
Dec-96	21.96	14.04	21.99	20.36	712.59	728.87	735	690	1	1
Jan-97	33.28	10.41	23.13	19.65	728.87	762.15	750	710	(1)	1
Feb-97	31.44	13.47	23.67	19.62	762.15	781.00	785	745	1	1
Mar-97	10.33	18.13	23.74	19.00	781.00	763.19	805	760	1	1
Apr-97	6.09	47.78	22.88	26.34	763.19	746.85	785	745	1	1
May-97	81.55	4.52	37.49	25.66	746.85	812.56	770	720	(1)	1
Jun-97	63.91	0.00	42.93	26.96	812.56	876.47	850	785	(1)	1
Jul-97	37.40	19.67	42.87	26.94	876.47	895.86	920	850	1	1
Aug-97	47.15	1.59	43.90	27.64	895.86	945.31	940	870	(1)	1

The last two columns show those months when the short Call (<sc) or the short Put (>sp) would have finished in-the-money rather than worthless. If the number shown is 1 the position finished safe, if it is (1) it finished in-the-money. The long Call and Put sides of the covered short spread are not shown in the table. Out of the 33 months, the 2 sigma short Call would have finished in-the-money 12 times, but the 2 sigma short Put would have finished in-the-money only once. This indicates that, in a strong bull market such as existed during this period, a Bull CvSS would have worked better than a two sided CvSS. So the best plan was to open just a Put CvSS and with the long Put 10 or more below the short Put rather than just 5. This strategy means you would have had only one month that required corrective action for the short Put and that the premium difference between the short Put and the long Put would have been at least 2 3/8 rather than 1 for the case of only 5 points between the short and long. Which means for the 10 point wide spread the amount of profit per month is more than 2.375 times greater than for the 5 point wide spread.

How much capital growth could you expect over 33 months starting with $5000 Capital using the 2 sigma Bear CvSS with the OEX long Put 2 strike prices (10 Points) below the short Put? During the one month that the 2 sigma short Put was threatened, it is assumed that the corrective action cost 50% more than the profit of the month before. All other months the Put CvSS finished safe. The capital growth is shown in Figure 5.5 below:

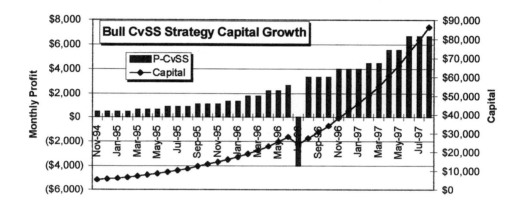

During the 33 months shown in this chart the profit grew at the rate of 100% return per year taking the initial capital from $5,000 to an ending capital of $86,000. Initially the capital was enough margin for 2 Put CvSS; at the end there was enough margin for 30 Put CvSS. This example used real data to produce the results shown in the graph. If you had started with more capital the results would have been similar but with bigger ending numbers.

How much capital growth could you expect over 33 months starting with $25,000 Capital using the 2 sigma Bear CvSS with the OEX long Put 2 strike prices (10 Points) below the short Put? A similar chart is shown in Figure 5.6 for the case assuming you started with $25,000 initial capital to use for the Bear CvSS strategy:

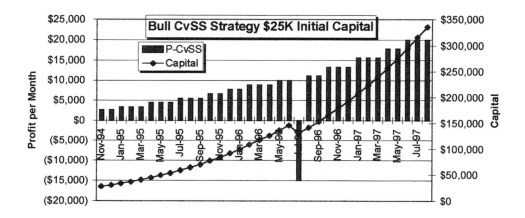

This chart shows that if you start out with 5 times more capital ($25,000) you end up with $336,000 capital or some 4 times more than if you started with $5,000. These two examples show you can make your capital grow safely in a Bull Market using the Bull CvSS strategy (using only Put options) with the only loss occurring when there is a downward market correction such as in the July 1996 option month.

How much capital growth could you expect over 56 months starting with £15,000 Capital using the 2 sigma Bull CvSS with the SEI long Put 2 strike prices (100 Points) below the short Put? The FTSE-100 was analyzed from Jan 93 to Aug 97 to determine how many months a CvSS would have finished worthless. The data for that analysis is shown in the accompanying Figure 5.7. The last two columns tell if the Call (<sc) or Put (>sp) side finished in-the-money. A 1 indicates it finished worthless, a (1) indicates it finished in-the-money.

Op Mo	MAX	MIN	C2sig13	P2sig13	SEI 1ST	SEI LST	Shrt Call	Short Put	<sc	>sp
Dec-92	14.4	1.8	16.21	13.66						
Jan-93	72.0	45.5	38.75	25.40	2788.5	2763.5	2,850	2,750	1	1
Feb-93	109.0	26.0	109.00	26.00	2763.5	2838.0	2,850	2,750	1	1
Mar-93	120.0	22.5	15.56	4.95	2838.0	2899.5	2,850	2,800	(1)	1
Apr-93	19.0	78.5	110.82	62.74	2899.5	2825.5	3,000	2,900	1	(1)
May-93	53.5	39.5	102.68	57.42	2825.5	2825.5	2,950	2,750	1	1
Jun-93	76.5	6.0	57.88	72.57	2825.5	2902.0	2,900	2,750	(1)	1
Jul-93	5.0	71.0	93.52	57.27	2902.0	2831.5	3,000	2,850	1	(1)
Aug-93	192.0	70.5	129.13	56.96	2831.5	3057.0	2,950	2,750	(1)	1
Sep-93	244.5	35.5	165.75	53.15	3057.0	3004.5	3,200	3,000	1	1
Oct-93	101.0	40.0	155.05	49.78	3004.5	3120.0	3,150	2,950	1	1
Nov-93	112.5	14.5	146.32	50.34	3120.0	3109.0	3,250	3,050	1	1
Dec-93	184.5	59.5	147.20	49.12	3109.0	3310.5	3,250	3,050	(1)	1
Jan-94	184.5	26.5	146.68	47.70	3310.5	3475.0	3,450	3,250	(1)	1
Feb-94	164.5	125.0	142.90	65.31	3475.0	3350.0	3,600	3,450	1	(1)
Mar-94	11.0	155.5	149.25	85.33	3350.0	3216.5	3,500	3,300	1	(1)
Apr-94	17.0	133.0	164.04	93.71	3216.5	3143.0	3,400	3,150	1	(1)
May-94	5.0	73.5	166.65	93.52	3143.0	3090.0	3,300	3,050	1	1
Jun-94	39.0	157.5	168.30	104.86	3090.0	2939.0	3,250	3,000	1	(1)
Jul-94	142.5	151.0	168.83	104.14	2939.0	3081.5	3,100	2,850	1	1
Aug-94	142.5	3.5	157.76	113.60	3081.5	3168.5	3,250	3,000	1	1
Sep-94	94.0	102.0	151.79	114.03	3168.5	3080.0	3,300	3,050	1	1
Oct-94	64.5	120.5	130.33	111.99	3080.0	3033.0	3,200	2,950	1	1
Nov-94	114.5	47.0	130.67	111.03	3033.0	3120.5	3,150	2,900	1	1
Dec-94	87.5	177.5	130.50	110.93	3120.5	3013.0	3,250	3,000	1	1
Jan-95	85.0	107.5	119.25	107.89	3013.0	2952.5	3,150	2,900	1	1
Feb-95	159.0	60.5	113.09	100.95	2952.5	3017.5	3,050	2,850	1	1
Mar-95	69.5	38.0	103.12	107.60	3017.5	3087.0	3,100	2,900	1	1
Apr-95	126.0	35.5	97.29	108.33	3087.0	3206.0	3,200	3,000	(1)	1
May-95	119.0	8.0	88.48	114.88	3206.0	3290.0	3,300	3,100	1	1
Jun-95	92.5	16.0	69.83	120.78	3290.0	3376.5	3,350	3,200	(1)	1
Jul-95	87.5	101.5	59.49	112.31	3376.5	3413.0	3,450	3,250	1	1
Aug-95	96.0	18.5	55.57	106.11	3413.0	3509.0	3,450	3,300	(1)	1
Sep-95	96.0	33.0	50.25	101.64	3509.0	3566.0	3,550	3,400	(1)	1
Oct-95	57.0	114.0	55.47	103.24	3566.0	3550.0	3,600	3,450	1	1
Nov-95	79.1	56.0	53.22	98.28	3550.0	3629.1	3,600	3,450	(1)	1
Dec-95	79.1	56.1	53.09	97.93	3629.1	3612.0	3,700	3,550	1	1
Jan-96	135.0	17.1	57.27	72.73	3612.0	3754.0	3,650	3,500	(1)	1
Feb-96	142.0	48.0	61.37	64.29	3754.0	3767.5	3,800	3,700	1	1
Mar-96	9.0	129.0	71.27	78.90	3767.5	3651.0	3,850	3,700	1	(1)
Apr-96	206.1	0.0	93.97	83.74	3651.0	3857.1	3,750	3,550	(1)	1
May-96	0.0	149.9	108.11	100.17	3857.1	3789.6	3,950	3,750	1	1
Jun-96	0.0	82.8	117.97	96.38	3789.6	3722.3	3,900	3,700	1	1
Jul-96	43.5	90.0	119.77	92.98	3722.3	3710.5	3,850	3,650	1	1
Aug-96	162.4	42.0	128.39	91.88	3710.5	3872.9	3,850	3,600	(1)	1
Sep-96	104.3	17.0	128.71	92.13	3872.9	3964.1	4,000	3,800	1	1
Oct-96	89.0	53.6	128.58	90.50	3964.1	4053.1	4,100	3,850	1	1
Nov-96	20.0	152.7	132.84	99.47	4053.1	3958.2	4,200	3,950	1	1
Dec-96	119.4	4.2	134.39	105.65	3958.2	4077.6	4,100	3,850	1	1
Jan-97	130.1	21.0	136.56	108.37	4077.6	4207.7	4,200	3,950	(1)	1
Feb-97	149.7	13.7	138.43	108.85	4207.7	4336.8	4,350	4,100	1	1
Mar-97	107.5	82.0	135.43	109.04	4336.8	4254.8	4,450	4,250	1	1
Apr-97	58.4	40.2	128.45	102.44	4254.8	4310.5	4,400	4,150	1	1
May-97	383.4	0.0	199.27	102.44	4310.5	4693.9	4,500	4,200	(1)	1
Jun-97	89.2	136.8	189.48	98.71	4693.9	4593.9	4,900	4,600	1	(1)
Jul-97	370.5	18.1	224.63	99.51	4593.9	4877.2	4,800	4,500	(1)	1
Aug-97	194.5	71.5	218.41	97.64	4877.2	5071.7	5,100	4,800	1	1

Examining the previous chart you will see that a Bull CvSS (short Put 2 sigma below the market and a long Put two strike prices below the short) should have been used from January 93 through January 94 when a Bear leg started and lasted for five months. During the Bear leg from February 94 through June 95, a Bear CvSS (short Call 2 sigma above the market and a long Call two strike prices above the short) should have been used. A Bull CvSS was appropriate from July 94 through August 97.

In Figure 5.8 below it was assumed you started with £15,000 initial capital, used the SEI Bull CvSS strategy for 51 out of the 56 months, and during the other 5 months used a Bear CvSS. The chart shows the monthly profit and the Capital growth in pounds sterling (£).

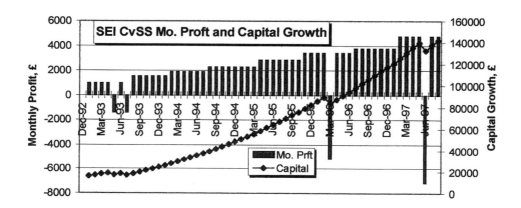

Starting with a capital of £15,000 I used 5 Put CvSS with the short Puts 2 sigma below the market and the long Puts two strike prices or 100 points below the short. With an average premium difference of 20 (which is conservative) this yields a monthly income of £950 in the beginning. As the capital increased I gradually increased the number of one sided CvSS until I reached the level of 25 yielding an average monthly income of £4,750. During those months where there was a loss caused by having to take corrective action, the loss was assumed to be 150% times the profit of the previous month. At the end the of the 56 months the capital grew from £15,000 to £142,000. This example of SEI trading shows you can make your capital grow safely in a Bull Market using the Bull CvSS strategy (using only Put options). When there was an extended Bear leg during the first half of 1994, I switched to a Bear CvSS with the short Call 2 sigma above the market and the long Call two strike prices or 100 points above the short. There were only 4 losses occurring during this 56 month period or an average of less than 1 per year. This is a capital growth of over 100% per year.

CHAPTER 6

GENERATING AND INTERPRETING MARKET SIGNAL CHARTS

The main charts that I use are the Stochastics %K-%D, MAD4, MAD9-4, and Welles-Wilder Relative Strength Indicator. I refer to these charts daily to judge which way the market is moving. The Stochastics chart is most sensitive to market changes and is the most complex to generate. The MAD4 (4 day exponential moving average difference chart) is next most sensitive to market swings and is the simplest to generate; the MAD9-4 (the difference between the 4 day and 9 day exponential moving average) is best for showing major switches in market direction. The WWI chart shows you when the market is overbought (meaning it's ready for a drop) or over sold (meaning its ready for a rise) and is the second most difficult to generate.

All the charts were generated and computed using EXCEL. In this chapter, I will discuss the steps I went through to generate (make) these charts and will explain the necessary formulas for the required computations.

The moving average for "n" days is the sum of the last "n" trading days of the OEX or SEI divided by "n." The exponential moving average is a mathematical approximation of the moving average that only takes 2 days worth of data to compute, no matter how many days the moving average is. For example, if the 22 day moving average for SEI is computed, it is necessary to sum the last 22 values of SEI and divide by 22. It is better to use the exponential moving average in market signal chart computations because only 2 days worth of data are needed as explained below.

The market indicator charts rely heavily on the exponential moving average which is simple to compute using Microsoft EXCEL workbooks. The moving average factor (MAF) depends on the number of days for the exponential moving average. For example, the MAF5 is the moving average factor for 5 days exponential moving average; MAF5 = 2/(5+1) = 0.3333. The MAF9 is the moving average factor for 9 days exponential moving average; MAF9 = 2/(9+1) = 0.20, etc. To compute the 9 day exponential moving average (Mav9) for the OEX, take a sequence of OEX for each trading day, OEX1, OEX2, OEX3, . . . OEXn (for the nth trading day). Start with OEX2 to compute the first value of the 9 day exponential moving average. The 9 day exponential moving average = MAF9 x OEX2 + Mav9-1 x (1 - MAF9), where Mav9-1 is the 9 day exponential moving average for the day before. If the sequence of values for OEX = 958.21, 959.32, 956.12, 957.64, then let's compute the 9 day exponential moving average for OEX using the exponential formula given above: for day 2, we will assume the exponential moving average for the day before is just the OEX; Mav9 = 0.2 x 959.32 + 958.21 x (1-0.2) = 958.43; for the next day Mav9 = 0.2 x 956.12 + 0.8 x 958.43 = 956.97; for the next day Mav9 = 0.2 x 957.64 + 0.8 x 956.97 = 957.10. That completes the 9 day exponential moving average computations for the 4 days of the OEX given above. It can be done with a hand held calculator, but it is much simpler with EXCEL!

In the next sections of this chapter we will examine each type of market indicator chart, describe what it shows about the market and describe how to compute it.

THE OEX STOCHASTICS %K-%D CHART

The Stochastics %K-%D chart predicts the short term direction of the market and I use it for both SEI and OEX. When the Stochastics is greater than zero (>0) this signals an up market; when it is less than zero (<0) it signals a down market. The Stochastics chart is shown in Figure 6.1 with the Stochastics %K-%D shown as bars and the OEX shown as a line:

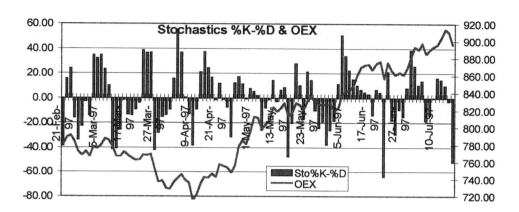

You may see that when the Stochastics switches from positive to negative, the OEX has a drop; the steeper the drop of the OEX, the more negative the Stochastics. When the Stochastics switches from negative to positive, the OEX rises. For example, in the chart above when the Stochastics switched negative on 9 April 97, the OEX had a sharp downward correction. When the OEX hit bottom at 720 and started back up the Stochastics switched from negative to positive. You can see the Stochastics is very sensitive to minor changes in direction of the OEX and follows the ups and down faithfully. Sometimes, during a day with many wild swings, the Stochastics switches from negative to positive repeatedly.

An interesting alternative to the Stochastics %K-%D chart is one that plots the %K and %D curves separately as a two line chart. When the two lines are greater than 80% the market is overbought; when the two lines are less than 20% the market is oversold. When the curves cross the 80% level descending, this is called a "death cross"; when the two curves cross the 20% level ascending this is called the "golden cross." This alternate curve is given as Figure 6.2.

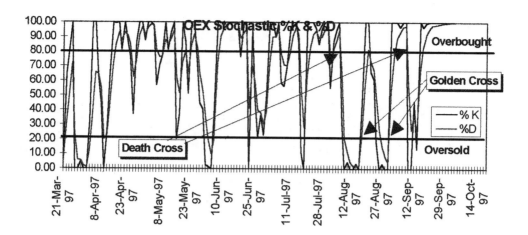

The Stochastics %K-%D computes a number of factors related to the OEX (or SEI) including the maximum and minimum value over the last 5 days. It then computes the 3 day moving average difference between the OEX and the 5 day minimum and 5 day maximum. Next it computes the 3 day moving average of the ratio of the moving average difference between the OEX and the 5 day minimum and the moving average difference between the OEX and the 5 day maximum. The Stochastics %K is computed as the ratio (in percent) between the difference between the OEX and the 5 day minimum and the difference between the 5 day maximum and the 5 day minimum. The Stochastics %D is calculated as the ratio (in percent) between the 3 day moving average difference between the OEX and the 5 day minimum and the 3 day moving average difference between the OEX and the 5 day maximum. Next the 5 day moving average of the %K is calculated, then the 5 day moving average of the %D is computed. Finally the Stochastics %K-%D is the difference between the Stochastics %K and the 5 day moving average of the Stochastics %D. Sounds complicated? It is, but, again, EXCEL makes it easy!

The equations and functions used by EXCEL for computing Stochastics %K-%D (shown above in Figure 6.1) and described above are presented below: The values of OEX are placed in a column next to the date of each trading day in an EXCEL worksheet (also referred to as a spread sheet). The spread sheet includes nine columns, whose headings are shown in Figure 6.3, for computing the necessary terms for the Stochastics %K-%D:

5da Max	5 da Min	MavDel1	MavDel2	dsStoch	% K	%D	DelStMa	Sto%K-%D

1. The first column computes the OEX maximum over the last 5 days and uses the following equation in the EXCEL cell (or box or rectangle) below the column heading: =MAX($B428:$B433), which is the EXCEL function MAX. The OEX value is in column B (the second column of the spreadsheet - out of sight here) with the most recent value in cell B433 and the OEX 5 days earlier is in cell B428. For those of you unfamiliar with EXCEL, the $ in the equation does not mean dollars; it is a signal to EXCEL to keep the column letter relatively the same as you move right and left from column to column.

2. The second column computes the OEX minimum over the last 5 days and uses the following equation in the EXCEL cell below the column heading: =MIN($B428:$B433), which is the EXCEL function MIN and the OEX is in column B with the most recent value in cell B433 and the OEX 5 days earlier is in cell B428.

3. The third column computes the 3 day exponential moving average difference between the OEX and the 5 day minimum and has the EXCEL equation: = ($B433-AB433) x sto2+AC432 x (1-sto2), where cell B433 contains the current OEX value, AB433 contains the 5 day minimum of the OEX, sto2 is the 3 day exponential moving average factor MAF3, or sto2 = 2/(3+1) = 0.5; AC432 contains the previous days computation of the 3 day exponential moving average difference between the OEX and the 5 day minimum. We talked about the equation for the exponential moving average several pages back.

4. The fourth column computes the 3 day exponential moving average difference between the 5 day maximum and the 5 day minimum and has the EXCEL equation: = (AA433-AB433) x sto2+AD432 x (1-sto2), where AA433 contains the current 5 day maximum, AB433 contains the 5 day minimum of the OEX, sto2 is the 3 day exponential moving average factor MAF3, or sto2 = 2/(3+1) = 0.5; AD432 contains the previous days computation of the 3 day exponential moving average difference between the 5 day maximum and the 5 day minimum.

5. The fifth column calculates the 3 day exponential moving average of the ratio between the numbers on this same line (433) in column 3 and column 4 given by the EXCEL equation: = sto2 x AC433/AD433+1-sto2 x

AE432, where AC433 contains the 3 day exponential moving average difference between OEX and the 5 day minimum and AD433 contains the 3 day exponential moving average difference between the 5 day maximum and the 5 day minimum; sto2 is the MAF3 = 0.5.

6. The sixth column computes the Stochastics %K which is the percent ratio between the difference between the OEX and the 5 day minimum and the difference between the 5 day maximum and the 5 day minimum, using the EXCEL equation: 100 x ($B433-AB433)/(AA433-AB433) , B433 is the current value of OEX, AB433 is the 5 day minimum of OEX, and AA433 is the 5 day maximum of the OEX.

7. The seventh column determines the Stochastics %D which is the percent ratio between column 3 and column 4 and is given by the EXCEL equation: = 100 x AC433/AD433, where AC433 contains the 3 day exponential moving average difference between OEX and the 5 day minimum and AD433 contains the 3 day exponential moving average difference between the 5 day maximum and the 5 day minimum.

8. The eighth column computes the 5 day exponential moving average of the Stochastics %K and is given by the EXCEL equation: = sto3 x AF433+AH432 x (1-sto3), where sto3 is the 5 day exponential moving average factor MAF5, or sto3 = 2/(5+1) = 0.3333; AF433 contains the current Stochastics %K AH432 contains the previous 5 day moving average.

9. The ninth column and the final computation gives the Stochastics %K-%D which is charted in Figure 6.1 and is computed with the EXCEL equation: =AF433-AH433, where AF433 contains the Stochastics %K and AH433 contains the 5 day exponential moving average of the Stochastics %K.

For those readers who are familiar with the power of EXCEL you know that it is only needed to enter the equations in the 8 columns across in one row, then use your mouse, cover the 8 columns, and pull down on the corner of the eighth column down to the end date for which you want the computations made and, voilá, you have all the columns and rows filled out to create the Stochastics %K-%D chart. To create the chart you merely cover those 8 columns plus the date and OEX columns, select *insert chart*, select *combination*, and in a few seconds you have the chart generated for your data just like Figure 6.1.

THE OEX WELLES-WILDER RELATIVE STRENGTH INDICATOR CHART

The Welles-Wilder relative strength indicator (RSI or WWI) chart is very useful for telling you when the market is overbought or oversold. When the value of the Welles-Wilder Indicator is greater than 80 (>80) for the 7 day WWI, then the market is overbought which means you can expect a downward correction at any time. When the WWI is less than 20 (<20), then the market is oversold and you can expect a bounce up in the market soon. The 7 day WWI chart is given below in Figure 6.4 which has the WWI and OEX plotted as two lines with the overbought line at 80 and the oversold line at 20:

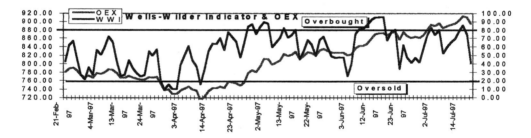

When the WWI was in the oversold region at the end of March 97 and the beginning of April 97 there was a recovery in the OEX until it dropped back on 14 April with the WWI again in the oversold region. Then a long up trend started on the OEX. When the WWI reached the overbought region in mid June 97 and stayed there for several days, there was a correction in the OEX that brought the WWI below the overbought region into the normal range between 20 and 80. You can see other examples of when the WWI hit the overbought region and OEX corrections brought it down to the normal region again.

The following equations and functions are used for computing the Welles-Wilder RSI (shown in Figure 6.4): The values of OEX are placed in a column next to the date of each trading day in an EXCEL worksheet (or spread sheet). The spread sheet includes the 5 columns shown in Figure 6.5 for computing the necessary terms for the Welles-Wilder RSI for generating the WWI chart:

UpDel	DnDel	UpMA	DnMA	*WWI*

1. The first column listed above (UpDel) carries on the calculations of determining if the OEX moved up on the current day and uses the following equation in the EXCEL cells in the column below the heading UpDel: = IF($C1027>0,$C1027,0), which is the EXCEL IF function. The OEX daily change (delta) is in column C (the third column in the worksheet from which the five headings above were copied) with the most recent value in cell C1027. If the delta is positive (>0), then that value of delta is placed in the cell below UpDel in line 1027, or else zero is placed in the cell.

2. The second column (DnDel) determines if the OEX moved down on the current day and uses the following equation in the EXCEL cells below the column heading DnDel: = IF($C1027<0,$C1027,0), which is the EXCEL IF function. The OEX daily change (delta) is in column C with the most recent value in cell C1027. If the delta is negative (<0), then the function places delta in the cell below DnDel, or else it places zero in the cell.

3. The third column listed above (UpMA) computes the 7 day exponential moving average of the UpDel column and has the EXCEL equation: =SFWS x V1027+(1-SFWS) x X1026, where V1027 contains the current value of UpDel, and SFWS is the 7 day exponential moving average factor MAF7, or SFWS = 2/(7+1) = 0.25; X1026 contains the previous days' computation of the 7 day exponential moving average of UpDel. This is the equation for the exponential moving average employed here.

4. The fourth column (DnMA) computes the 7 day exponential moving average of the DnDel column and has the EXCEL equation: =SFWS x W1027+(1-SFWS) x Y1026, where W1027 contains the current value of DnDel, and SFWS is the 7 day exponential moving average factor MAF7, or SFWS = 0.25; Y1026 contains the previous days computation of the 7 day exponential moving average of DnDel.

5. The fifth column (WWI) calculates the 7 day Welles-Wilder Indicator which is the ratio between the UpDel exponential moving average and the sum of the UpDel exponential moving average and the DnDel exponential moving average given by the EXCEL equation: $=100 \times X1027/(X1027-Y1027)$, where X1027 contains the 7 day exponential moving average of the UpDel and Y1027 contains the 7 day exponential moving average of the DnDel, with the factor 100 making the maximum value of WWI = 100. The main thing to remember about the Welles-Wilder chart is *when WWI is greater than 80, then the market is overbought, and when WWI is less than 20, the market is oversold.*

THE OEX 9 DAY - 4 DAY MOVING AVERAGE DIFFERENCE CHART

The 9 day minus 4 day exponential Moving Average Difference (MAD9-4) chart is very useful for showing you major changes in direction of the market. When the value of the 9 day minus 4 day exponential moving average difference is greater than zero (>0), then the market is in an up trend. When the MAD9-4 is less than zero (<0), then the market is in a down trend. The MAD9-4 chart is given below in Figure 6.6 which has the MAD9-4 plotted as bars and the OEX plotted as a line:

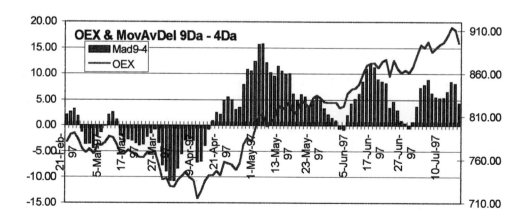

When a downward correction of the OEX began in mid-March 97 the MAD9-4 switched negative; when the correction ended in mid-April 97 the MAD9-4 changed back to positive. You can see this was a definite signal for an up trend in the OEX.

The equations and functions used for computing the MAD9-4 (shown in Figure 6.6) are given below: The values of OEX are placed in a column next to the date of each trading day in an EXCEL worksheet (or spread sheet). The spread sheet includes the 3 columns shown in Figure 6.7 for computing the necessary terms for the MAD9-4 for generating the MAD9-4 chart:

mav 4da	mav 9da	Mad9-4

1. The first column (mav 4da) computes the OEX 4 day exponential moving average and uses the following equation in the EXCEL cell below the column: =sfa x $B1175+(1-sfa) x D1174, where sfa is the 4 day exponential moving average factor MAF4, or sfa = 2/(4+1) = 0.40; B1175 contains today's value of OEX and D1174 is yesterday's value of the 4 day exponential moving average.

2. The second column (mav 9da) determines the OEX 9 day exponential moving average and uses the following equation in the EXCEL cell below the column: =sfb x $B1175+(1-sfb) x E1174, where sfb is the 9 day exponential moving average factor MAF9, or sfb = 2/(9+1) = 0.20; B1175 contains today's value of OEX and E1174 is yesterday's value of the 9 day exponential moving average.

3. The third column (Mad9-4) computes the difference between the OEX 4 day exponential moving average and the 9 day exponential moving average and has the EXCEL equation: =D1175-E1175, where D1175 contains the current value of the 4 day exponential moving average, and E1175 has the current value of the 9 day exponential moving average. As for all the moving average computations, the exponential moving average is used because of its simplicity - it only needs 2 days of data.

THE OEX 4 DAY MOVING AVERAGE DIFFERENCE CHART

The 4 day exponential moving average difference chart (MAD4) is a good intermediate term indicator for market direction changes. When the value of the MAD4 is greater than zero (>0) then the market is in an up trend. When the MAD4 is less than zero (<0) then the market is in a down trend.. The 4 day exponential moving average difference chart (MAD4) is given below in Figure 6.8 which has the MAD4 and OEX plotted as two lines. The death crosses are when the MAD4 switches from positive to negative indicating a change from an up trend to a down trend; the golden crosses are when the MAD4 switches from negative to positive indicating a switch from down to up trend:

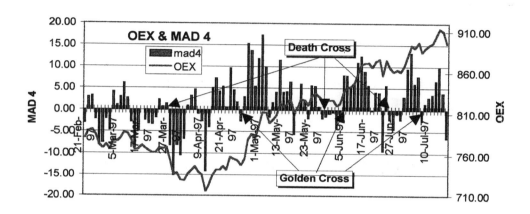

The MAD4 is a more sensitive indicator than the MAD9-4; in mid-March 97 the MAD4 switched to negative when the OEX downward correction began, but had two positive regions when the OEX had up ticks. Remember the MAD9-4 stayed negative this whole period until the strong up recovery began in mid-April 97. The MAD4 is a good indicator to use when you want to use long Calls and long Puts for several days rather than for intraday trading. The golden cross indicates you should buy Calls, the death cross indicates you should buy Puts. If you are using such a multi-day strategy, you need to be aware that the value of your Call or Put may vary considerable during a given trading day because of the intraday volatility. I personally prefer to use the delta strategy for long Calls and Puts described in Chapter 4, where you only have an open position for an hour or so.

The equations and functions used for computing the 4 Day exponential Moving Average Difference (MAD4) (shown in Figure 6.8) are given below: The values of OEX are placed in a column next to the date of each trading day in an EXCEL worksheet (or spread sheet). The spread sheet includes the 2 columns shown in the following Figure 6.9 for computing the necessary terms for the MAD4 chart:

ma4	mad4

1. The first column (ma4) computes the OEX 4 day exponential moving average and uses the following equation in the EXCEL cell below the column: =B657 x sfi+AF656 x (1-sfi), where sfi is 4 day exponential moving average factor MAF4, or sfi = 2/(4+1) = 0.40; B657 contains today's value of OEX and AF656 is yesterday's value of the 4 day exponential moving average.

2. The second column (mad4) computes the difference between the OEX and the 4 day exponential moving average and has the EXCEL equation: = B657-AF657, where B657 has today's value of OEX and AF657 contains the current value of the 4 day exponential moving average.

SEI CHARTS USED FOR DECISION MAKING

The SEI American style options based on the FTSE-100 index traded on the London LIFFE market use the same charts for trading as the OEX uses. There is one great difference between the New York markets and the London markets: New York has much greater intraday volatility than London. The volatility on the New York market is caused by the program traders who buy or sell a huge number of baskets of stocks in a matter of minutes which can cause the OEX to drop a whole percentage point in 5 minutes. The buy and sell programs in London move in a much more leisurely fashion. For example, a London sell program may last an hour or two instead of mimicking the few-minute turnarounds characteristic of the New York market. There are only a few reversals in direction during a trading day in London, compared with a dozen or more about-faces in New York. For example, in New York the Stochastics %K-%D signal may change direction several times within a single day, whereas in London a change in direction of the Stochastics %K-%D would be rare. I mention the Stochastics since it is the most sensitive of the indicators to market direction changes.

If you want to do day trading I strongly urge you to use the SEI rather than the OEX because it is easier to determine which direction the market is moving by watching a real time quote system such as the Satellite channel SkyNews which updates the FTSE-100 and the DJIA once per minute.

The FTSE-100 often opens in sympathy with the close of the DJIA the night before - if the DJIA closed down strongly, then the FTSE-100 will open down strongly and vice versa. There is a two hour overlap between the New York market opening and the London market close, and during this time period the London market often moves in accord with the New York open. If the DJIA opens up strongly, it will pull the FTSE-100 up with it. It should be remembered that the LIFFE options close 20 minutes before the London market closes, so the SEI options close 1 hour and 40 minutes after the New York open. The London market opens 6 hours before the New York market. A further advantage of trading in London is that you can trade both the OEX and the SEI options; if you trade in the USA you can not trade SEI. Also, I have found the discount brokers in London charge lower commissions than US discount brokers. This is true even though OEX trades involve transatlantic telephone calls or fax messages.

THE SEI STOCHASTICS %K-%D CHART

The Stochastics %K-%D chart predicts the short term direction of the SEI market. When the Stochastics is greater than zero (>0) this signals an up market; when it is less than zero (<0) it signals a down market. The Stochastics chart is shown below in Figure 6.10 with the Stochastics %K-%D shown as bars and the SEI shown as a line:

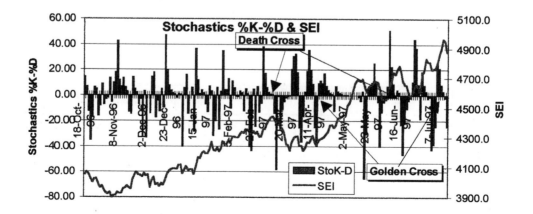

The death cross is when the Stochastics switches from positive to negative, which is a signal for opening a SEI long Put. The golden cross is when the Stochastics switches from negative to positive, which indicates a SEI long Call may be profitable. For example, in the chart above when the Stochastics switched negative in mid-March 97, this signaled the beginning of a strong downward correction when long Puts made money. When the SEI bounced back several days later, the Stochastics switched from negative to positive. The Stochastics is very sensitive to minor changes in direction of the SEI and both the Stochastics and SEI switch direction at the same time.

The Stochastics %K-%D for the SEI uses the same equations as those in the Stochastics chart for the OEX and therefore can be found earlier in this chapter. I use different EXCEL workbooks for SEI charts than for the OEX charts This SEI EXCEL chart workbook is named Ftschrts.

THE SEI WELLES-WILDER RELATIVE STRENGTH INDICATOR CHART

The Welles-Wilder relative strength indicator (RSI) chart is very useful for telling you when the market is overbought or oversold. The SEI version is very similar to the OEX chart. When the value of the Welles-Wilder Indicator (WWI) is greater than 80 (>80) for the 7 day WWI, then the market is overbought which means you can expect a downward correction at any time. When the WWI is less than 20 (<20), then the market is oversold and you can expect a bounce up in the market soon. The 7 day WWI chart is given below in Figure 6.11 which has the WWI and SEI plotted as two lines with the overbought line at 80 and the oversold line at 20:

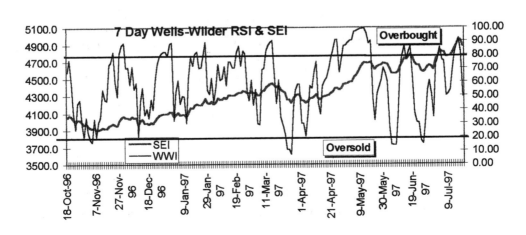

When the WWI was in the oversold region at the end of March 97 it only required a slight recovery in the SEI to move the WWI out of the oversold region. A long up trend moved the SEI into the overbought region where it remained for almost 2 weeks - an unusual event. Finally there was a downward correction in the SEI that took the WWI out of the overbought region back to the normal range between 20 and 80.

The equations and functions used for computing the SEI Welles-Wilder RSI (shown in Figure 6.11) are the same as for the OEX and will not be repeated here. I should point out however, that I also use a 14 day WWI chart which has the overbought region above 70 and the oversold region below 30. The 14 day chart is generated using the same equations and functions as the 7 day WWI chart, except the 14 day exponential moving average is used instead of the 7 day moving average for the UpDel and DnDel. The 14 day WWI chart for SEI (FTSE-100) is given in Figure 6.12:

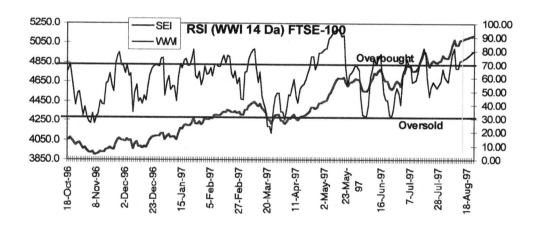

THE SEI 9 DAY - 4 DAY
MOVING AVERAGE DIFFERENCE CHART

The SEI 9 day - 4 day exponential moving average difference (MAD9-4) chart is very useful for showing you major changes in direction of the FTSE-100. When the value of the 9 day - 4 day Moving Average difference is greater than zero (>0), then the market is in an up trend. When the MAD9-4 is less than zero (<0), then the market is in a down trend. The MAD9-4 chart is given in the following Figure 6.13 which has the MAD9-4 plotted as bars and the SEI plotted as a line:

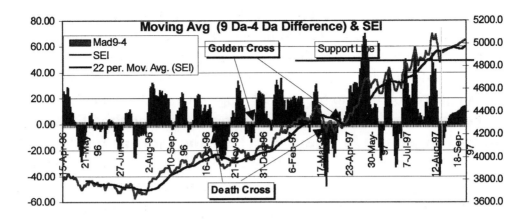

The death cross is a signal to open a long Put and a golden cross is a signal for a long Call. The MAD9-4 is excellent for showing when the SEI is in an up cycle and when there is a significant correction taking place. It doesn't have all the changes in sign that the Stochastics %K-%D has so it is better for telling when to open a multi-day long Call or Put. Note that the chart shows a support line at about 4875 indicating that strong market forces keep the SEI from dropping below this level. The chart also shows a 22 day moving average which is a trend line inserted by EXCEL. Note that when the SEI drops below the 22 day moving average during a downward correction, later as the SEI rises again the SEI moves above the 22 day moving average. I used 22 days, since this is the approximate length in trading days of the option month.

The equations and functions used for computing the MAD9-4 (shown in Figure 6.13) are the same as for the OEX and don't need to be repeated here.

CHAPTER 7

INTERNET OPTION QUOTE SYSTEMS FOR TRADING

The use of Internet option quote systems and market news can be a great aid to all kinds of market trading. In fact, sometimes I wonder how I ever managed to trade with only a once a day BBC (British Broadcasting Corporation) radio report of the Dow Jones close for the day and option prices from the Wall Street Journal delivered at least two days late. Now Internet delivers any information I could possibly want at the touch of a few keys. You don't have to be a computer wizard. In fact, you don't have to know anything about programming a computer. Your screen gives you a list of choices to show you the path to whatever you are searching for.

WHAT INTERNET BRINGS YOU

To access the Internet you need a personal computer (PC) with a modem and a subscription to an Internet server. The PC should be a 486 or better with a gigabyte hard disk and 16K random access memory; the modem should be 33.6 kilobaud rate for fast access. An Internet provider (or server) costs about $15 per month and hooks up to your phone line which ties your computer to the Internet. When you sign up with a server you select a user name and a code word and the server will tell you if you can't use that particular name or code word. CompuServe and America On Line are well known servers, but you can probably find a server close to your home or office at a cheaper rate. You can still use your present phone line to send and receive regular telephone calls or faxes. The other cost is telephone connect time at the local phone rate. I emphasize LOCAL phone rate - you can connect with someone on the other side of the Earth and it still costs only the local rate.

Normally your Internet server supplies software such as Netscape Navigator to let you browse through the Internet. Microsoft Explorer comes free with Windows 95. If you have an older version of one of these browser software programs you can usually download a later version from the Internet free. Each browser has add-ons that permit it to do specialized tasks required by various programs. If a program needs an add-on it will tell you to download it from the Internet. Both Netscape Navigator and Microsoft Explorer include everything necessary for sending and receiving e-mail with their browser.

When you click on the net search button while using Netscape Navigator a list of search services, also called search engines, comes up. The four most popular search engines are Lycos, Yahoo, Excite, and Infoseek. I like Lycos best because it seems to supply more relevant items when I ask for information. Also on Netscape's list are AOL.NetFind, CNET, SEARCH.COM, HOTBOT, LookSmart, and WebCrawler.

After choosing Lycos, I typed *Index Option Quotes* in the box headed SEARCH: and a notice appeared saying items 1 to 10 out of 2245 relevant results were displayed on my screen. Here are the first two items on the list:

1) Datatrack Network Inc. Stock & Option Quotes
Developers of: The fastest, most efficient Stock & Option quote system on the Internet. Designed with the emphasis on speed and substance. Automatic u.
http://www.dniquote.com/ [100%]

2) StockNvest Home Page
Welcome to StockNvest Stocks and Investment Information Financial Page
Index Stock Quotes Charts/Indexes Foreign Exchanges Stock Financials Stock
Rese.
http://www2.interaccess.com/abeweb/ [99%]

If none of the first ten items are interesting, you can click on next page and the next ten items out of the 2245 available will come up on your screen. When you want to investigate an item more thoroughly, you just click on the item.

REGISTERING WITH A QUOTE SYSTEM

There are two types of option quote systems available on the Internet: free ones, which give 20 minute delayed quotes, and real time quote systems that cost about $35 per month. Both systems require that you register with them. This is done right on your computer screen. The quote system will ask for your user name and your user password. These do not have to be the same name and password as you used with your server, in fact, you could use different ones for each web page you sign up with. BUT, it will quickly become very confusing and cumbersome for you if you have to keep track of a lot of different user names and passwords. I recommend you use the same user name and password that are registered with your server.

CODES FOR CBOE OPTION QUOTE SYSTEMS

The Internet quote systems require that you enter your option information request for U.S. options by using the code established by the CBOE (Chicago Board of Trade). The code is 3 letters for the type of option (OEX for the S&P 100) followed by a letter that designates the Call or Put expiration month and a second letter that designates the strike price. A table of these codes is given in the following Figure 7.1:

Option Codes

EXPIRATION MONTH CODES													
	Jan	Feb	Mar	Apr	May	Jun	Jul	Aug	Sep	Oct	Nov	Dec	
Calls	A	B	C	D	E	F	G	H	I	J	K	L	
Puts	M	N	O	P	Q	R	S	T	U	V	W	X	

STRIKE PRICE CODES												
Key	A	B	C	D	E	F	G	H	I	J	K	L
Strike	5	10	15	20	25	30	35	40	45	50	55	60
Prices	105	110	115	120	125	130	135	140	145	150	155	160
	205	210	215	220	225	230	235	240	245	250	255	260
	305	310	315	320	325	330	335	340	345	350	355	360
	405	410	415	420	425	430	435	440	445	450	455	460
	505	510	515	520	525	530	535	540	545	550	555	560
	605	610	615	620	625	630	635	640	645	650	655	660
	705	710	715	720	725	730	735	740	745	750	755	760
	805	810	815	820	825	830	835	840	845	850	855	860
	905	910	915	920	925	930	935	940	945	950	955	960

M	N	O	P	Q	R	S	T
65	70	75	80	85	90	95	100
165	170	175	180	185	190	195	200
265	270	275	280	285	290	295	300
365	370	375	380	385	390	395	400
465	470	475	480	485	490	495	500
565	570	575	580	585	590	595	600
665	670	675	680	685	690	695	700
765	770	775	780	785	790	795	800
865	870	875	880	885	890	895	900
965	970	975	980	985	990	995	1000

For example, the code for the OEX June Call 930 would be OEX FF; the OEX April Put 875 would be OEX PO. Sometimes when there is a wide range of strike prices available that span more than one hundred points, then for the lower strike prices you would use OEX and for the higher group of strike prices you would use OEW.

THE LOMBARD QUOTE SYSTEM
for U.S. OPTIONS, INDEXES & STOCKS

Lombard: http://www.lombard.com/cgi-bin/PACenter/PAQuote

Lombard is a free quote system supplied by Lombard brokerage in San Francisco that provides 20 minute delayed quotes for any option, index or stock. Lombard also provides almost real time charts of the OEX (or other indices) during the trading day. I often look at the OEX chart during the trading day and always print it out at the end of the trading day. This chart makes it easy to find all the ups and downs for each trading day caused by the program traders. You can see the Buy programs as nearly vertical jumps in the value of OEX; the Sell programs look like precipitous drops in the OEX. Typically there are more than a dozen of these program trades per day, and the intraday volatility that can be seen on the chart typically causes a daily swing of the OEX of 2%. See following copy of the Lombard Intraday OEX chart as Figure 7.2:

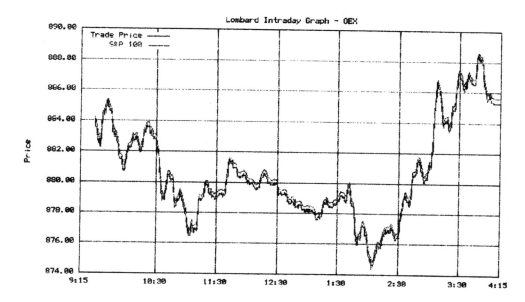

Here is an example of the free (20 minute delayed) quote from Lombard. It was taken after option month close on 15 August 97, so the numbers are the actual closing numbers for the Lombard free quote for the OEX September 870 Call, Figure 7.3 below:

S&P 100 INDEX SEP 870 CALL:

Last	28	Change	- 15 1/2
Bid	26 ½	Ask	28
Volume	726	Date/Time	8/17/97 8:09 EST
Last Size	30 %	Change	-35.63
Bid Size	0	Ask Size	0
Stock Symbol OEX.X Option Chain Symbol OEXIN (Sep Call 870)			
Exchange	OPRA		
Open	39 ¾	Prev. Close	43 ½
Day Low	26 ½	Day High	39 3/4
Open Interest	1541	Expiration	9/20/97 Tick Trend ——
	=+-	Fundamentals	

THE INTERQUOTE QUOTE SYSTEM
for U.S. OPTIONS, INDEXES & STOCKS

Interquote: http://www.interquote.com/cgi-bin/qs

The Interquote quote system is easier to use than the Lombard for option quotes because Interquote allows you to define a personalized portfolio with all the Indexes, OEX option Strike Prices and other stocks and stock options you want to track. Below in Figure 7.4 are the closing values and other values such as highs and lows for the day for the portfolio I defined at the beginning of the September option month in 1997:

Interquote Day Quotes							kk=	1.94			
17-Aug-97		22:30	Time of quote								
Symbol	Last	Change	Bid	Ask	High	Low	Volume	Call Sp	Put Sp	URP	
										inq ss	
OEX.X	869.36	-27.8			897.16	869.36	0				
SPX.X	900.81	-23.96			924.77	900.81	0				
$INDU	7694.66	-247.37			7939.01	7694.66	534412				
VIX.X	28.14	2.15			29.39	25.81	0	SP-OEX	SP-OEX		
SPY	89.7812	-2.8438	89.6562	89.8125	92.125	89.625	4907100				
OEX IL	32.5000	-16.3750	32.8750	33.8750	45.0000	32.5000	228	860		-9.36	
OEX IM	42.0000	-28.5000	30.0000	31.0000	42.0000	42.0000	10	865		-4.36	
OEX IN	28.00	-15.5	26.5000	28.0000	39.7500	26.5000	726	870		0.64	
OEX IO	25.0000	-13.375	24.6250	25.6250	36.5000	27.0000	135	875		5.64	
OEX IP	28.0000	-9.0000	22.1250	23.1250	34.0000	22.0000	2543	880		10.64	
OEX IQ	27.5000	-7.3750	19.8750	20.6250	31.5000	19.0000	6208	885		15.64	
OEX IR	19.0000	-11.7500	17.7500	18.5000	29.0000	18.0000	2820	890		20.64	
OEX IS	16.0000	-9.8750	15.5000	16.5000	26.0000	15.0000	585	895		25.64	
OEX IT	94.7500	-6.2500	78.0000	79.0000	94.7500	94.7500	1	900		30.64	
OEX UH	15.0000	7.7500	15.0000	15.5000	15.5000	8.0000	1340		840	29.36	
OEX UI	0.0000	0.0000			0.0000	0.0000	0		845	24.36	
OEX UJ	14.0000	4.6250	18.8750	19.2500	19.0000	1.0000	1926		850	19.36	
OEX UK	13.0000	2.0000	21.0000	22.0000	13.5000	12.7500	75		855	14.36	
OEX UL	22.0000	10.0000	22.2500	24.2500	22.6250	12.6250	933		860	9.36	
OEX UM	23.0000	10.0000	23.5000	24.5000	23.0000	14.5000	243		865	4.36	
OEX UN	28.0000	14.5000	26.0000	26.6250	26.8750	2.0000	1741		870	-0.64	
OEX UO	27.0000	10.75	28.125	29.1250	28.0000	17.2500	685		875	-5.64	
OEX UP	26.0000	8.5	30.75	31.7500	30.0000	18.0000	1956		880	-10.64	
$COMPX	1562.03	-24.66			1586.71	1561.85	0	OEW UT	29.1250		
$DVOL	0.0000	0.00			431822	0	0	OEW IA	23.5000		
$UVOL	0.0000	0.00			86076	0	0	10.000	3.7500		
HWP	66.0625	-3.8125	65.5625	66.0625	69.5	66	3841700				
IBM	99.9375	-3.6875	100	100.25	104.5	99.875	4602600				
IBM IQ	19.0000	-4.75	15.625	16.375	19	19	10				
MSFT	132.8750	-3.375	132.875	132.9375	136	132.75	6384800				
MSQ IE	11.1250	-2.875	10.5	11	13.125	11.125	36				
INTC	92.1250	-3.75	92.125	92.1875	95.75	92	16655900				
INQ IO	19.6250	-2.625	17.5	18.25	21	19.625	262				
INQ UQ	2.0625	0.8125	1.875	2.125	2.0625	1.25	1004				
OEW IE	6.5	-7.25	6.5000	7.5000	13.0000	7.0000	170				
OEW IG	5.5000	-3.5	5.25	5.7500	9.7500	5.0000	208				
OEX UM	23.0000	10	23.5	24.5	23	14.5	243				
OEX UK	13.0000	2	21	22	13.5	12.75	75				

THE LIFFE QUOTE SYSTEM for
U.K. STOCKS, OPTIONS, COMMODITIES, ETC.

LIFFE: http://www.liffe.com

This web page covering the London market normally gets updated for the latest trading day about 2 or 3 hours after the London market closes, unless there is unusual volatility such as happened on 15 August 97 when the FTSE-100 plunged 125.5 points, or over 2.5%. The LIFFE web page gives the information in text format, which makes copying to an EXCEL worksheet easy, then I use the Data, Text to Column function to convert the data to spread sheet format.   Below in Figure 7.5 is a copy of the EXCEL SEI Premiums (sei_prms) work sheet contained in my FTSE market variations (Ftsmkv2) work book:

This spread sheet includes the settlement prices for Call and Put premiums for a wide range of strike prices. It also includes the volatility and delta for each strike price. The delta is the slope of the Put and Call premiums at each strike price. With the FTSE at 4873.6 and the Call at 4850, the delta (slope) is 0.50, meaning that for each point the FTSE rises, the C4850 premium increases by 0.50; with the Put at 4850, the Delta is -0.51, meaning that for each point the FTSE drops, the P4850 premium increases by 0.51. See the FTSE settlement price quotes for 17 August 97 in Figure 7.5:

17-Aug-97				Sep CCvSS	Sep PCvSS		
FTSE =	4873.6	-117.7		£850	£1,500	C5050/P4650	
			Tot Init Crdt =	£2,350	1.608	$3,779	
+++ FTSE 100 Index (SEI) (SE			I/O) +++				
	CALLS					PUTS	
Settlement	Volatility	Delta	Expiry	Strike	Settlement	Volatility	Delta
————	————	———	———	———	————	————	———
926	25.53	0.99	Sep-97	3950	3.5	32.78	-0.01
876	25.53	0.99	Sep-97	4000	4	31.92	-0.02
826	25.53	0.99	Sep-97	4050	4	30.25	-0.02
776	25.53	0.98	Sep-97	4100	4.5	29.05	-0.02
726	25.53	0.97	Sep-97	4150	6	28.29	-0.03
676	25.53	0.96	Sep-97	4200	7	27.17	-0.04
626	25.53	0.95	Sep-97	4250	9.5	27.19	-0.05
576	25.53	0.94	Sep-97	4300	11.5	26.44	-0.06
526	25.53	0.92	Sep-97	4350	14.5	25.51	-0.08
476	25.53	0.89	Sep-97	4400	18.5	25	-0.1
426	25.53	0.87	Sep-97	4450	22.5	24.48	-0.12
379.5	25.53	0.83	Sep-97	4500	28.5	23.73	-0.14
337.5	24.97	0.8	Sep-97	4550	36	23.15	-0.18
295.5	24.43	0.77	Sep-97	4600	44	22.68	-0.22
259	23.85	0.72	Sep-97	4650	55.5	22.09	-0.26
222.5	23.29	0.67	Sep-97	4700	70.5	21.87	-0.32
186.5	22.74	0.62	Sep-97	4750	86.5	21.69	-0.38
157	22.16	0.56	Sep-97	4800	107	21.14	-0.44
128	21.69	0.5	Sep-97	4850	129	20.78	-0.51
101	20.97	0.44	Sep-97	4900	155.5	20.42	-0.58
80	20.55	0.38	Sep-97	4950	185.5	20.05	-0.65
59	20.06	0.31	Sep-97	5000	218.5	19.8	-0.72
45	19.59	0.25	Sep-97	5050	256.5	19.46	-0.79
33	19.55	0.2	Sep-97	5100	296.5	19.18	-0.86
23.5	19.11	0.15	Sep-97	5150	341.5	19.13	-0.91
16	18.85	0.11	Sep-97	5200	388	0.5	-1
10.5	18.5	0.08	Sep-97	5250	438	0.5	-1
7	18.37	0.05	Sep-97	5300	488	0.5	-1
4	17.94	0.03	Sep-97	5350	538	0.5	-1
3	18.27	0.02	Sep-97	5400	588	0.5	-1
1.5	18.27	0.01	Sep-97	5450	638	0.5	-1
1	18.27	0.01	Sep-97	5500	688	0.5	-1
0.5	18.27	0	Sep-97	5550	738	0.5	-1
0.5	18.27	0	Sep-97	5600	788	0.5	-1

THE ESI QUOTE SYSTEM for SEI TRADING

ESI: http://www.esi.co.uk/esioption/option.cgi?O,SEI,SEP97

This web page (Figure 7.6 on the following page) gives you SEI option premiums before open each day and then updates the premiums each 20 to 30 minutes during the trading day. About 30 minutes after FTSE-100 close it gives you the end of trading day premiums for the SEI options.

17-Aug-97					Sep CCvSS	Sep PCvSS		
FTSE =	4873.6	117.7			£1,800	£950	C5050/P4650	
			Tot Init Crdt =		£2,750	1.6108	$4,430	
+++ FTSE 100 Index (SEI) (SE			I/O) +++					
	CALLS					PUTS		
Settlement	Volatility	Delta	Expiry	Strike	Settlement	Volatility	Delta	
--------	--------	-----	-------	----	--------	---------	-----	
1391	297.54	0.98	Sep-97	3600	H	236.1	0	
1341	286.19	0.98	Sep-97	3650	H	227.37	0	
1291	275	0.98	Sep-97	3700	H	218.76	0	
1241	263.95	0.98	Sep-97	3750	H	209.63	0	
1191	253.06	0.98	Sep-97	3800	H	200.33	0	
1141	242.31	0.98	Sep-97	3850	H	191.15	0	
1091	231.69	0.98	Sep-97	3900	H	182.08	0	
1041	221.22	0.98	Sep-97	3950	H	173.14	0	
991	210.88	0.98	Sep-97	4000	H	164.31	0	
941	200.67	0.98	Sep-97	4050	H	155.59	0	
891	190.59	0.97	Sep-97	4100	H	146.97	0	
841	180.63	0.97	Sep-97	4150	H	138.46	0	
676	170.8	0.97	Sep-97	4200	9.25	130.06	0	
626	161.08	1	Sep-97	4250	8.5	121.75	0	
576	151.47	1	Sep-97	4300	11.25	113.54	0	
526	141.98	1	Sep-97	4350	16	105.43	0	
476	132.61	1	Sep-97	4400	15.5	97.42	0	
426	121.96	1	Sep-97	4450	17.5	89.49	0	
379.5	111.38	0.93	Sep-97	4500	30.5	81.66	0	
337.5	100.91	0.84	Sep-97	4550	33	73.92	0	
295	90.55	0.85	Sep-97	4600	43	66.26	0	
258.5	80.31	0.73	Sep-97	4650	53	58.69	0	
222	70.19	0.73	Sep-97	4700	67	55.15	-0.01	
186	60.18	0.72	Sep-97	4750	80.5	46.64	-0.02	
159.5	50.28	0.53	Sep-97	4800	109	38.24	-0.02	
127.5	39.3	0.64	Sep-97	4850	131	31.44	-0.04	
101	27.76	0.53	Sep-97	4900	152	26.73	-0.1	
80	22.24	0.42	Sep-97	4950	181.5	22.89	-0.26	
57	21.01	0.46	Sep-97	5000	214	21.01	-0.59	
48.5	19.99	0.17	Sep-97	5050	253	20	-0.88	
29.5	24.55	0.38	Sep-97	5100	291	0.1	-0.99	
25	29.47	0.09	Sep-97	5150	339.5	0.1	-0.99	
16.5	37.22	0.17	Sep-97	5200	388	0.1	-0.99	
12.5	44.89	0.08	Sep-97	5250	438	0.1	-0.99	
5	51.62	0.15	Sep-97	5300	488	0.1	-0.99	
3.5	58.15	0.03	Sep-97	5350	538	0.1	-0.99	
2.5	29.93	0.02	Sep-97	3950	587.5	33.1	0	

When the LIFFE doesn't have the SEI closing premiums at 2 or 3 hours after FTSE-100 close, I often use the ESI quotes and hand copy them into the Ftsmktv2 workbook on the sei_prms worksheet. The reason I have to copy the Call and Put premiums by hand is that ESI doesn't have a text format that EXCEL can convert to worksheet format such as LIFFE has. When a premium has a letter "H" this means half and must be changed manually or else EXCEL doesn't know what to do with it and gives such error messages as "VALUE?" if used in a computation. The premiums for September 97 at close on 17 August is given in Figure 7.6.

The two columns marked Delta under the Call and Put areas of the chart are the Call and Put slopes. The slope -0.59 for the Put at strike price 5000 means that for each drop of one point in the FTSE-100 the P5000 premium will increase by 0.59 point. The slope 0.53 for the Call at strike price 4900 means that for an increase of one point in the FTSE-100 the C4900 premium will rise by 0.53 point.

Also note that to change to a different option month, just change the web page address. The http address above ended with SEP 97 because that was the option month when I obtained the data in that chart. To obtain the premiums for the OCT 97 options change the address to: http://www.esi.co.uk/esioption/option.cgi?O,SEI,OCT97.

CNN FINANCIAL NEWS for NEW YORK & LONDON

CNN: http://cnnfn.com/

The CNN Financial News web page (on the Internet) cnnfn.com has at the top right side the DJIA, the NASDAQ and the 30 year US Treasury bond (Long Bond) which is updated frequently during the trading day and after close gives the closing numbers. I find this page very useful during the trading day, since it is the only place on the Internet where I've found Long Bond price and yield updated every few minutes. Since the DJIA and the OEX tend to follow the Long Bond - when the price of the Long Bond is up (the %yield moves in the opposite direction - down), the stock market normally rises. It is useful for predicting which way the stock market is going to move. On this main page cnnfn.com, there are other pieces of information than can be clicked on to read details of the market. Below is an example of market news that is helpful in understanding what is happening in the market. This is an excerpt of the market news wrap-up of

August 15, 1997, when the stock market had a major sell off. It was copied from the CNN web page on that date: cnnfn.com

Sharp sell off rocks Dow /
Blue chips record second-biggest point drop in history
August 15, 1997: 5:18 p.m. ET

NEW YORK (CNNfn) — Weak leadership in the bond market, earnings warnings and concerns about the U.S. Dollar on Friday sent the Dow Jones industrial average to the second-worst point decline in its history. In a sell-off that left few broader markets unscathed, the Dow lost 247.37 points to close at 7,694.66. The 3.11 percent plunge, while less significant in percentage terms, was the largest point drop since the 508-point loss on Oct. 19, 1987: . . . this report continued for another page or so . . .
— David Ryneck (CNN editor of this market wrap-up article)

INTERACTIVE WALL STREET JOURNAL
MARKET NEWS for U.S. & U.K.

WSJI: http://interactive6.wsj.com/bin/login?Tag=/&URI =/edition/current/summaries/front.htm:
The interactive Wall Street Journal on the Internet describes what happened to the market during the trading day. This page, like the CNN page above, is updated several times a day, with the closing data given 20 minutes or so after the NY market close. Here is an excerpt from the WSJI end of the day market report for August 15, 1997, the same day as the CNN report above:

Sunday, August 17, 1997
Industrials Plunge To Second-Largest One-Day Decline
By DAVE PETTIT
INTERACTIVE WALL STREET JOURNAL

Stocks plunged on Friday, pushing the Dow Jones Industrial Average to its second-largest drop on record, as investors continued to fret about the prospect for higher interest rates. Bonds recovered from an early slump, while the dollar eased against the mark and yen. After struggling all day, the market's losses doubled in the final half-hour of trading. Throughout the period, aggressive sell programs arrived on the New York

Stock Exchange floor, pushing prices steadily lower. At the closing bell the industrial average was down 247.37, or 3.1%, to 7694.66 — its lowest close since June 30. The Dow's point decline was the second only to the 508 points it lost in the 1987 market crash. Friday's percentage decline — although far narrower than the 23% lost in the crash — also was notable. It was the largest since Nov. 15, 1991, the day of a memorable 3.9% tumble triggered by plunging biotechnology stocks and worries that bank profits would be crushed by a proposal floated at the time to cap the interest rates charged on credit-card debt. The Standard & Poor's 500-stock index fell 23.96 to 900.81, the New York Stock Exchange Composite Index lost 10.56 to 469.10 and the Nasdaq Composite Index skidded 24.66 to 1562.03. "It just got ugly during the last half hour," said Michael Lyons, a senior trader at Morgan Stanley, Dean Witter . . . report continued for a few pages . . .

The type of market report copied from CNN and the Wall Street Journal Interactive with excerpts shown above are very helpful in giving an overall perspective to the market movements at the end of each trading day for the New York markets. CNN and the Wall Street Journal Interactive also have pages daily that describe the London Market movements and give me perspective on the FTSE-100 market changes.

BARRON'S WALL STREET MARKET REPORTS

Barron's http://interactive.wsj.com/edition/current/summaries/barrons.htm

This page is accessed from the Wall Street Journal Interactive front page and is included free with the WSJI subscription price. I read the Barron's market reports weekly to give an overview of what happened in the New York markets during the past week. Below is an excerpt from a regular weekly report about what happened on Wall Street:

Monday, August 18, 1997
Black and Blue Chips
By Alan Abelson

Definitely an 8. Possibly a 9. Friday's market, that is. And we're not talking in terms of comeliness. We're talking strictly Richter scale, man. Quakes like that just don't come along every day, and, commiserate as we do with the victims — we haven't seen so many wailing widows and screaming orphans since way back in '87 — we felt the same rush we get from viewing an eclipse of the sun.

The 247-point drop was, as you're by now probably sick and tired of being reminded, the greatest since the Big One just a couple of months shy of 10 years ago. There was something nice and total about the rout. Not just that three times as many stocks went down as went up. But for once, the big names were sucking air just as frantically as the mass of shares. In fact, last week was a thorough downer for the blue chips.

Explanations abound. A group of eminent technicians, after close study of their charts, insist it's the Friday Curse, which they identify as the evil workings of stock-deprived gypsies or jealous Wall Street drones bent on taking revenge on their betters, lolling on the beaches or teeing off on the lovely greens, by marking down stock prices when no one was around to counter their dastardly deeds . . . the report continues for several more pages . . .

I find these weekly Barron's reports useful in understanding the NY market dynamics of the week before. The update appears each Saturday for the previous week.

TEMPLE WILLIAMS' DAILY ELLIOTT WAVE REPORT

http://www.concentric.net/~sellnow/general.shtml

This free Internet page provides a prediction of which way the market will move the next trading day. Mr. Williams adds his Ewave (Elliott Wave) for the previous trading day by 9 AM New York time at the beginning of each trading day; in other words, 30 minutes before New York market open. Fortunately you don't have to understand Ewave theory to get a useful prediction from his executive summary which examines eight Ewave curves of the SPX for eight different time periods with Temple William's assessment as to whether the Ewave is Neutral, Bullish or Bearish. Below is his executive summary for Thursday 21 Aug 1997:

1	90 months	Neutral
2	90 weeks	Bearish
3	90 days	Bearish
4	1 hour	Bearish
5	30 minutes	Bearish
6	30, 15, and 10 minutes	Bearish
7	10 and 5 minutes	Bearish
8	1 minute	Bearish

The bearish or bullish assessment is listed under the column to the far right of his executive summary called "My Comments." The period of the Ewave chart is listed under the second column to the far left called "Chart Visibility." The executive summary has five columns as shown in Figure 7.7:

Degree	Chart Visibility	Preferred Count	Confidence Level	My comments

The first column refers to the Ewave degree, the third column refers to the Ewave count he assigned to each chart, the fourth column refers to his % confidence level in his prediction of Bearish or Bullishness. For the sample case above for Thursday 21st August, his overall assessment was "Bearish" for the next day, 22 August. On this day the U.S. market opened down over 100 points, stayed deep in negative territory all day long and during the last half hour had a dramatic recovery when the OEX rose from 884 to 896.91, or some 12.9 points in 30 minutes. So his assessment of a down day was accurate, but he didn't predict the dramatic recovery. His executive summary is not always accurate, since his Thursday executive summary didn't predict the huge drop on Friday, August 15,1997, when the OEX dropped 27.80 points. Nevertheless, it is an easily accessed Web page that gives one more view of which direction the market may move the next trading day. Mr. Williams says his Ewave charts are only good for predicting the next 20 to 40 minutes. He uses the Ewave charts for day trading and he says in day trading the focus is 20 minutes into the future. Following is one of his Ewave charts for Fri 12 Aug 97 as Figure 7.8:

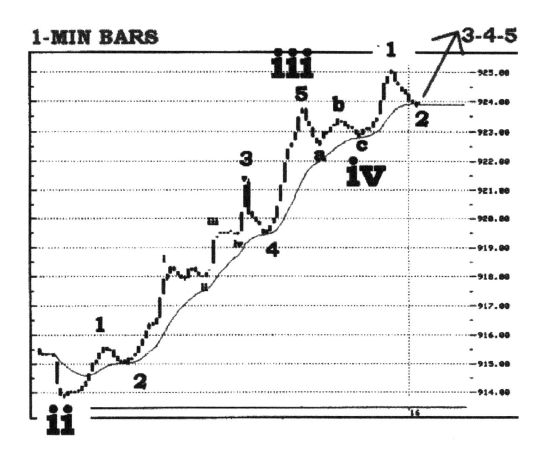

FIEND'S SUPERBEAR MARKET REPORT

Another interesting daily market report is given by FIEND'S SUPERBEAR MARKET REPORT which is given on web page: http://home.sprynet.com/sprynet/fiendbea   This daily market report is available the day after the market closes. It includes a list of all major indices and a few less well known including the close, change for the day and even the date of the all time high among other factors. This web site also has a multiple page market commentary for the most recent trading day as well as a one minute tick Dow Jones Industrial Average chart. An except from the daily market report for Friday 15 Sep 97 for which there was a good market rise is given below:

Market Commentary

Despite a huge bond rally and an initial jump of over 50 points, the Dow managed to trade down 50 points before a late afternoon rally finally erased the Friday jinx. The

Dow has now made at least three trips to the 7600 level and has bounced off of it every time so far. The Dow had a lot of help from bonds and it apparently needed it to make only its 5th significant gain since reaching its peak back on August 6th. The gains are not coming easy for the Dow, but breadth on the NYSE was overwhelmingly positive by almost a 3 to 1 margin. Volume was moderate on the NYSE and up volume was also ahead of down volume by about a 3 to 1 margin . . . *this market commentary continued for another couple of pages . . .*

Fiend's daily index report is shown as Figure 7.9 below:

Market Summary

Index	09/12/97	Change	High	Date	Record	Date	Record Low Since 09/05/97	08/29/97
Dow30	7742.97	+81.99	8259.31	08/06/97	7622.42	08/29/97	7822.41	7622.42
Trans	3038.98	+11.76	3038.98	09/12/97	3038.98	09/12/97	2959.53	2870.17
Utils	239.60	+3.83	*240.85	01/22/97	209.47	04/25/97	235.52	231.77
S&P500	923.91	+11.32	960.32	08/06/97	899.47	08/29/97	929.05	899.47
Nasdaq	1649.33	+9.47	1656.22	09/09/97	1639.25	09/10/97	1635.77	1587.32
NYSE	483.30	+6.24	497.00	08/06/97	469.10	08/15/97	484.64	470.48
Rus2000	440.09	+4.16	440.09	09/12/97	440.09	09/12/97	433.04	423.43
Amex	672.31	+5.47	672.31	09/12/97	672.31	09/12/97	667.55	650.16
30Yr Tr	65.86	-0.87	*59.49	12/29/95	71.86	07/08/96	66.38	66.01
Bnk Idx	690.50	+7.75	713.87	07/31/97	670.28	08/29/97	689.72	670.28
MSH 35	509.47	+0.93	532.00	08/20/97	500.24	08/29/97	521.88	500.24
Consumr	398.79	+6.80	426.91	07/31/97	391.99	09/11/97	401.73	392.31
Cyclicl	502.24	+3.28	522.17	08/07/97	498.96	09/11/97	509.50	499.64
Airline	537.85	-4.99	542.84	09/11/97	537.85	09/12/97	509.88	489.71
Retail	515.53	+8.75	515.53	09/12/97	515.53	09/12/97	505.88	483.36

*52 week records; all time records are 256 and 5.78% from late 1993.

NYSE Advances 2,089 Declines 769 NASDAQ Advances 2,528 Declines 1,856

NYSE Total Volume: 544 million NASDAQ Total Volume: 701 million Up Vol: 391 mil;

Down Vol: 130 mil Up Vol: 402 mil; Down Vol: 245 mil

The daily overall market outlook given by this web site is given in the following Figure 7.10:

Overall Outlook		
Short Term (< 1 week):	Neutral	(Upgrade on 09/15/97)
Intermediate Term (1-3 mths):	Bearish	(Downgrade on 08/11/97)
Long Term (3-9 mths):	FiendUltraPermaBear	(Downgrade on 02/08/96)

This web site also gives the closing prices for all 30 DJIA stocks daily.
This web site also gives a daily 5 minute tick chart for the DJIA as shown in Figure 7.11:

JOHN BOGGIO'S REAL TRADER MARKET REPORT

The Real Trader's Market Report by John Boggio is based on symmetrical wave analyses and is given on web page: http://www.realtraders.com/boggio/disc7_toc.htm. On this Web Page the information is free and requires no log-in. He writes reports based on his type of analysis, which he calls SymWave Analysis. Here is an excerpt from a report he posted on his web site on 17 Sep 97 that did a good job of predicting a big rally:

Symmetry SPZ7 15 Min. 9/17/97

Last week (9/12/97), I wrote a post titled, "GEN: Tech Stocks - Expect Beating for 9/12/97" and in that post, I wrote:

* * *

So, as I said earlier, tomorrow can be a very important day. If we convincingly exceed the recent lows, then I suspect the market is in the process of forming a major top in which a decline of 20% should be expected. If we do not break down tomorrow or Monday, and rally, then based on my style of analysis, we will have averted any further declines for some time. Hence, we will rally and exceed the Aug. 7th high, as we continue this phenomenal bull market rally.

* * *

Well, we DID NOT break below the recent lows and subsequently rallied. Thus, IMO we have averted the decline for the time being.

The purpose of this post is to give you a idea of where you might be able to enter this market on a pullback, or the stock market in general, since we have had such an explosive rally over the last few days.

Using symmetry wave analysis, we have only 1 wave structure that we can follow over the last few days . . . *this report continues for another page or so . . .*

John Boggio has a page on his Web Site that explains his symmetrical wave theories.

A SURVEY OF REAL TIME QUOTE SYSTEMS ON THE INTERNET [1]

There are now a number of real time quote systems on the Internet which vary greatly in price and features. Those listed below came from Kathy Yakal's article in Barrons weekly Internet report. Many require special software downloaded from the internet as part of the service to use the real time quote system. There are two types (1) the snapshot type where you get a set of quotes when you ask for it, and (2) the real time scrolling quote where you can see one or more quotes continuously scrolling on your screen. Sometimes the snapshot quote may be delayed by a few seconds to a minute. The scrolling type quote is generally more expensive and usually requires special downloaded software. As I mentioned above, I use the InterQuote snapshot type real time quote system that does not require special software. InterQuote also has the scrolling type. Barron's in the referenced article gives InterQuote a 3 star rating with which I concur.

The star ratings assigned by Barron's pertain to the sites' real-time quote feature, not the site as a whole. The monthly charges for the site normally do not include the monthly exchange fees which are about $4/exchange.

At Quote.com (http://www.quote.com), Rating: * 1/2, you're allowed 1,000 real-time quotes per exchange, per day, for $19.95 a month, as part of the company's Premium Service. The quotes are snapshot quotes, where the user has to click a button to update prices. Scrolling quotes are planned in future.

PC Quote (http://www.pcquote.com), Rating: ***, charges $75 a month or $750 annually — for its basic service, which waives exchange fees for nonprofessional investors for Nasdaq, NYSE and Amex quotes. It requires PC Quote 6.0 software, downloadable, free, at the site, which provides scrolling quotes from all U.S. and Canadian exchanges. The software is extremely flexible, providing tools to view and manipulate the instant data in order to enhance users' ability to act on market moves and sudden changes. Using PC Quote 6.0 at the $75-a-month level, allows multiple symbols, custom alarms (based on volume, price limits and highs or lows), open multiple quote windows to follow more than one issue at a time and uses Excel. Templates.

Data Broadcasting Corp.'s MarketWatch (http://www.dbc.com), Rating: **, provides snapshot quotes. For a flat fee of $29.95 a month, you get unlimited snapshot real-time quotes from the three major exchanges. DBC also offers delayed data for futures and equity options, mutual and money-market fund quotes, and prices on international exchanges, plus enhanced historical. For $99 per month you get scrolling real-time quotes using software StockEdge Online, downloaded free. Using the software, you can monitor securities' prices continuously using personalized scrolling symbols and export 50 symbols at a time into Excel.

Paragon Software's InterQuote (http://www.interquote.com), Rating: ***, I use the snapshot quotes which costs about $30/mo. It's scrolling quotes costs $69.96/mo. or $629.55 annually, plus exchange fees and includes unlimited real-time quotes from the major stock and options exchanges plus the OTC Bulletin Board.

S&P Comstock (http://www.spcomstock.com) Rating: **, has scrolling quotes $175 a which uses downloadable software for real-time quotes on over 256,000 stocks, options, foreign exchanges, commodities and indexes. For $225 a month, you get several enhancements, including advanced charting and multiple-windows capability. International Access through Internet feed costs another $50 a month.

Telescan (http://www.telescan.com), Rating: *, costs $50/mo. for unlimited snapshot, 90-second-delayed quotes from NYSE, Amex, Nasdaq and OPRA (Options Price Reporting Authority), plus $13.50 a month for exchange fees.

WallStreetCity (http://www.wallstreetcity.com), costs $9.95/mo. to $34.95*/mo. for different levels of access to news, analysis and data plus an online charge, starting at $9.95 for one hour a month ($4.80 an hour for each additional hour). You need to buy a data-retrieval and technical-analysis program available from Telescan called Investor's Platform for Windows, which costs $199. Additional search modules are available, ranging from $100 to $395.

North American Quotations (http://www.naq.com), Rating: **. Costs $30/mo. plus exchange fees, for unlimited streaming real-time quotes for stocks only from all North American (including Canadian) exchanges. The Real Time Trader software (downloadable free) includes charts and news from Reuters. Options and commodities futures prices will be available later, which will cost extra per month.

Which is the best quote provider? They're all reasonably good, but InterQuote and PC Quote probably are the best all-around choices. They're all improving with time as technology improves. *End of Kathy Yakal's list.*

This is just a small sample of the trading aids available on the Internet and more are being added every day. Information on almost any subject can be collected at your leisure. Before I had Internet I couldn't understand why people liked it so much. Now that I have it, I wouldn't think of giving it up. It really changed my life! For the better! It's usefulness is why the number of users is growing exponentially.

[1] Reference Barron's 8 Sep 97, article by KATHY YAKAL

CHAPTER 8

SEI TRADING SYSTEM USING EXCEL WORKBOOKS FTS-1

During the time I have been trading SEI Options on the London Exchange (FTSE) I have developed some EXCEL workbooks to organize my trading in a logical and easy-to-read fashion. I started with some OEX workbooks I had developed for OEX Index Option trading and converted them to fit the parameters of the SEI market. These 3 EXCEL workbook provide me with the information I need to trade SEI, the American style options that allow exercises at any day of the option month. I don't use the European style options as they can only be exercised on expiration Friday.

The EXCEL workbooks, and the worksheets contained in each, are discussed below. The first workbook, Ftsmkv2, keeps track of the daily variations in the FTSE market and computes the 2 sigma numbers needed for covered spread positions. The second workbook, Ftscharts, generates and updates several market signal charts using SEI data from a main work sheet called SEIMADC. The market signal charts available are the MADC9-4 chart, the Stochastics %K-%D chart, and the WWI 7 day and 14 day relative strength indicator charts. This workbook has other charts, but I find the four mentioned above most useful in trading. The third workbook called Ftstrfrm keeps track of all the SEI trades and the profit or loss made on each trade with the basic sums in pounds sterling (£). This work-book also includes the current exchange rate between U. S. Dollars and the British Pound so the profit is calculated in dollars as well as pounds.

THE FTSMKV2 WORKBOOK

- Ftsmkv2 (FTSE market variations, second version) contains the daily spread sheet called SEIMKTV for entering FTS-100 and the DJIA and the premiums for any open CvSS. There is a chart to show how closely the London and New York indexes track each other. The worksheet SEIMKTV also computes the 13 month Call 2 sigma (standard devia-tion) and Put 2 sigma. You can find the area of the spreadsheet where the 2 sigma computation are made by going to EDIT, GOTO, 2 sigma calculation. For example, for August 97 the Call 2 sigma = 224.63 and the Put 2 sigma = 99.51 (for the last day of the previous month); the 2 sigma computation results are following in Fig 8.1:

2 Sigma Calculation
FTSE-100, FTS

Op Mo	MAX	MIN	ABS Mx Del	2 Sigma (Lst 13 Mo) Call	Put
Apr-96	206.1	0	206.10	93.97	83.74
May-96	0.00	149.87	149.87	108.11	100.17
Jun-96	0.00	82.80	82.80	117.97	96.38
Jul-96	43.50	90.00	90.00	119.77	92.98
Aug-96	162.40	42.00	162.40	128.39	91.88
Sep-96	104.30	17.00	104.30	128.71	92.13
Oct-96	89.00	53.60	89.00	128.58	90.50
Nov-96	20.00	152.70	152.70	132.84	99.47
Dec-96	119.40	4.20	119.40	134.39	105.65
Jan-97	130.10	21.00	130.10	136.56	108.37
Feb-97	149.70	13.70	149.70	138.73	110.60
Mar-97	107.50	82.00	107.50	132.54	106.44
Apr-97	58.40	40.20	58.40	128.45	102.44
May-97	383.40	0.00	383.40	199.27	102.44
Jun-97	89.20	136.80	136.80	189.48	98.71
Jul-97	370.50	18.10	370.50	224.63	99.51
Aug-97	209.60	71.50	209.60	219.54	97.64
Sep-97	112.20	30.80	112.20	220.61	98.15

The equation for computing the Call 2 sigma is: Call 2 sig. = 2 x STDEV(AE75:AE87), where column AE (headed MAX) contains the monthly maximum value of the SEI (American style options using the FTSE 100).   Therefore, the letters and numbers inside the parentheses AE75: AE87 mean the thirteen "boxes" from AE75 through AE87 which hold the maximum values for the last 13 months. The computer uses the STDEV formula which is part of EXCEL to calculate the standard deviation (sigma) of the 13 numbers. When multiplied by 2 it is 2 sigma. The equation for computing the Put 2 sigma is: Put 2 sig. = 2 x STDEV(AF75:AF87) where column AF (headed MIN) contains the monthly minimum, and AF75: AF87 are the minimum values for the last 13 months. The Call 2 sigma for August 97 = 224.63 and the Put 2 sigma = 99.51, the values at expiration in July 97.

This worksheet has a section for computing and keeping track of covered short spreads (Strangles) in columns H through U. Columns H through J contain the short Call (Call Strike Price short = CSPs), short Put (PSPs), Long Call (CSPL), Long Put (PSPL), Call Premium for Long Call (CPRL), Put Premium for Long Put (PPRL), Call Premium for short Call (CPRs), Put Premium for short Put (PPRs), Number of Options (NO), Unearned Profit (URPR) on the covered short spread, Initial Credit (Init Crdt) received for opening the covered short spread, and finally the margin (Margin) required for the SEI covered short spread in Figure 8.2 below:

CSPs	PSPs	CSPL	PSPL	CPRL	PPRL	CPRs	PPRs	NO	URPR	Profit	Init Crdt	Margin
5050	4700	5100	4650	14	62	20.5	76	10	(£200)		£1,850	£9,590
5050	4700	5100	4650	0.0	0.0	0.0	0.0	10		£0		

The equation (on line 1166 of the worksheet) for computing the short Call strike price (CSPs) of a covered short spread is = ROUND((C1166+224.63)/50,0) x 50 = 5050, where ROUND is the EXCEL round-off function, C1166 contains the value of SEI for the day the CvSS is opened, 224.63 is the Call 2 sigma for the previous option month (the latest mo.), and the 50 causes the strike price to be rounded to the nearest 50 as SEI strike prices are 50 points apart. The long Call strike price (CSPL) = 5100 is 50 higher than the short Call strike price (CSPs). Similarly, the equation for computing the short Put strike price (PSPs) is =ROUND((C1166-99.51)/50,0) x 50 = 4700, where 99.51 is the Put 2 sigma for the previous month. The long Put strike price (PSPL) = 4650 is 50 lower than the short Put strike price (PSPs). The premiums are entered in the four columns indicated. The equation for Init Crdt (the initial credit received when the covered short spread is opened) is given by: = Q1166 x 10 x (O1166+P1166-M1166-N1166)-Q1166 x 5 x 4 = £1,850, where column Q contains the number of options (10), and columns O and P contain the short premiums and columns M and N contain the long premiums on the day the CvSS is opened, and the last term computes the commission for the ten CvSS opened. The equation for computing the margin required for opening the same CvSS discussed above is given by: = Q1166 x (500-O1166+M1166-P1166+N1166) x 2 = £9,590, where Q1166 =10 is the number of options, and columns O and P contain the short premiums and columns M and N contain the long premiums on the day the CvSS is opened. The equation for the unearned profit (URPR) on the covered short spread is given by: = T1166-Q1166 x 10 x (O1166+P1166-M1166-N1166) = -£200 where T1166 is the cell (box on the spread sheet) that contains the initial credit received and the other term in the formula computes the value (URPR) of the covered short spread on any given day using the premium values for that day.

At expiration on the very last day of the option month, all the premiums that are out-of-the-money go to zero; any premiums that are in-the-money are worth the Index expiration value minus the strike price (for a Call) or the strike price minus the Index expiration value (for the Put).

If the covered short spread finishes safely, with the SEI value below the short Call and above the short Put, the values of all the components of the CvSS are zero and you get to keep the money you received when you first opened the CvSS. Otherwise the premiums are computed by the worksheet. One equation for the last day for the short Call strike price (CPRs) is given by the equation: = IF(C1185<H1185,0,C1185-H1185); this logic equation tells the cell that the premium is zero if the SEI is less than the short Call strike price in column H. If the premium is not zero, it is the difference between the SEI at expiration and the short Call strike price. Similar logic equations are used for the premiums of the other three positions in the covered short spread on expiration day. If the expiration premiums all finish the month with zero value, then the unearned profit (URPR), also called the profit for the month, is the same as the initial credit (in this example, £1,850) or at an exchange rate of 1.6108 dollars per pound, $2,980. Since the margin for this covered short spread is £9,500, then the return for this month on margin = 1850/9590 = 19.3% or annualized = 231%. But since I recommend using only half your capital for your covered short spread margin, the annualized return on capital = 0.5 x 231% = 115%. The example in this spread sheet is typical of the return you can expect when trading SEI covered short spreads.

In the Ftsmkv2 workbook, there is a spread sheet called sei_prms for entering the daily end-of-day quotes provided by LIFFE for SEI strike prices with both Call and Put premiums included and other data, as shown in the figure 8.3 below, including volatility and delta (the slope for each Call and Put). Settlement means the closing premiums for SEI for each strike price. An example of a sample day's closing premiums is shown in the following Figure 8.3:

CALLS					PUTS		
Settlement	Volatility	Delta	Expiry	Strike	Settlement	Volatility	Delta
348	28.53	0.85	Sep-97	4500	23	27.58	-0.13
306.5	27.92	0.81	Sep-97	4550	30.5	26.71	-0.17
264.5	27.17	0.78	Sep-97	4600	38	25.84	-0.21
226.5	26.61	0.73	Sep-97	4650	47.5	24.88	-0.26
190.5	25.94	0.67	Sep-97	4700	61.5	24.24	-0.32
155.5	25.37	0.61	Sep-97	4750	77	23.74	-0.39
127	24.76	0.54	Sep-97	4800	99.5	23.31	-0.47
98	24.06	0.47	Sep-97	4850	122	22.69	-0.55
76	23.49	0.4	Sep-97	4900	152.5	22.33	-0.64
55	22.83	0.32	Sep-97	4950	186	22.23	-0.72
40	22.35	0.26	Sep-97	5000	225	22.08	-0.8
27	21.9	0.19	Sep-97	5050	266	21.71	-0.88
19	21.73	0.14	Sep-97	5100	312.5	21.91	-0.94
12	21.44	0.1	Sep-97	5150	361	0.4	-1
8	21.32	0.07	Sep-97	5200	411	0.4	-1

The columns are as follows: the first column *Settlement* is for Call premium closing (or settlement) prices. The next column is a measure of Call volatility. The next column *Delta* is the Call slope in terms of premium increase per increase in SEI points. The middle column *Expiry* is the expiration month, in this case September 97. The next column shows the Put settlement premium. The next column is the Put volatility. The last column is the Put premium slope or *Delta*, which is listed with a minus sign in front of the number to show the slope is negative, since Put premiums increase when the SEI drops. This worksheet is used to generate the Call and Put premium charts that show how the premiums vary as the distance from at-the-money increases or decreases. A Call premium chart is given the following Figure 8.4. If you look along the vertical x-axis labeled zero, the at-the-money premium = 85:

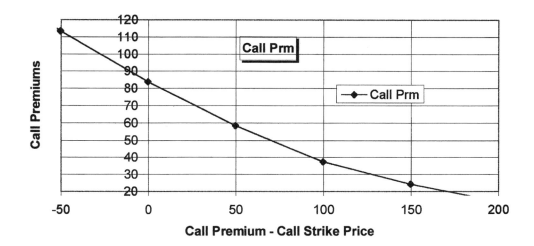

A Put premium chart is given below in Figure 8.5. When the x-axis is zero this at-the-money premium = 80

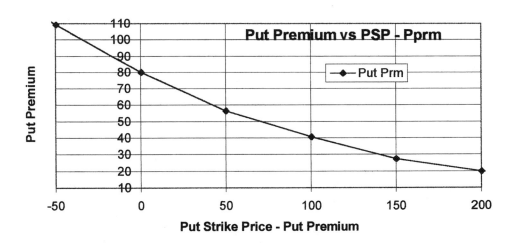

There are also two spread sheets called Call_statistics and Put_statistics. This is where I enter the daily Internet quotes I get from LIFFE for the SEI. Three lines of sample Call data are shown in Figure 8.6 below:

Close Bid	Close Offer	Settle Price	Delta	Vola-tility	Daily High	Daily Low	Est. Vol	Open Int.	Exer-cises
150	158	155	0.65	24.3	170	150	156	1012	0
115	122	121.5	0.58	23.47	160	113	74	537	0
90	95	92	0.5	22.57	140	84	537	3359	0

The data are for Call strike prices, 4900, 4950 and 5000 from top to bottom and include closing bid, closing offer, settlement price, Delta (slope), volatility, high and low for the day, estimated volume, open interest and any exercises (closing of positions demanded by the LIFFE Exchange) for the day. Of course, LIFFE supplies me with much more data than the three lines given here; on the same day I received the data shown in Figure 8.6, they gave me data for all the SEI strike prices from 3950 to 5600. I copy this data off the Internet and into the spread sheet page daily. There is a similar spread sheet for entering the LIFFE Put statistics.

THE FTSCHRTS WORKBOOK

- Ftschrts (FTSE market signal charts) is the workbook for generating and updating the market signal charts for SEI. The main work sheet for all the chart computations is called SEIMADC. From SEIMADC all the following charts are generated: the MADC9-4 chart, the Stochastics %K-%D chart, and the WWI 7 day and 14 day relative strength indicator charts. This work book has additional charts, but I find the four mentioned above most useful in trading. The first chart, MADC9-4, is shown below in Figure 8.7:

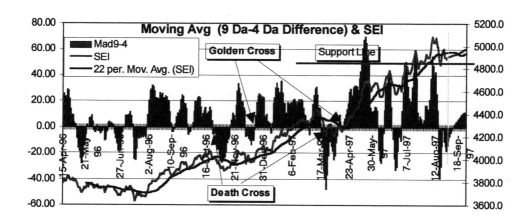

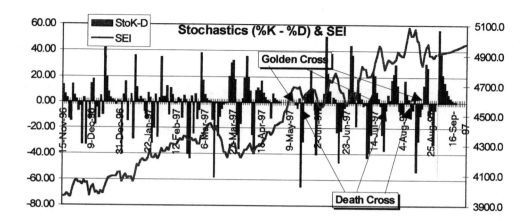

Below is the Welles-Wilder Indicator(WWI) or Relative Strength Indicator (RSI) chart for 7 days in Figure 8.9:

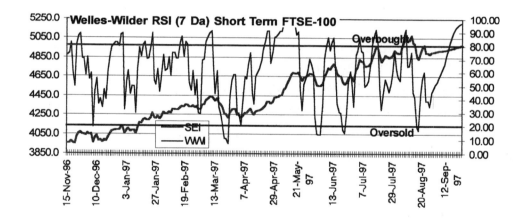

With these three charts you can get a good view of what is happening to the market by studying them at the end of the day. The Mad9-4 chart shows you major changes in market direction; the Stochastics %K-%D chart shows you shorter term switches in market direction, and the Welles-Wilder (RSI) chart tells you when the market is oversold or overbought. All these charts are updated with a single entry of the current value of FTSE-100 (SEI) in the SEIMADC workbook. After making the entry daily after the close of trading, then you should examine the charts. If you want to make trading decisions intraday, then you can make interim entries of the current value of SEI during the day and see how the charts are moving.

THE FTSTRFRM WORKBOOK

- Ftstrfrm (FTSE trading forms) is the workbook for keeping track of all your SEI trades and the profit and loss made on each trade with the basic sums in pounds (£). The workbook also includes a column where you can enter the current ratio of dollars to pounds ($/£) and another column with formulas that use this entry so the profit is automatically calculated and displayed in dollars as well as pounds. The column headings for the worksheet called sei_trds are given below in Figure 8.10:

Date	Opt	Mkt Pr	NOPS	CSPL	BS	cPRML	CSPs	PRM	cPRMs

The next column headings continuing across the same worksheet are given in Figure 8.11:

PSPL	BS	pPRML	PSPs	BS	pPRMs	Com	MyFee	Credit	CumCrdt	Lon Cap	Action

The column headings are somewhat abbreviated to fit within the widths of the columns. They are fully expanded in the next section.

How to use worksheet sei_trds in a typical long trade for Calls. Assume that on 26 August you open a long Call position for 5 Calls at 4950 and pay a premium of 83 and later during the day sell the 5 C4950 for 95. You would make the following entries for the buy transaction in the worksheet on the next row after last trade:

- 26 Aug 97 under **Date**

- SEI under **Opt** (for option type)

- 4910 under **Mkt Pr** (for market price of FTSE-100, the underlying instrument)

- 5 under **NOPS** (for number of options which are always multiplied by 10 when using SEI options and by 100 when using OEX options, for the number of shares per option. This is done automatically by the formulas embedded in the worksheet.)

- 4950 under **CSPL** (for Call Strike Price Long)

- -1 under **BS** (for Buy or Sell: for Buy, enter -1, or for Sell, enter a +1)

- 83 under **cPRML** (for Call Premium Long)

No other entries are required for the option transaction. EXCEL computes all other quantities and displays them automatically. The following quantities are calculated by EXCEL:

- Under **Com** (for commission) = NOPS x £5 = 5 x £5 = £25

- Under **Credit** = NOPS x BS x cPRML - Com = 5 x (-1) x 83 x 10 -£25 = -£4,175

- Under **CumCrdt** (for Cumulative Credit) = £Previous CumCrdt + £Credit = £25,000-£4175 = £20,825.

When you sell the 5 long Calls we discussed above, you would make the following entries in the worksheet, on the next row below the buy transaction:

- 26 Aug 97 under **Date**

- SEI under **Opt** (for option type)

- 4930 under **Mkt Pr** (for market price of FTSE-100, the underlying instrument)

- 5 under **NOPS** (for number of options)

- 4950 under **CSPL** (for Call Strike Price Long)

- +1 under **BS** (for Buy, enter -1, or for Sell, enter a +1)

- 95 under **cPRML** (for Call Premium Long)

No other entries are required for the Sell transaction. EXCEL computes all other quantities and displays them automatically. The following quantities are calculated by EXCEL:

- Under **Com** (for commission) = NOPS x £5 = 5 x £5 = £25

- Under **Credit** = NOPS x BS x cPRML - Com = £5 x (+1) x 95 x 10 -£25 = £4,725

- Under **CumCrdt** (for Cumulative Credit) = £Previous CumCrdt + £Credit = £20,825 + £4,725 = £25,550

- The profit for the round trip trade = £550; at an exchange rate of 1.6098 = $885

Above is an example of how to use the sei_trds worksheet of the Ftstrfrm for a long Call round trip transaction (buy and sell). It is a very handy form for keeping track of your SEI trades.

How to use worksheet sei_trds in a typical long trade for Puts. Use the same procedure as for Calls except use the Put columns: For buying the Long Put position:

- 4950 under **PSPL** (for Put Strike Price Long)

- -1 under **BS** (for Buy or Sell: for Buy, enter -1, or for Sell, enter a +1)

- 83 under **pPRML** (for Put Premium Long)

For selling the Long Puts use:

- 4950 under **PSPL** (for Put Strike Price Long)

- +1 under **BS** (for Buy, enter -1, or for Sell, enter a +1)

- 95 under **pPRML** (for Put Premium Long)

How to use worksheet sei_trds in a typical Call or Put Covered Short Spread. You can use the same form for entering the strike prices and premiums for a Call or Put CvSS. For a Call CvSS you would enter the number of options NOPS only once (do not multiply by 2 as the spread sheet will do that for you). Then enter the Long Call Strike Price (CSPL) and Premium (cPRML) with a -1 to indicate Buy under the BS column (after the CSPL column), then enter the short Call Strike Price (CSPs) and Premium (cPRMs). You do not need to enter a +1 to indicate Sell as the worksheet assumes this for you. The worksheet automatically examines all the columns where you made entries and computes the initial credit received for the Call CvSS. For example, if you opened 10 Call CvSS with a short Call at 5000 and the long Call at 5050 using the premiums from figure 8.3 above, the cPRMs = 40 and the cPRML = 22, then the worksheet computes the credit = 10 x 10 x (40-22) -5 x 10 x 2 = £1,800 - £100 = £1,700 or at an exchange rate of 1.6218 $/£ = $2,757.

If you wanted to use the sei_trds worksheet of the Ftstrfrm for a Put covered short spread you would use the Put columns.

Long Put Strike Price =   PSPL and following BS column.

Long Put Premium = pPRML

Short Put Strike Price = PSPs and following BS column.

Short Put Premium = pPRMs

Purpose of the remaining columns in worksheet sei_trds.

There are three remaining columns. *My fee* which factors in your fee if you are doing trading for others. *Lon Cap* means London capital, to keep funds invested in the London markets differentiated from funds invested in other markets. *Action* is a column where you can enter a reminder or note to yourself to identify the trade made based on that line in the worksheet, such as *open CvSS* or *close CvSS*.

Additional worksheet oex_Trds for trading OEX from London.

The Ftstrfrm workbook also has a worksheet oex_Trds for keeping track of your OEX trades, if you want to trade both OEX and SEI options. This cannot be done through a US broker. But you can do it if you have an account with a broker in London, such as Union Cal Ltd. (a discount brokerage open 24 hours a day since they handle options all over the world). This OEX worksheet has similar columns and requires similar entries for buy and sell transactions and makes similar computations to the SEI worksheet discussed above so the explanation won't be repeated here.

HOW TO DO SEI DAY TRADING USING THE DELTA STRATEGY

To do SEI day trading you need a satellite receiver to receive SkyNews and its associated Teletext to obtain real time data about the FTSE-100 during the trading day that opens at 08:30 London time or 02:30 New York time. Most delta day trades can be opened and closed with a profit during the first hour to hour and a half of trading since London makes most its market moves during the first 1½ hours and the last 1½ hours. First you need to look at the charts of Ftschrts workbook described above to get a feeling for whether it will be an up day, meaning a long Call, or a down day, meaning a long Put. In addition you should look at 3SAT, a German satellite channel on its Teletext page 156, just after London's open, to obtain the FTSE-100 futures price to see its value compared with the opening Cash price. If it is well above the cash price, then for the first hour expect an up market, if it is the same or less, then for the first hour expect a falling market   (The S&P 500 futures and Spot (Cash) prices being traded in Frankfurt, Germany, are also shown long before the New York open, which is very handy if you are trading OEX.) The first reading is given at 08:31 London time or 09:31 German time or 03:31 New York time. In other words, the first futures reading is available immediately after the London market opening. If the futures price is way above the closing cash price from the night before this indicates an up market and a Call position; if it is about the same or below the cash price, this indicates a down market or a Put position. The SPX Spot (cash) price is available on 3SAT teletext page 163; if the SPX spot is higher than the close the night before it indicates a rising market; if below, it indicates a falling market during the first half hour of New York trading. Since the FTSE moves in sympathy with the New York market, this data tells you what to expect during the last 1½ hour of London option trading.

But the most important indicator is the actual movement of the FTSE-100 from open to about the first 20 to 30 minutes. If it opens high and then starts dropping at, say, 1 point per minute, this is a sign for a long Put. If the market opens low and then starts rising at a point per minute or more, this is a sign for a long Call. For example, on Friday 29 August, the 3SAT FTSE-100 futures reading was much lower than the futures close on 28 August. The FTSE-100 opened down 18, rose slightly for 10 minutes and then started dropping. With the cash price at 4831, I placed an order to buy 5 September SEI Puts at 4900 at market and I included a sell order at a delta of 20 points more than received. At 0900 London time I received confirmation that I had bought 5 SEI P4900 at 140 and 15 minutes later I was notified that the 5 SEI P4900 were sold at 160. This delta strategy day trade yielded a profit = 5 x 10 x (160-140)-5 x 5 x 2 = £1000 - Comm = £950 or at an exchange rate of 1.6218 $/£ = $1,541. This is a good example of a successful day trade using the delta strategy with SEI.

If the market continues moving down slowly and you have time, increase your profit by increasing your requested delta. Keep your mental stop loss rising also, in case the market suddenly turns around. On 29 August the market continued falling so a larger delta could have been obtained. My selection of a delta of 20 was based on the fact that the after hours trading of the DAX (the German index) had dropped a great deal after the floor trading ended on 28 August, so I expected a big sympathetic drop in the FTSE-100 on 29 August. My reading of the DAX after hours trading drop, the big drop in the DJIA of 92 points on the 28th and the low FTSE-100 futures all convinced me to use the large delta of 20 for the SEI long Put at 4900.

However, in day trading using the delta strategy, if the market moves against you, close out as soon as possible. Don't hope, act to cut your losses. If you get too greedy, you will lose instead of win. On 29 August, the market had continued to sink, so I had opened a Put position for a second time that day. At 23 minutes before 4 London time, the market was down a comfortable (for me) 60 points. However, the market suddenly started zipping up. I knew SEI options closed 10 min after 4 PM London time, and I quickly abandoned my hopes of another large delta that day and sent in an order to close at market. I was able to get out with a small profit. By market close the FTSE-100 was only down 27.9. In the last twenty minutes the market had gone up more than thirty points. Note: the London market is similar to the New York market in that the first and last hours often show much more activity than the middle of the trading day.

NON-DIRECTIONAL LONG STRADDLE STRATEGY

The delta strategy in the previous section is a directional strategy - meaning that you must be able to determine which direction the market is going to move before taking a position. If you are right you will make money; if you are wrong you will lose money. It takes skill and lots of work to make directional strategies work. If you can't spend a large part of the trading day on these directional strategies it is better not to use them. The use of non-directional strategies takes less time and less skill than the use of the delta strategy. For this reason the non-directional long straddle strategy is an excellent way to make money no matter which direction the market moves as long as it moves sharply up or down.

The non-directional long straddle strategy works as follows: Buy far-out-of-the-money Calls above the market and Buy far-out-of-the-money Puts below the market. If the market moves up the Calls will become more valuable and the Puts will become less valuable. If the market moves down the Puts will become more valuable and the Calls will become less valuable. Let's take two examples for the SEI:

Example 1

- On 18 July 97 FTSE-100 (SEI) closed at 4877. Just before options close we buy 10 Calls about 250 points above the market at strike price 5100 for a premium of 17 and we buy 10 Puts about 250 points below the market at strike price 4500 for a premium of 19; the total premium = 17 + 19 = 36. The cost for the 10 C5100 and 10 P4500 = 36 x 10 x 10+5 x 10 x 2 = £3,700 including commissions. At an exchange rate of 1.6769 = $6,204.

- On 8 August 97, fifteen trading days later, the FTSE-100 closed at 5022, and just before market close, we sell the 10 C5100 and 10 P4500 and receive the following premiums: C5100 = 54.5, P4500 = 1 for a total premium = 55.5. The credit for the close-out sale = 55.5 x 10 x 10 - 5 x 10 x 2 = £5,450 net after commissions. At an exchange rate of 1.5816 $/£ = $8,619.

- The net profit for the round trip trade = £5450 - £3700 = £1,750 = $2,768 and we didn't have to predict the direction of the market. We would have made a profit whether the market rose or fell as long as it had a good movement. In this case the market rose.

Example 2

- On 20 August 97 the FTSE-100 (SEI) closed at 4958.4. Just before options close we buy 10 Calls 300 above the market at strike price 5250 for a premium of 19 and buy 10 Puts 300 below the market at strike price 4650 for a premium of 20.5; the total premium = 19 + 20.5 = 39.5. The cost for the 10 C5250 and 10 P4650 = 39.5 x 10 x 10+5 x 10 x 2 = £4,050 including commissions. At an exchange rate of 1.6081 = $6,513.

- On 29 August 97, seven trading days later, the FTSE-100 closed at 4817, and just before market close, we sell the 10 C5250 and 10 P4650 and receive the following premiums: C5250 = 4.5, P4650 = 47.5 for a total premium = 52. The credit for the close-out sale = 52 x 10 x 10 - 5 x 10 x 2 = £5,100 net after commissions at an exchange rate of 1.6218 $/£ = $8,271.

- The net profit for the round trip trade = £1,050 = $1,703 and we didn't have to predict the direction of the market. All we needed was good market movement. In this case the market fell.

In the two examples of the Long Straddle Strategy, why did we close out before options expiration? We had a good profit and the premiums always decay at the end of the option month, so we wanted to lock in our profit after a good market move.

NON-DIRECTIONAL COVERED SHORT SPREAD (CvSS) STRATEGY, 1 and 2 SIDED

The Covered Short Spread (CvSS) is another excellent non-directional strategy to use for SEI. The non-directional covered short spread strategy is an good way to make money no matter which direction the market moves as long as it doesn't move above your short Call or below your short Put, which are chosen to make this possibility a low probability.

The non-directional covered short spread strategy works as follows:

The two sided CvSS is opened by Selling 10 Calls 2 sigma above the market and Buying 10 Calls one strike price higher than the short Calls. The initial credit for the Call CvSS is equal to the premium difference times the number of options times ten (for SEI), less commission; and also Selling 10 Puts 2 sigma below the market and Buying 10 Puts one strike price lower than the short Puts. The initial credit for the Put CvSS is equal to the premium difference times the number of options times ten, less commission. Now if the market moves up less than 2 sigma during the option month, the Calls finish worthless and you get to keep your initial credit on the Call side. If the market moves down less than 2 sigma during the option month, the Puts finish worthless and you get to keep the Put CvSS initial credit. So the net profit for the 2 sided covered short spread is equal to the initial credit for the Call side plus the initial credit for the Put side as long as the market finishes between the Short Call and Short Put. Let's take two examples for the SEI:

Example 1: Two sided covered short spread

- On 18 July 97 FTSE-100 (SEI) closed at 4877, and the Call 2 sigma = 224.45 and the Put 2 sigma = 99.57. The short Call = 224.45+4877 = 5101, round off to SC5100, the long Call = 5150. The premiums are: C5100 = 17 and C5150 = 10.5, so the initial credit for the 10 Call CvSS = 10 x 10 x (17-10.5) -Comm = £650 - £100 = £ 550; the short Put = 4877 - 99.57 = 4777, round off to 4800, and the long Put = 4750. The premium for SP4800 = 83.5 and the LP4750 = 65, so the initial credit for the 10 Put CvSS = 10 x 10 x (83.5-65) -Comm = £1,850 - £100 = £1,750. So the total initial credit for both sides of the CvSS = £550 + £1750 = £2,300. Just before options close we sell 10 Calls 5100 and buy 10 Calls 5150 and sell 10 Puts at 4800 and buy 10 Puts at 4750 for which we received the premiums stated above and ended with the initial credit of £2,300. The margin for the 10 two sided CvSS = 10 x 2 x (500 - 17 - 83.5 + 10.5 + 65) = £9,500. So the initial credit/margin = 24.2%. This margin formula is a good approximation to the SEI margin requirements (for a further discussion of SEI margin requirements, see Chapter 5, under Margin for CvSS). 500 is the 50 point difference between strike prices on the SEI times the number of stocks per option (10) on the SEI.)

- During the August option month that expired on 15 August, the maximum the SEI reached was 5086.8, which was below the short Call at 5100, and the minimum was 4865.8, which was above the short Put at 4800. So the Puts and Calls finished worthless and the initial credit of £2,300 became the profit for the month.

Example 2: one sided covered short spread

- An alternative to the two sided Covered Short Spread is the one sided covered short spread. For example, open only a Put CvSS if you expect the market to rise strongly (more than 2 sigma), or open only a Call CvSS if you expect the market to drop strongly (more than 2 sigma). All indications were that the August 97 option month was to be a down month, so I decided to open a Call CvSS with the long Call 2 strike prices higher than the Short Call; choosing a strike price two instead of one higher than the short Call increases the premium difference and therefore the initial credit. As long as the market stays below the short Call the initial credit becomes profit at month end. The Call 2 sigma = 224.63 for August. On Monday, 21 July 97, the FTSE-100 (SEI) closed at 4805.7, a drop of 71.5 for the day. Just before options close we sell 10 Calls = 4805.7 + 224.63 = 5030.33, round off to 5050. The premium for C5050 = 20.5. At the same time we buy 10 Calls at 5150, the premium C5150 = 10.5. The initial credit received for the 10 one sided Call CvSS = 10 x 10 x (20.5 - 10.5) - Comm = £1000 -£100 = £900.

The highest the SEI got was 5086.8 which was above the short C5050 for one day and then fell back. Then three days before expiration it hit 5075.8 and then fell back again. At expiration on 15 Aug 97 the SEI was at 4973.1 (the SEI expires at 10:30 LON time) well below the short Call at 5050, so the initial credit became profit at the end of the month. The margin for the one sided Call CvSS = 10 x (1000 - 20.5 + 10.5) = $9,900; this margin equation has the factor 1000 rather than the 500 (used in the CvSS example above) because the difference between the short Call and long Call was 100 points rather than 50. So the monthly return on Margin = £950/£9900 = 9.6%, about half the return as for the 2 sided CvSS.

In the two examples of the Covered Short Spread (Strangle), in one case we used a two sided covered short spread with the short Call 2 sigma above the market and the short Put 2 sigma below the market; in the other case we used a single sided Call covered short spread with the short Call 2 sigma above the market and the long Call 2 strike prices higher than the short Call; this strategy generated less initial credit, but the margin is about the same as a 2 sided covered short spread. If there is a strong up market, then the one sided Put covered short spread works well; in this case the long Put would be 2 strike prices below the short Put.
Of course, there is the possibility that the market may not move the way you expect it to. In this case, the corrective actions listed in Chapter 5 should be followed.
The SEI options traded on the London Stock Exchange are an excellent

vehicle for option trading using both the non-directional covered short spread and one sided short spread strategies and also the directional delta strategy. The advantage of the covered short spread (strangle) is the initial credit goes into your account at the beginning of the month. As long as your short position(s) do not get into the money at expiration, the initial credit becomes the profit for the month. The advantage of the directional delta strategy is that you can make small profits during a short period of time during the trading day. If you use this strategy successfully a few times a month, you can augment the profit from the covered short spread strategy, which should be the basic strategy for SEI trading to build capital. The advantage of the non-directional long straddle strategy is it requires a small investment at the beginning of an option month and as long as there is a good market move either up or down, you will realize a good profit in two or three weeks time. If you use a combination of these strategies described in this chapter you can make your capital grow without too great a risk of loss.

CHAPTER 9

HOW TO BUILD YOUR CAPITAL SAFELY

DIRECTIONAL AND NON-DIRECTIONAL STRATEGIES

There are two basic approaches to option trading: the non-directional strategies in which you depend on market statistics to make a profit and the directional strategies in which you depend on market volatility and being able to predict on a short term basis which direction the market is going to move. If you have a lot of time to devote to directional trading, the use of the directional delta strategy can be quite profitable. If you have a limited amount of time to devote to option trading, I recommend the non-directional strategies.

The non-directional strategies include:

- The 2 sigma covered short spreads (strangles) in which the minimum capital to start is about $5,000. The covered short spreads (CvSS) can be either 2 sided or one sided. During a strongly up (bull) market it is better to use the one sided Put CvSS often called the Bull CvSS. During a down (bear) market it is better to use the one sided Call CvSS often called the Bear CvSS. When you're not sure whether the market is going up or down use both the Put and Call CvSS with the short Put 2 sigma below the market and the short Call 2 sigma above the market. Normally the 2 sided CvSS means selling Calls 2 sigma above the market and buying the same number of Calls at the next strike price higher; and at the same time the 2 sided CvSS means selling Puts 2 sigma below the market and buying the same number of Puts at the next strike price below the market. With this strategy about 90% of the time your initial credit when the position is opened will become your profit at expiration. One big advantage of the CvSS is the margin requirement is small, allowing the use of this strategy with a small amount of capital (e.g. $5,000). The Bull and Bear CvSS can use a long Position 2 strike prices below or above the short Position in order to more than double the premium difference with about the same margin as for the 2 sided CvSS.

- The long straddle in which the minimum capital to start is about $3,000. For this strategy buy far-out-of-the-money Calls at a small premium and buy an equal number of far-out-of-the-money Puts at a small premium. If the market rises sharply the Calls become a lot more valuable and the Puts become slightly less valuable; conversely, if the market drops sharply the Puts become much more valuable and the Calls become slightly less valuable. It is important to close the long straddle 2 to 3 weeks into the option market to lock in your profit. During the last week of the option month the premiums decay so fast, your profit might evaporate.

- The 2 sigma naked short spread (strangle) has a CBOE requirement of a minimum margin of $50,000 to trade this strategy. For this strategy you sell Calls 2 sigma above the market and sell Puts 2 sigma below the market and 90% of the time your initial credit becomes your profit at expiration. The advantage of the naked short spread over the covered short spread is that if corrective action must be taken when the short Call or short Put is threatened, the cost of the corrective action is normally less for the naked SS than for the CvSS.

The principal directional strategy is the Delta Strategy:

- If the market indicators say the market is going to rise, the delta strategy buys Calls in-the-money at the market with a sell order included to sell the Calls at a delta above the premium paid when the Calls were bought. For the OEX normally the delta is 1; so if you buy 3 OEX Calls at 20 with a delta of 1, when the OEX rises enough (about 2 points) for the premium to increase to 21, then you will sell the 3 OEX Calls for a profit of $300 less commission. Not much profit, but normally the close out is within an hour of the opening of the long Call position.

- If the market indicators say the market is going to drop, the delta strategy buys Puts in-the-money at the market with a sell order included to sell the Puts at a delta above the premium paid when the Puts are bought. For the OEX normally the delta is 1; so if you buy 3 OEX Puts at 20 with a delta of 1, when the OEX rises enough (about 2 points) for the premium to increase to 21, then you will sell the 3 OEX Calls for a profit of $300 less commission. Not much profit, but normally the close out is within 30 minutes of the opening of the long Put position, since market drops are usually more rapid than market rises.

THE TWO SIDED COVERED SHORT SPREAD STRATEGY

In the following capital growth example, we will assume you have only $5,000 initial capital and that you only use one half of your capital for OEX 2 sigma two sided covered short spreads (strangles). The period of capital growth will be 36 months and each tenth month it is assumed you lose because the short Put or short Call is penetrated and corrective action had to be taken.

Figure 9.1 shows that by starting out with an initial capital of only $5,000, at the end of three years with occasional corrective action being necessary, the capital grows to $89,600. In the beginning the margin requirements are close to the capital available, but later only 50% or less of the capital is used for margin. This projection of profits from covered short spread trading shows this is the only strategy needed to make your profits grow safely, but fairly rapidly. The covered short spread strategy requires decision making at the beginning of the option month when opening the position, then little worry during the option month, unless either your short Call or short Put is threatened by an unusually large market movement. By choosing the short Call 2 sigma above the market and the short Put 2 sigma below the market, you reduce the probability of a threat to your Call or Put to less than 10% during a month. In other words, the probability of the initial credit becoming your monthly profit is about 90% or more.

Figure 9.1 below shows the spread sheet for the monthly profit using the two sided 2 sigma OEX covered short spread strategy.

Two sided 2 sigma Covered Short Spread Strategy

| | | | Initial Capital | $5,000 | | |
| | | | Comm/Opt | $7.50 | | |
Opt Mo.	Call Prm Diff	Put Prm Diff	NOPS	Init Crdt	Margin	Capital
Dec-97	1.0000	1.0000	3	$510	$4,400	$5,510
Jan-98	1.1250	1.0000	3	$548	$4,363	$6,058
Feb-98	1.0000	1.2500	3	$585	$4,325	$6,643
Mar-98	1.0000	1.0000	3	$510	$4,400	$7,153
Apr-98	1.1250	1.0000	3	$548	$4,363	$7,700
May-98	1.0000	1.3125	3	$604	$4,306	$8,304
Jun-98	1.0000	1.0000	3	$510	$4,400	$8,814
Jul-98	0.9375	1.0625	3	$510	$4,400	$9,324
Aug-98	1.0000	1.0000	3	$510	$4,400	$9,834
Sep-98	1.0000	1.0000	4	$680	$5,200	$10,514
Oct-98	-2.0000	1.0000	4	($520)	$6,400	$9,994
Nov-98	1.0000	1.0000	5	$850	$6,000	$10,844
Dec-98	1.0000	1.2500	6	$1,170	$6,650	$12,014
Jan-99	1.0000	1.0000	6	$1,020	$6,800	$13,034
Feb-99	1.1250	1.0000	6	$1,095	$6,725	$14,129
Mar-99	1.0000	1.0625	7	$1,234	$7,556	$15,363
Apr-99	1.0000	1.0000	8	$1,360	$8,400	$16,723
May-99	1.0000	1.0000	9	$1,530	$9,200	$18,253
Jun-99	1.0000	1.0000	10	$1,700	$10,000	$19,953
Jul-99	1.0000	1.0000	11	$1,870	$10,800	$21,823
Aug-99	1.0000	-1.5000	12	($960)	$14,600	$20,863
Sep-99	1.0000	1.0000	13	$2,210	$12,400	$23,073
Oct-99	1.0000	1.0000	14	$2,380	$13,200	$25,453
Nov-99	1.0000	1.0000	15	$2,550	$14,000	$28,003
Dec-99	1.0000	1.0000	16	$2,720	$14,800	$30,723
Jan-00	1.0000	1.0000	18	$3,060	$16,400	$33,783
Feb-00	1.0000	1.0000	20	$3,400	$18,000	$37,183
Mar-00	1.0000	1.0000	22	$3,740	$19,600	$40,923
Apr-00	1.0000	1.0000	24	$4,080	$21,200	$45,003
May-00	1.0000	1.0000	26	$4,420	$22,800	$49,423
Jun-00	1.0000	1.0000	28	$4,760	$24,400	$54,183
Jul-00	-1.3125	1.0000	32	($1,960)	$35,000	$52,223
Aug-00	1.0000	1.0000	36	$6,120	$30,800	$58,343
Sep-00	1.0000	1.0000	40	$6,800	$34,000	$65,143
Oct-00	1.0000	1.0000	44	$7,480	$37,200	$72,623
Nov-00	1.0000	1.0000	48	$8,160	$40,400	$80,783
Dec-00	1.0000	1.0000	52	$8,840	$43,600	$89,623

The chart in Figure 9.2 below shows how starting with only $5,000 capital you can make your capital grow using only the 2 Sigma Covered Short Spread (Strangle) Strategy.

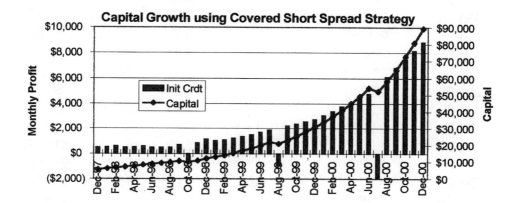

The occasional losses indicate months when corrective action had to be taken because of a threat to either a short Call or Put.

THE BULL COVERED SHORT SPREAD STRATEGY

In the capital growth example below, we will assume you have only $5,000 initial capital and that you only use one half of your capital for the OEX one sided 2 sigma Bull CvSS. The period of capital growth will be 36 months and only once do you lose because the short Put is penetrated and corrective action had to be taken.

The capital grows more rapidly using this strategy for two reasons: (1) the premium difference between the short Put and long Put are greater than the sum of the premium differences for the 2 sided CvSS because the long Put is two strike prices lower than the short Put. A premium difference of 2.375 is typical but occasionally the premium difference will be 2½ or 2¾. And (2) since we are in a Bull leg of the market with only occasional corrections downward, the short Put required corrective action only once during the time period examined.

Figure 9.3, on the following page, shows the spread sheet for the monthly profit using the one sided 2 sigma Bull CvSS below in which Puts are sold 2 sigma below the market and the same number of Puts are bought 2 strike prices lower:

Opt Mo.	Bull Put Prm Diff	NOPS	Init Crdt	Margin	Capital
Dec-97	2.3750	3	$668	$4,288	$5,668
Jan-98	2.3750	3	$668	$4,288	$6,335
Feb-98	2.3750	3	$668	$4,288	$7,003
Mar-98	2.5000	3	$705	$4,250	$7,708
Apr-98	2.3750	3	$668	$4,288	$8,375
May-98	2.3750	3	$668	$4,288	$9,043
Jun-98	2.3750	3	$668	$4,288	$9,710
Jul-98	2.6250	4	$990	$4,950	$10,700
Aug-98	2.3750	4	$890	$5,050	$11,590
Sep-98	2.3750	4	$890	$5,050	$12,480
Oct-98	2.3750	5	$1,113	$5,813	$13,593
Nov-98	2.2500	5	$1,050	$5,875	$14,643
Dec-98	2.3750	7	$1,558	$7,338	$16,200
Jan-99	2.3750	8	$1,780	$8,100	$17,980
Feb-99	2.3750	8	$1,780	$8,100	$19,760
Mar-99	2.3750	10	$2,225	$9,625	$21,985
Apr-99	2.0000	10	$1,850	$10,000	$23,835
May-99	2.3750	12	$2,670	$11,150	$26,505
Jun-99	2.3750	14	$3,115	$12,675	$29,620
Jul-99	2.3750	16	$3,560	$14,200	$33,180
Aug-99	2.3750	19	$4,228	$16,488	$37,408
Sep-99	2.3750	22	$4,895	$18,775	$42,303
Oct-99	2.3750	25	$5,563	$21,063	$47,865
Nov-99	2.7500	28	$7,280	$22,300	$55,145
Dec-99	-3.0000	32	($10,080)	$43,600	$45,065
Jan-00	2.3750	27	$6,008	$22,588	$51,073
Feb-00	2.3750	30	$6,675	$24,875	$57,748
Mar-00	2.3750	35	$7,788	$28,688	$65,535
Apr-00	2.3750	40	$8,900	$32,500	$74,435
May-00	2.3750	45	$10,013	$36,313	$84,448
Jun-00	2.3750	50	$11,125	$40,125	$95,573
Jul-00	2.3750	58	$12,905	$46,225	$108,478
Aug-00	2.3750	64	$14,240	$50,800	$122,718
Sep-00	2.3750	70	$15,575	$55,375	$138,293
Oct-00	2.3750	75	$16,688	$59,188	$154,980
Nov-00	2.3750	80	$17,800	$63,000	$172,780
Dec-00	2.3750	90	$20,025	$70,625	$192,805

The chart showing the monthly profit and capital growth are given below in Figure 9.4:

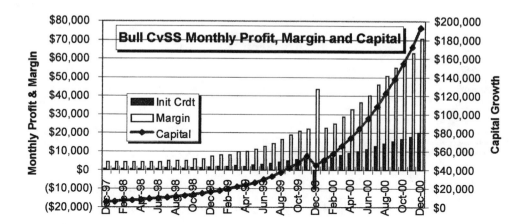

The chart above illustrates that the margin remains below 50% of the capital after the first few months, and that the monthly profit grows steadily until at the end of the chart it reaches $20,000 per month. Only one month is there a loss when the OEX dropped below the short Put and corrective action was required that caused a loss for that month.

THE SEI LONG STRADDLE STRATEGY

In the following capital growth example, we will assume you have only $5,000 initial capital and that you only use about half of your capital for buying SEI far-out-of-the-money Calls and Puts to execute the Long Straddle Strategy near the beginning of the option month. The period of capital growth will be 7 months and sometimes you lose a small amount because the market doesn't change much during the time the straddle is open, but the times you win the profit is quite large considering the modest investment. The following Figure 9.5 shows the spread sheet for the monthly profit using the Long Straddle in which the same number of far out-of-the-money SEI Calls and Puts are bought:

SEI Long Straddle - Buy Calls & Puts Far-Out-Of-The-Money

Init_Capital   £3,000 $4,987

Date	SEI	Call Sp	Put Sp	Call Prm	Put Prm	NOPS	Crdt	Strad Prft	Capital	Exch $/£	$ Capital
11-Mar-97	4444.3	4700	4200	1	2	5	(£200)				
14-Mar-97	4424.3	4700	4200	1	1.5	5	£75	(£125)	£2,875	1.6622	$4,779
14-Apr-97	4251.7	4400	4100	1	1.5	5	(£175)				
17-Apr-97	4298.9	4400	4100	1	1	5	£50	(£125)	£2,750	1.6622	$4,571
22-Apr-97	4346.1	4500	4200	9.5	18.5	5	(£1,450)				
13-May-97	4691	4500	4200	195	1	5	£9,750	£8,300	£11,050	1.6622	$18,367
16-May-97	4693.9	4850	4550	16.5	26.5	5	(£2,200)				
12-Jun-97	4757.2	4850	4550	8.25	2.25	5	£475	(£1,725)	£9,325	1.6622	$15,500
30-Jun-97	4596.3	4850	4350	13.5	19.5	5	(£1,700)				
16-Jul-97	4964.2	4850	4350	149	1	5	£7,450	£5,750	£15,075	1.6877	$25,442
18-Jul-97	4877.2	5150	4650	17	39.5	5	(£2,875)				
8-Aug-97	5022.9	5150	4650	31.5	1	5	£1,575	(£1,300)	£13,775	1.581	$21,778
19-Aug-97	4914.2	5150	4650	39.5	34	5	(£3,725)				
29-Aug-97	4817.5	5150	4650	12	47.5	5	£2,925	(£800)	£12,975	1.6218	$21,043

The chart showing the straddle profit in pounds sterling (£) and the profit growth in U.S. Dollars ($) for seven option months from March 97 through September 97 is shown in Figure 9.6 below:

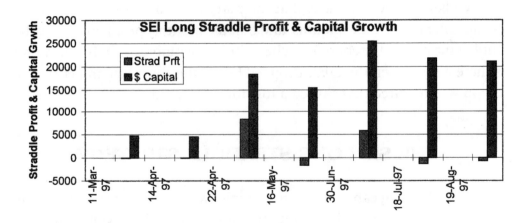

As you may see from the chart, the strategy doesn't work every month but for the months it works, it generates a lot of profit for a relative small investment. In each case only 5 Calls and Puts were bought and then sold. The initial capital was $5,000 (£3,000). At the end of the seventh option month the capital had grown to $21,043 (£12,975). The strategy should work equally well for OEX, but I had better historical data to paper trade it for the SEI.

THE DIRECTIONAL DELTA STRATEGY

In the following capital growth example, we will assume you have only $5,000 initial capital and that you only use about half of your capital for buying OEX in-the-money Calls when the market indicators say the market is going up or buying OEX in-the-money Puts when the market indicators signal a down market. The period of capital growth shown is 36 months; it is assumed that you do eight round trip delta trades per option month (about two per week) and that the average delta you use is one more than the premium you receive. Sometimes you receive a higher delta, but these higher deltas offset the occasional loss, so the average delta is only one. If the market signals a rise you buy Calls; if the market signals a drop, you buy Puts. The number of options start at 3 when you have $5,000 and gradually increase in number as your capital grows. Figure 9.7 shows the spread sheet for the monthly profit using the Delta Strategy:

Delta Strategy: Buy Calls or Puts, Sell at Delta more
Initial Capital = $5,000

Opt Mo.	#DelStrgy	NOPS	Avg Delta	Delta Prft	Capital
Dec-97	8	3	1	$2,040	$7,040
Jan-98	8	3	1	$2,040	$9,080
Feb-98	8	3	1	$2,040	$11,120
Mar-98	8	3	1	$2,040	$13,160
Apr-98	8	3	1	$2,040	$15,200
May-98	8	3	1	$2,040	$17,240
Jun-98	8	3	1	$2,040	$19,280
Jul-98	8	3	1	$2,040	$21,320
Aug-98	8	3	1	$2,040	$23,360
Sep-98	8	3	1	$2,040	$25,400
Oct-98	8	3	1	$2,040	$27,440
Nov-98	8	3	1	$2,040	$29,480
Dec-98	8	3	1	$2,040	$31,520
Jan-99	8	5	1	$3,400	$34,920
Feb-99	8	5	1	$3,400	$38,320
Mar-99	8	5	1	$3,400	$41,720
Apr-99	8	5	1	$3,400	$45,120
May-99	8	5	1	$3,400	$48,520
Jun-99	8	5	1	$3,400	$51,920
Jul-99	8	5	1	$3,400	$55,320
Aug-99	8	5	1	$3,400	$58,720
Sep-99	8	5	1	$3,400	$62,120
Oct-99	8	5	1	$3,400	$65,520
Nov-99	8	5	1	$3,400	$68,920
Dec-99	8	5	1	$3,400	$72,320
Jan-00	8	5	1	$3,400	$75,720
Feb-00	8	8	1	$5,440	$81,160
Mar-00	8	8	1	$5,440	$86,600
Apr-00	8	8	1	$5,440	$92,040
May-00	8	8	1	$5,440	$97,480
Jun-00	8	8	1	$5,440	$102,920
Jul-00	8	8	1	$5,440	$108,360
Aug-00	8	8	1	$5,440	$113,800
Sep-00	8	8	1	$5,440	$119,240
Oct-00	8	8	1	$5,440	$124,680
Nov-00	8	8	1	$5,440	$130,120
Dec-00	8	8	1	$5,440	$135,560

The chart showing the delta strategy profit and the profit growth in dollars for the trades made is shown in Figure 9.8 below:

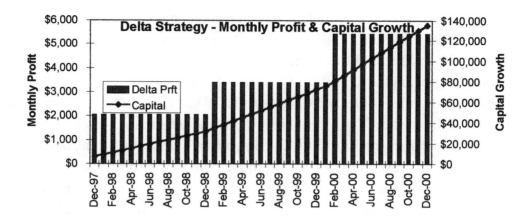

As you may see from the chart, the strategy works quite well on the average. Starting with $5,000 your capital grows to $135,000 after 36 months. I must warn you this type of trading is very time consuming and you must limit losses. If the market moves against your Call or Put, you must close it out quickly and take your small loss. If you picked the wrong direction for the market and sit around holding on to your position while you hope for a turn-around, you could realize large losses. The above delta strategy figures assume you are well disciplined and cut your losses when you select the wrong direction (i.e. a Put when the market is rising or a Call when the market is falling). The strategy should work equally well for SEI, and in some regards SEI option trading using the delta strategy is easier on the London market, since the ups and downs last longer than on the New York market. The wild moves caused by the New York program traders hasn't yet arrived in London.

SUMMARY OF CAPITAL GROWTH STRATEGIES

The capital growth examples above show that by concentrating on one strategy you can make your capital grow surely and safely. The strategy requiring the least attention to the market is the non-directional Covered Short Spread (Strangle) strategy. It requires careful market watching at the beginning of the option month when you are opening the position and at any time during the option month that your short Calls or Puts are threatened. Otherwise the CvSS strategy is relatively carefree and, as you can see from the above sections, can make your capital more than double each year.

The Covered Short Spread (Strangle) strategy has two options: (1) a two sided CvSS with both a Call side and a Put side with the short Call 2 sigma above the market and the short Put 2 sigma below the market when you open the position and with the covering long positions 1 strike price beyond the short positions and (2) the one sided CvSS or Bull CvSS using Put CvSS with the short Put 2 sigma below the market and the long Put 2 strike prices lower than the short Put. During a Bull Market this is the best strategy to use because the vigorous up movement will never threaten a short Call, since you don't open one. During a Bear market you would use only the Call CvSS or Bear CvSS with the short Calls 2 sigma above the market and the long Calls 2 strike prices above the short Call. I had one reader ask how you know when to use the Bull CvSS or the Bear CvSS. The answer is you look at the market signal charts to see when the market is in a Bull leg or a Bear leg. Normally the chart showing OEX and the Moving average difference 9 day - 4 day (MAD9-4) is the best chart to study when looking for a Bull or Bear leg. The MAD9-4 will be positive during Bull legs and negative during Bear legs.

The Long Straddle Strategy is another non-directional strategy that will allow good capital growth starting with a modest amount of capital. To execute this strategy you buy far-out-of-the-money Calls and buy an equal number of far-out-of-the-money Puts. The Calls and Puts will have small premiums so the investment is modest. If the market moves vigorously either up or down you will make a good profit. By repeating the strategy during each option month you can make your capital growth nicely. When you lose the amount is small, but when you win the profit is large, thus the net capital growth is good. For the example given above, in 7 months using SEI, the initial capital of $5,000 grew to $21,000. The strategy should work equally well for OEX, provided there is strong market movement either up or down. If the market doesn't move much, you will lose with this strategy, but the amount of loss is small.

The delta strategy is the easiest strategy to use, but it requires a lot of daily attention to the market to be successful. If you don't have sufficient time during the trading day to watch the market almost minute by minute don't use this directional strategy, but stick with one of the non-directional strategies such as the CvSS one or two sided or the Long Straddle.

It is, of course, possible to combine the strategies and make your capital grow even faster. But by using multiple strategies you increase your work load and requirement for attention to the market and also increase your risk of a big loss since you may become overloaded watching the market and make a mistake in judgment that could be very costly.

CHAPTER 10

EQUATIONS IN OPTION TRADING

This chapter summarizes the equations used in option trading, first explaining how Call and Put 2 sigmas are calculated and followed by the remainder of the equations organized by the trading strategy used and in the order below:

- Two sided 2 sigma Covered Short Spreads

- Bull one sided 2 sigma Covered Short Spreads

- Bear one sided 2 sigma Covered Short Spreads

- Naked 2 sigma Short Spreads

- The Long Put or Call delta strategy

EXCEL IS A BIG HELP
IN GENERATING OPTION EQUATIONS

The EXCEL formulas on your Personal Computer do all the *dog work* for option trading and perform the computations needed to execute the trading strategies described in this book. In addition EXCEL can generate charts to aid you in option trading. The principal market signal charts described in other chapters include:

• The MAD 9-4 Chart for signaling major changes in market direction

• The Stochastics %K-%D chart for signaling more frequent market turn-arounds

• The Welles-Wilder Relative Strength Indicator chart for signaling over-bought or oversold market conditions. Since the equations for these charts were thoroughly covered in other chapters they won't be repeated here.

EQUATIONS FOR STANDARD DEVIATION
(2 SIGMA) COMPUTATIONS

Standard Deviation (sigma) is used for all the covered short spread strategies as well as the naked short spread strategies. Since standard deviation is such a basic tool for the non-directional strategies described in the book, descriptions of standard deviation and "2 sigma" will be covered in the first part of this chapter. Standard deviation is a statistical function which computes the distribution of random market values, and is a measure of how probable the market is to move a given amount during the option month. For a purely random function the data points (market values) are grouped under a "bell-shaped curve" which puts most of the data in a big lump in the middle with fewer and fewer data points (market values) above the center of the bell on the positive outer edges (for a rising market) and fewer and fewer market values below the center of the bell on the negative outer edges for a falling market. See Figure 10.1.

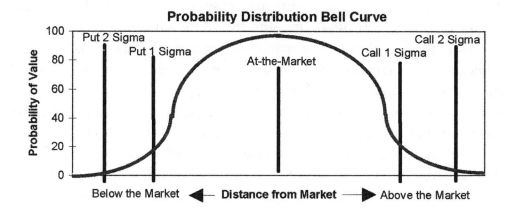

If the market movements were purely random, two times the standard deviation would be a distance from the center where only 5% of the market values would fall, that is, the area above 2 standard deviations from the center or the area below 2 standard deviations from the center. For the purely random market movements, if matching vertical lines are set at one standard deviation above the center and one standard deviation below the center, then some two thirds of the market values would fall between these "one standard deviation" or "sigma" lines. If two more vertical lines are drawn two sigma above the center and 2 sigma below the center, then about 90% of the market movements are contained between the 2 sigma lines This leaves about 5% of the market movements above the + 2 sigma line and 5% of the market movements below the -2 sigma lines.

Market movements are not purely random, but fortunately the EXCEL standard deviation function (formula) computes a value based on the actual distribution of market values. Normally during a Bull market the values are skewed towards the high side of the bell curve; during a Bear market the values are skewed towards the low side of the bell curve. Because of this skewing effect, I compute a Call standard deviation for the rising market and a Put standard deviation for the falling market. I label the plus 2 sigma the Call 2 sigma and the minus 2 sigma the Put 2 sigma. These skewed values computed by EXCEL are used for determining the Short Call 2 sigma above the market and the Short Put 2 sigma below the market.

The number of months of market movement data to use is another fundamental parameter for computing the Call 2 sigma and the

Put 2 sigma. I normally use 13 months of market movement data. However, when there is a rapidly rising market such as we had during the May 97 through August 97 option months, the 13 month Call 2 sigma was too small compared to the extreme market movements. In other words, during a period of big jumps in the market the market moves up more than 2 sigma, thus putting the short Call in jeopardy. I have used 6 month 2 sigmas and 3 month 2 sigmas to try to compensate for this Bull Market effect, but over the long haul, the 13 month 2 sigma computations have given the most reliable results. The descriptions below will be for OEX, but they are equally applicable to SEI or any other index option. The few differences between OEX and SEI are explained in the relevant paragraphs.

Market variations for computing the 2 sigmas require entering the daily value of OEX in a spread sheet, which is the *main* work sheet of my market variation workbook. The daily delta or change in OEX is computed by taking the difference between today's value and yesterday's value. The equation is: delta = OEX(today) - OEX(yesterday). The EXCEL equation is =B625-B624, where column B contains the OEX and row 625 is the current trading day and row 624 is the previous trading day.

The next step is to compute the cumulative delta or Cumdel for the option month. In a column called Cumdel, on the first day of the new option month Cumdel = delta (the change in OEX value from close at option expiration on Friday and the OEX value at close on Monday). The EXCEL equation is =C604, column C contains delta and row 604 is the first trading day of the new option month. For the next day and subsequent days Cumdel = delta(today) + Cumdel(yesterday), so the EXCEL equation is =D604+C605, where column C contains delta and column D contains Cumdel, and row 605 is today and row 604 is the previous trading day. The Cumdel equation is extended down from the second trading day to the expiration day of the current option month. The result is Cumdel goes up when the market goes up and down when the market goes down; the biggest positive number in the Cumdel column for the option month is the highest the market went up from last month's expiration; the most negative number is the biggest drop in the market from last month's expiration.

The next step is to scan the Cumdel column and find the Maximum rise and the Minimum drop of OEX during the option month. This could be done manually by just looking, but it is easier if you use the automated EXCEL MAX (maximum) and MIN (minimum) functions. The MAX scan equation is given by =IF(MAX(D604:D627)>0,

MAX(D604:D627),0) where MAX is the EXCEL function which scans the range of cells from D604 (the spread sheet cell in the Cumdel column telling the amount the OEX close changed from the day before on the first day of the option month) to D627 (the Cumdel cell on the last day or expiration day of the option month). The logic IF equation tells EXCEL to place the maximum value for the option month in the cell containing the equation if there is a maximum value greater than zero, or else to place a zero in the cell. The cell containing this logic IF equation is in the column called Max Cumdel that computes the maximum cumulative delta for the month and the row is that of the expiration day of the last option month.

The MIN scan equation is given by =ABS(IF(MIN(D604:D627)<0, MIN(D604:D627),0)) where ABS is the EXCEL function that takes the absolute value of the quantity within the parentheses; in other words, if the value is negative, ABS makes that value positive. The MIN function scans the same range of cells as the MAX function to determine the largest drop during the option month. The IF equation is used to determine if there is a negative value, if so it places the greatest negative value in the cell, otherwise it places a zero in the cell. For the month of this example the cumulative delta value never went negative, only positive, so the value placed in this cell was zero.

The next step is to place the MAX and MIN determined by the scanning equations above in an area of the spread sheet that computes the 2 sigma values. For each option month the value of MAX is computed as described above and moved to a cell in column W labeled with the name of the month. Then the 13 month Call 2 sigma is computed from the EXCEL equation =2 x STDEV(W26:W39) where STDEV is the EXCEL standard deviation function and the cells W26 through W39 contain the last 13 months of MAX data under column W. Row 39 is the month August 97 and the value computed for the Call 2 sigma is 43.43.

The 13 month Put 2 sigma is computed from the EXCEL equation =2 x STDEV(X26:X39) where STDEV is the EXCEL standard deviation function and the cells X26 through X39 contain the last 13 months of MIN data under column X. Row 39 is the month August 97 and the value computed for the Put 2 sigma is 27.01.

As you may see from the above details of 2 sigma computation, the only effort is setting up the spread sheet to compute the Cumdel, the MAX and the MIN for each month, and then make the daily entry of the closing

OEX price. All the rest of the computation is done automatically - no work on your part. The EXCEL worksheet that makes all the 2 sigma computations has a GO TO function under EDIT to allow you to find the 2 sigma computation area easily when you want to check the current value of the Call and Put 2 sigmas. It also has a GO TO function to get you back to the current option month for entering the closing OEX values. EXCEL automates the process and makes it easy for you, the option trader, to know what the latest 2 sigma values are.

EQUATIONS FOR 2 SIGMA
2 SIDED COVERED SHORT SPREADS

To open a 2 sigma 2 sided Covered Short Spread (Strangle) you need to compute a safe strike price for the short Call and a safe strike price for the short Put. Use the latest Call and Put 2 sigmas for the option month for which the position is being opened. The short Call position is computed on the first day of the new option month using the EXCEL equation which for the short Call is =ROUND((C1185+AH87)/5,0) x 5 = 910, where ROUND is the EXCEL round-off function, C1185 contains the value of OEX at expiration of the last option month and AH87 contains the Call 2 sigma value applicable to this month. The factor 5 divided into the sum of the OEX plus the Call 2 sigma makes the round off to the nearest 5, since the OEX strike prices are each even 5 points. (If you are trading SEI you must change this last 5 to be 50 since SEI strike prices are 50 points apart.) The 5 (or 50 for SEI) is multiplied outside the ROUND parentheses to compute the nearest strike price.

The short Put position is also computed on the first day of the new option month using the EXCEL equation for the short Put which is =ROUND((C1185-AI87)/5,0) x 5 = 845, where ROUND is the EXCEL round-off function, C1185 contains the value of OEX at expiration of the last option month and AI87 contains the Put 2 sigma value applicable to this month. The factor 5 divided into the sum of the OEX minus the Put 2 sigma, makes the round off to the nearest 5 since the OEX strike prices are each even 5 points. (If you are trading SEI you must change this last 5 to be 50 since SEI strike prices are 50 points apart.) The 5 (or 50 for SEI) is multiplied outside the ROUND parentheses to compute the nearest strike price.

The long Call for the 2 sided CvSS is computed from the EXCEL equation =H1186+5 = 915, just one strike price higher than the short Call, where H1186 contains the value of the short Call.

The long Put for the 2 sided CvSS is computed from the EXCEL equation =J1186-5 = 840, just one strike price lower than the short Put, where J1186 contains the value of the short Put.

The initial credit received for the 2 sided CvSS is computed using the EXCEL equation =Q1186 x 100 x (O1186-M1186+P1186-N1186) - Q1186 x 7.5 x 4, which, continuing with the same example as in the paragraphs above, equals \$2,075, where Q1186 is the number of options =10 which is multiplied by 100 for OEX positions (because there are 100 shares for each OEX option position) or by 10 for SEI positions (because there are 10 shares for each SEI option position), O1186 is the cell containing the short Call bid premium = 16, M1186 is the cell containing the long Call ask premium = 14.625, P1186 is the cell containing the short Put bid premium = 8.5, N1186 is the cell containing the long Put ask premium = 7.50. The last term - Q1186 x 7.5 x 4 calculates the commission on the CvSS where Q1186 is the number of options =10 and 7.5 is the commission per option and 4 is the number of different types of options (LC, SC, SP, LP). Of course, if your broker uses a different commission per option than \$7.50, then you would use his rate.

The margin required for the 2 sided OEX CvSS is found using the EXCEL equation =2000 x 2+Q1186 x 100 x (10-O1186+M1186-P1186+N1186) = \$11,625, where 2000 is the fixed margin per CvSS and the 2 is because there are both a Call and a Put side to the CvSS, and the other term added to the fixed margin is the variable margin depending on the number of CvSS (Q1186 = 10), multiplied by 100 for OEX positions (because there are 100 shares for each OEX option position) or by 10 for SEI positions (because there are 10 shares for each SEI option position), the 10 is the double spread width of 5 for the Call CvSS and the Put CvSS and the other terms within the parenthesis are the Call and Put premiums as defined above (the bid price for the short positions and the ask price for the long positions).

The OEX return on margin = Initial Credit/Margin = \$2075/\$11625 = 17.85% for the month, or = 12 x 17.85% = 214% on an annualized basis. Since I recommend using no more than 50% of your capital for margin, the annual return on capital = 0.5 x 214% = 107%.

If the OEX stays below the Short Call at 910 and above the

Short Put at 845, at expiration the initial credit of $2,075 becomes profit for the month.

The SEI margin rule is much more complex and variable and depends on risk matrices which vary with the market. These risk matrices are given after close each day on the LIFFE Internet page. Margin requirements are set by the London Clearing House (LCH), an entity that guarantees all option transactions by brokers, that considers such factors as volatility and how deep the premiums are out-of-the-money. The margin for 10 SEI two sided CvSS = 10 x 2 x (500 - SCPrm -SPPrm + LCPrm + LPPrm), where SCPrm = Short Call Premium, SPPrm = Short Put Premium, LCPrm = Long Call Premium, and LPPrm = Long Put Premium. The 500 is the 50 point difference between strike prices on the SEI 2 sided CvSS times the number of stocks per option (10) on the SEI. The numbers inside the parenthesis must be multiplied by two because there are 2 sides to this covered short spread. A typical value for normal premiums = £9,500. See Chapter 5 under Margin for CvSS for more information about SEI margins.

EQUATIONS FOR BULL ONE SIDED PUT COVERED SHORT SPREADS

The Bull one sided Covered Short Spread (Strangle) uses only Put covered short spreads. The short Put safe strike price needs to be computed using the latest Put 2 sigma for the option month for which the position is being opened. The short Put position is computed on the first day of the new option month using the EXCEL equation for the short Put which is =ROUND((C1185-AI87)/5,0) x 5= 845, where ROUND is the EXCEL round-off function, C1185 contains the value of OEX at expiration of the last option month and AI87 contains the Put 2 sigma value applicable to this month. The factor 5 divided into the sum of the OEX minus the Call 2 sigma, makes the round off to the nearest 5 since the OEX strike prices are each even 5 points. (If you are trading SEI you must change this last 5 to be 50 since SEI strike prices are 50 points apart.) The 5 (or 50 for SEI) is multiplied outside the ROUND parentheses to compute the nearest strike price.

The long Put for the Bull CvSS is computed from the EXCEL equation =J1186-10= 835, two strike prices lower than the short Put, where J1186 contains the value of the short Put.

The initial credit received for the Bull CvSS is computed using the EXCEL equation =Q1186 x 100 x (P1186-N1186)- Q1186 x 7.5 x 2 = $1,850, where Q1186 is the number of options =10, which is multiplied by 100 for OEX positions (because there are 100 shares for each OEX option position) or by 10 for SEI positions (because there are 10 shares for each SEI option position), P1186 is the cell containing the short Put bid premium = 8.5, N1186 is the cell containing the long Put ask premium = 6.50. The last term - Q1186 x 7.5 x 2 calculates the commission on the Bull CvSS where Q1186 is the number of options =10 and 7.5 is the commission per option and 2 is the number of different types of options (SP, LP). Of course, if your broker uses a different commission per option than $7.50, then you would use his rate.

The margin required for the Bull CvSS is computed using the EXCEL equation =2000+Q1186 x 100 x (10-P1186+N1186) = $10,000, where 2000 is the fixed margin per CvSS, and the other term added to the fixed margin is the variable margin depending on the number of CvSS (Q1186 = 10), multiplied by 100 for OEX positions (because there are 100 shares for each OEX option position) or by 10 for SEI positions (because there are 10 shares for each SEI option position), the 10 is the width of 10 points on the OEX between the short Puts and the long Puts, and the other terms within the parenthesis are the Put premiums as defined above. For London traders, the margin for 10 SEI Bull CvSS = 10 x (1000 - SPPrm + LPPrm), where SPPrm = Short Put Premium, , and LPPrm = Long Put Premium, a typical value for normal premiums = £9,500. The 1000 is the 100 point difference between strike prices on the SEI Bull CvSS multiplied by the number of stocks per option (10) on the SEI. The SEI margin algorithm was discussed above under 2 sided CvSS and is also found in Chapter 5 under Margin for CvSS.

The return on margin = Initial Credit/Margin = $1850/$10000 = 18.50% for the month, or = 12 x 18.50% = 222% on an annualized basis. Since I recommend using no more than 50% of your capital for Margin, the annual return on Capital = 0.5 x 222% = 111%.

If the OEX stays above the Short Put at 845, at expiration the initial credit of $1,850 becomes profit for the month.

EQUATIONS FOR BEAR ONE SIDED
CALL COVERED SHORT SPREADS

The Bear one sided Covered Short Spread (Strangle) uses only Call covered short spreads. The short Call safe strike price position must be computed using the latest Call 2 sigma for the option month for which the position is being opened. The short Call position is computed on the first day of the new option month using the EXCEL equation for the short Call which is =ROUND((C1185+AH87)/5,0) x 5 = 910, where ROUND is the EXCEL round-off function, C1185 contains the value of OEX at expiration of the last option month and AH87 contains the Call 2 sigma value applicable to this month. The factor 5 divided into the sum of the OEX plus the Call 2 sigma, makes the round off to the nearest 5 since the OEX strike prices are each even 5 points. (If you are trading SEI you must change this last 5 to be 50 since SEI strike prices are 50 points apart.) The 5 (or 50 for SEI) is multiplied outside the ROUND parentheses to compute the nearest Strike price.

The long Call for the Bear CvSS is computed from the EXCEL equation =H1186+10 = 920, two strike prices higher than the short Call, where H1186 contains the value of the Short Call

The initial credit received for the Bear CvSS is computed using the EXCEL equation =Q1186 x 100 x (O1186-M1186)- Q1186 x 7.5 x 2 = $3,225, where Q1186 is the number of options =10, which is multiplied by 100 for OEX positions (because there are 100 shares for each OEX option position) or by 10 for SEI positions (because there are 10 shares for each SEI option position), O1186 is the cell containing the short Call bid premium = 16, M1186 is the cell containing the long Call ask premium = 12.625. The last term - Q1186 x 7.5 x 2 calculates the commission on the CvSS where Q1186 is the number of options =10 and 7.5 is the commission per option and 2 is the number of different types of options (LC, SC). Of course, if your broker uses a different commission per option than $7.50, then you would use his rate

The margin required for the Bear CvSS is computed using the EXCEL equation =2000+Q1186 x 100 x (10-O1186-M1186) = $8,625, where 2000 is the fixed margin per CvSS, and the other term added to the fixed margin is the variable margin depending on the number of CvSS (Q1186 = 10), multiplied by 100 for OEX positions (because there are 100 shares for each OEX option position) or by 10 for SEI positions (because there are 10 shares for each SEI option position), the 10 is the width of 10 points on the OEX between the short Puts and the long Puts and the other terms within the parenthesis are the Put premiums as defined above. For London traders, the margin for 10 SEI Bear CvSS = 10 x (1000 - SCPrm + LCPrm), where SCPrm = Short Call Premium, LCPrm = Long Call Premium, a typical value for normal premiums = £9,500. The 1000 is the 100 point difference between strike prices on the SEI Bear CvSS multiplied by the number of stocks per option (10) on the SEI. The SEI margin algorithm was discussed above under 2 sided CvSS and is also found in Chapter 5 under Margin for CvSS.

The return on margin = Initial Credit/Margin = $3225/$8625 = 37.39% for the month, or = 12 x 37.39% = 449% on an annualized basis. Since I recommend using no more than 50% of your capital for margin, the annual return on capital = 0.5 x 449% = 225%.

If the OEX stays below the Short Call at 910, at expiration the initial credit of $3,225 becomes profit for the month.

EQUATIONS FOR
2 SIGMA NAKED SHORT SPREADS

For the 2 sigma Naked Short Spread (Strangle) you need to compute a safe strike price position for the short Call and a safe strike price position for the short Put using the latest Call and Put 2 sigmas for the option month for which the position is being opened. The short Call position is computed on the first day of the new option month using the EXCEL equation for the short Call which is =ROUND((C1185+AH87)/5,0) x 5 = 910, where ROUND is the EXCEL round-off function, C1185 contains the value of OEX at expiration of the last option month and AH87 contains the Call 2 sigma value applicable to this month. The factor 5 divided into the sum of the OEX plus the Call 2 sigma, makes the round off to the nearest 5 since the OEX strike prices are each even 5 points. The 5 is multiplied outside the ROUND parentheses to compute the nearest strike price.

The short Put strike price is also computed on the first day of the new option month using the EXCEL equation for the short Put which is =ROUND((C1185-AI87)/5,0) x 5 = 845, where ROUND is the EXCEL round-off function, C1185 contains the value of OEX at expiration of the last option month and AI87 contains the Put 2 sigma value applicable to this month. The factor 5 divided into the sum of the OEX plus the Put 2 sigma, makes the round off to the nearest 5 since the OEX strike prices are each even 5 points. The 5 is multiplied outside the ROUND parentheses to compute the nearest Strike price.

The initial credit received for the 2 Sigma Naked Short Spread is computed using the EXCEL equation =Q1186 x 100 x (O1186+P1186) - Q1186 x 7.5 x 2 = \$9,740, where Q1186 is the number of options =4, which is multiplied by 100 for OEX positions (because there are 100 shares for each OEX option position), O1186 is the cell containing the short Call bid premium = 16, P1186 is the cell containing the short Put bid premium = 8.5. The last term - Q1186 x 7.5 x 2 calculates the commission on the naked short spread where Q1186 is the number of options = 4 and 7.5 is the commission per option and 2 is the number of different types of options (SC, SP). Of course, if your broker uses a different commission per option than \$7.50, then you would use his rate.

The margin required for the 2 Sigma Naked Short Spread is computed using the EXCEL equation =Q1186 x 100 x (C1186) x 0.15 = \$53,266, where Q1186 = number of options = 4, multiplied by 100 for OEX positions (because there are 100 shares for each OEX option position), and C1186 is the value of OEX on the day the short spread is opened = 887.78, and 0.15 is the margin requirement imposed by the CBOE; **the minimum margin required to trade Naked Short Spreads = \$50,000.** I don't recommend the SEI naked short spread for London traders.

The return on margin = Initial Credit/Margin = \$9740/\$53266 = 17.78% for the month, or = 12 x 17.78% = 213% on an annualized basis. Since I recommend using no more than 50% of your capital for margin, the annual return on capital = 0.5 x 213% = 106.5%.

If the OEX stays below the short Call at 910 and above the short Put at 845, at expiration the initial credit of \$9,740 becomes profit for the month.

EQUATIONS FOR DELTA STRATEGY USING LONG CALLS OR PUTS

The Delta Strategy uses either long Calls or long Puts depending on whether the market is rising (long Calls) or is dropping (long Puts).

The delta strategy is a day trading method in which in a rising market long Calls are bought with an order to sell at a premium "delta" more than paid; in a falling market long Puts are bought with an order to sell at a premium "delta" more than paid. The position is normally open for just a short time, typically an hour or less. The long Call or long Put is selected in the money (long Call below the market or long Put above the market). The delta for OEX is usually 1. If a delta of 1 is used, then typically a change in the OEX of 2 points in the right direction (up for the Calls or down for the Puts) is enough to execute the sell order. For SEI the delta is normally 5; if the SEI moves 10 points in the right direction, this would be enough to execute the sell order.

The premium slope for an in-the-money Call or Put is typically 0.5 or greater. Premium slope = premium difference/strike price difference. On 22 September 1997 the OEX Call 915 = 26.25, the OEX Call 910 = 29.5; slope = (29.5-26.25)/5 = 0.65. With this slope for the C915, a delta = 1 would require an OEX rise = delta/slope = 1/0.65 = 1.54. The slope equation applies to the SEI also.

The OEX long Put buy transaction is given by the EXCEL equation in workbook Oextrd in the worksheet My_Trades as: =(P6 x O6+M6 x L6+J6 x I6+G6 x F6) x 100 x D6-Q6 = -$7,038, the cost of buying the Puts, where all terms in the parenthesis are blank except M6 which contains the value of the long Put premium = 14 and L6 which is the buy/sell indicator = -1 for a buy, D6 = number of options = 5 and Q6 = Commission = $38 = number of options x 7.5, where 7.5 is the commission per option.

The SEI long Put buy transaction for trading the delta strategy in London uses the Ftstrfrm workbook and the My_Trades worksheet. The equation for the cost of buying long Puts is given by: =(P105 x O105+M105 x L105+J105 x I105+G105 x F105) x 10 x D105-Q105 where all columns within the parentheses are blank except K, L, and M; K is the long Put strike price = 4800, L is the BS code for buying or selling = -1 for buying, and K = 68 the premium paid for the long Put. Column D contains the number of options traded = 5; Q is the column for the commission for 5 options = £25.

The OEX long Put sell transaction is given by the EXCEL equation in workbook Oextrd in the worksheet My_Trades as: =(P7 x O7+M7 x L7+J7 x I7+G7 x F7) x 100 x D7-Q7 = $7,963, the amount received selling the Puts, where all terms in the parenthesis are blank except M7 which contains the value of the long Put premium = 16 and L7 which is the buy/sell indicator =+1 for a sell, D7 = number of options = 5 and Q7 = Commission = \$38 = number of options x 7.5, where 7,5 is the commission per option. In this example delta = 2, since the long Put was sold at a premium 2 more than the purchase price.

The SEI long Put sell transaction is given by the following EXCEL formula: =(P105 x O105+M105 x L105+J105 x I105+G105 x F105) x 10 x D105-Q105= £3625; all columns are blank except K, L, and M which have the values 4800 for the Put strike price, 1 to indicate a sale, and 73 for the Put premium received on selling, which gives a delta of 5 for the round trip transaction.

The Profit for the OEX Put Delta = \$7,963 - \$7,038 = \$925. No margin required, just the cost of the long Puts.

The Profit for the SEI Put Delta = £3625 -£3425 = £200 = \$338 at 1.6880 \$/£.

The OEX long Call buy transaction is given by the EXCEL equation in workbook Oextrd in the worksheet My_Trades as follows: =(P8 x O8+M8 x L8+J8 x I8+G8 x F8) x 100 x D8-Q8 = -\$4,038, the cost of buying the Calls, where all terms in the parenthesis are blank except G8 which contains the value of the long Call premium = 8 and L8 which is the buy/sell indicator = -1 for a buy, D8 = number of options = 5 and Q8 = Commission = \$38 = number of options x 7.5, where 7,5 is the commission per option.

The SEI long Call buy transaction for trading the delta strategy in London uses the Ftstrfrm workbook and the My_Trade worksheet. The equation for the cost of buying long Calls is given by: =(P107 x O107+M107 x L107+J107 x I107+G107 x F107) x 10 x D107-Q107 = -£3825, where all columns within the parentheses are blank except E. F, and G where E is the Call strike price = 4800, F is the code for buying = -1, and G is the premium paid for the long Call = 76.

The OEX long Call sell transaction is given by the EXCEL equation in workbook Oextrd in the worksheet My_Trades as follows: =(P9 x O9+M9 x L9+J9 x I9+G9 x F9) x 100 x D9-Q9 = \$4,713, the amount received selling the Calls, where all terms in the parenthesis are blank except G9 which contains the value of the long Call premium = 9.5 and F9 which is the buy/sell indicator = +1 for a sell, D9 = number of options = 5 and Q9 = Commission = \$38 = number of options x 7.5, where 7.5 is the commission per option. In this example delta = 1.5, since the long Call was sold at a premium 1.5 more than for which it was bought.

The SEI long Call sell transaction is given by the following EXCEL formula:: =(P108 x O108+M108 x L108+J108 x I108+G108 x F108) x 10 x D108-Q108= £4975; all columns are blank except E, F, and G which have the values 4800 for the Call strike price, 1 to indicate a sale, and 100 for the Call premium received on selling, which gives a delta of 24 for the round trip transaction. I only asked for a delta of 10 but the market was rising so fast my order was actually executed at 24 more, a bonus not often received.

The Profit for the OEX Call Delta = $4,713 - $4,038 = $675. No margin required, just the cost of the long Calls.

The Profit for the SEI Call Delta = £4975 - £3825 =£1,150 = $1,938 at an exchange rate of 1.648 $/£. No margin required, just the cost of the long Calls.

SUMMARY

EXCEL has all the mathematical functions required for option trading. I have written a set of three EXCEL workbooks for OEX trading called OPTRADE5, and three workbooks for SEI trading called FTSDATA1 which contain all the equations (EXCEL functions) that you need for option trading using the strategies described in this book. You don't have to be a math wizard - just enter the daily value of OEX and SEI in the main worksheets and these formulas will do all the computations for you - instantly! Once per month the dates, equations, and charts have to be extended for the next month so the daily entries are once again computed for all the equations and the market signal charts are updated. Normally, this up-date of the spread sheets and charts is a half hour job. (The steps are explained in Appendix A).

The option trading equations are scattered through the various sections of this book, but this Chapter 10 integrates them in logical sections based on the option trading strategies to make them easier to find when you may have need to refer to or use them. Of course EXCEL is not absolutely necessary for option trading - you could use a hand held calculator to make all the computations. EXCEL just makes everything easier and forces you to organize your data so that you have an expanding data base. Appendix B "Option Trading EXCEL Workbooks available from the Author" gives a short description of the three OPTRADE5 workbooks and the three

FTSDATA1 workbooks. Appendix A describes the OEXSTRGY6 work-book which is set up to enter automatically the portfolio of option quotes obtained from Interquote on the Internet. This workbook includes all the necessary option trading equations which are updated as many times per day as you copy portfolio quotes and enter them into the main spread sheet of this workbook. I use this workbook daily and find it is a great aid to option trading, especially day trading, because of this constant updating capability.

APPENDIX A

OEXSTRGY6™
AN OEX TRADING SYSTEM WITH
AUTOMATIC ENTRY OF INTERNET OPTION
QUOTES AVAILABLE FROM AUTHOR

The OEX (S&P 100) index options are the best trading vehicles because of the large open interest and daily trading volume. Typically the open interest of the calls and puts together is over a million options and the daily volume is between 20% and 30% of the open interest or 200 to 300 thousand options. This large trading volume assures good liquidity, allowing you to change positions at will. I have developed an automated OEX trading system called **OEXSTRGY6** for 2 sigma short spreads and covered short spreads as well as long position (Calls and Puts) trading strategies. The key to this automated strategy is the updating of the Index Option market values and option premiums using data copied from your unique Interquote portfolio containing your own choice of portfolio data on the Internet WWW (World Wide Web) page. Once copied into the spread sheet Da_Quot by clicking on the **Entr Quote** button, the real time values are converted to spread sheet format and automatically linked to the other spread sheets and charts in the EXCEL 5 workbook using the Excel Visual basic Code in Figure A.1 below:

```
entr_quot Macro
' Macro recorded 3/4/96 by Jon Schiller
Sub entr_quot()
    Range("A3").Select
    ActiveSheet.Paste
    Selection.TextToColumns    Destination:=Range("A3"),
DataType:= _
        xlFixedWidth, FieldInfo:=Array(Array(0, 1), Array(6, 1), Array(16, 1), _
        Array(26, 1), Array(36, 1), Array(46, 1), Array(56, 1), Array(66, 1))
End Sub
```

This simple action of clicking on the Entr Quote button then updates all the charts and spread sheets in real time. Also certain parameters such as unearned profit (URP) for short spreads or covered short spreads and the value of long positions are computed automatically. With a magic click on this Entr Quote button, all your spread sheets and charts are automatically updated. You have instantaneous knowledge of the value of all your open positions (or paper traded positions) within seconds! This strategy uses the same algorithms for computing trading signals as used by the program traders in New York that drive the market daily by dumping in or extracting billions of dollars, causing the market to jump or drop. The program traders are particularly active during the first hour and again during the last 15 to 20 minutes of the New York market session. The principle market signal indicators used are:

1. The Stochastics %D-%K (special moving average indicators) difference

2. The difference between the 9 Day and 4 Day Moving Averages

3. The 7 day Welles-Wilder Indicator (WWI), which is a Relative Strength Indicator (RSI)

4. The 4 day Moving Average Difference

5. The oex-midc (Samn's indicator) which is similar to Stochastic %D-%K

There are charts for the first four market signal indicators which are generated by the oex_var and oex_qwkprft6 work sheets and the oex-midc indicator is computed automatically on the Da_quot spread sheet. The oex_qwkprft6 sheet is used for keeping track of any open long Calls or long Puts including the initial cost, unrealized profit or loss (URP) and a profit summary. The charts are also used to determine when a threat to your covered short spread is real or when it is temporary and will disappear.

The WWI or RSI chart shows when the market is *overbought* or *oversold* and many of the program traders use this chart to decide when to close a long Call or Put. When the RSI is greater than 80%, then the market is overbought and ready for a drop, so close your open long Call position. When the RSI is less than 20% the market is oversold and ready for a rise so close your open long Put position.

The Stochastics %D-%K, 4 Day moving average difference (MAD) and the 9 Day-4 Day MAD charts are used to determine when the market is rising or when the market is falling. When the indicator on any of these charts switches from negative to positive, this is called a *golden cross* (rising market) and when the indicator switches from positive to negative, this is called the *death cross* (falling market). On the Stochastics %D-%K chart, the *golden cross* is the signal for opening a long Call; close the long Call when you are happy with the profit or when the RSI (on the Welles-Wilder chart) reaches the *overbought* area. Also, on the Stochastics %D-%K chart, the *death cross* is the signal for opening a long Put; close the long Put when you are happy with the profit or when the RSI reaches the *oversold* area. The Da_quot spread sheet has logic equations in cell E55 to signal a L Call (long Call) and in cell F55 to signal a L Put (long Put). In addition, oex-midc, computed on the Da_quot worksheet in cell D54, tells when it is safe to open a long Call based on the OEX open, high, low, close and a parameter kk (=1.94). There are times when cell E55 and D54 both indicate a long Call, there are other times when E55 indicates a long Call but D54 doesn't; and there are times when D54 indicates a long Call and E55 doesn't. The best opportunity for long Calls is when both E55 and D54 indicate a long Call. Then you have the greatest probability for profit.

STOCHASTICS MARKET INDICATOR

The most useful market timing signal is the stochastics market indicator which indicates when to open a long Call or long Put. The stochastics market indicator is a rather complex set of algorithms that are implemented in columns AA thru AI of the worksheet oex_qwkprft6 in the OEXSTRG6.XLS workbook. The STO%D-%K (difference between the Stochastics %D and %K parameters) is computed in column AI of that spread sheet and is used to generate the short term signal for long Calls and Puts shown from the oex_sto%k-%d_chrt sheet (in the same workbook) Figure A.2 on the following page:

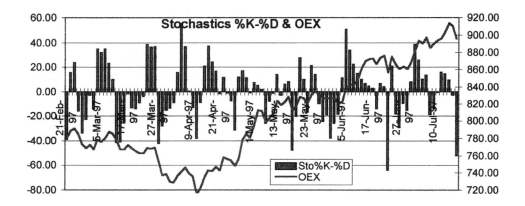

MOVING AVERAGE DIFFERENCE MARKET INDICATORS

- **MAD9-4**

  The MAD9-4 market indicator is the moving average difference between 4 days and 9 days to show the overall market trend. The moving average indicator is computed in columns D through F of the spread sheet oex_qwkprft6 in the OEXSTRG6.XLS workbook. The MAD9-4 (difference between the 9 day and 4 day moving averages) is computed in column F of this spread sheet. This last column is used to generate a longer term signal for long Calls and Puts shown in the mad9-4_chrt sheet (in the same workbook) in Figure A.3 below:

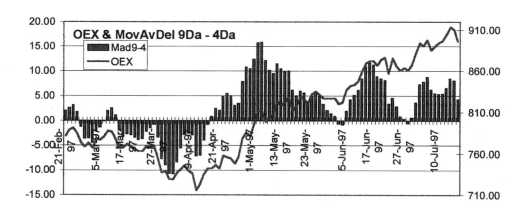

- **MAD4**

  Another moving average difference market indicator which is also used to indicate when to open a long Call or a long Put is the MAD4, but it is less sensitive to switches in market direction than the stochastics indicator. This mad indicator is computed in columns AD and AE of the spread sheet oex_var in the OEXSTRG6.XLS workbook. The MAD4 (difference between the OEX and 4 day moving average) is used as another short term signal for long Calls and Puts shown in the oex_mad4 chart sheet (in the same workbook) in Figure A.4 below:

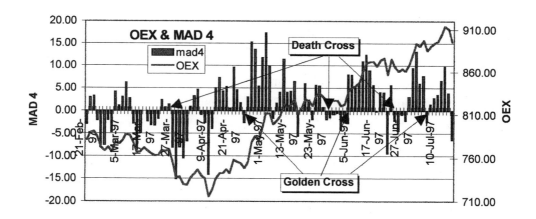

WELLES-WILDER (RSI) MARKET INDICATOR

The Welles-Wilder Relative Strength Indicator (called WWI or RSI) shows when the market is overbought or oversold. When it shows overbought, a downward correction is imminent meaning a long Put could be profitable. An oversold indication means the market is ready to rise and a long Call may be used. The RSI uses exponential moving averages of the ups and downs of the market to compute the RSI in columns V through Z of the spread sheet oex_qwkprft6 in the OEXSTRG6.XLS workbook. The chart WWI_CHRT is shown Figure A.5 below:

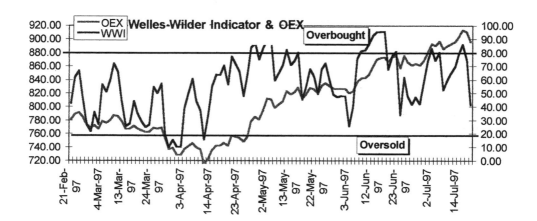

WHEN TO OPEN A LONG CALL OR LONG PUT

The stochastics indicator and the two moving average indicator charts shown above all try to tell you when to open a long Call or long Put position. The stochastics indicator changes direction more often, but when all three agree, then that is a good time to open a long position, provided the 7 Day WWI (relative strength indicator) is between 20 and 80 (i.e. not in the **overbought** or **oversold** area). To aid you in the decision making during a trading day, the spread sheet Da_Quot has logic equations that examine the four indicators (by a linkage to the values for today) and, if the signs are right, puts the words "L Call" in cell E55 or "L Put" in cell F55. If you want to be more confident it is the right time to open a long Call, Samn's indicator in cell D54 will indicate "L Call" when the oex-midc indicator so signals. In other words (provided you have linked the indicators to the cells) when *both* cell E55 and cell D54 indicate "L Call" then the probability of profiting on a long Call close to the market is amplified.

USE OF THE WELLES-WILDER
RELATIVE STRENGTH INDICATOR (RSI) SIGNAL

The RSI chart, also shown above, indicates when the market is in an overbought (RSI>80) or oversold region (RSI<20)and thus is ripe for a drop or a rise.

- When in the overbought area, this means the market is ready to drop so, if you have a long Call, close it out; or if at the same time the stochastics or moving average indicator signals a long Put this would be a confirmation that the long Put strategy is ready for profit.

- When in the oversold area, this means the market is ready to jump so, if you have a long Put, close it out; or if at the same time the stochastics or moving average indicator signals a long Call this would be a confirmation that the long Call strategy would make money.

TRADING RULES FOR OEXSTRG6™

The trading rules for the OEXSTRG6™ trading system based on the 2 sigma short spreads, the covered short spread and the long Call and Put position strategies are summarized below:

1. Open OEX 2 sigma short spreads (if you have capital over $50,000 in your trading account) or OEX 2 sigma covered short spreads (if you have less than $50,000 capital) at the beginning of each option trading month. Use the Trd_Frms worksheet to compute the strike prices, margin, initial credit and expected profit for the long and short Calls and Puts for your new short spread position. Use the EDIT/GOTO to find which form you want to use (both are shown below), see the Figure A.6 trading form below for opening a new OEX short spread and Figure A.7 for opening a new OEX Covered Short Spread:

OPEN NEW OEX SHORT SPREAD				Two Sigma Shrt Sprd Stgy		
25-Dec-96	Today's Date		OEX Sh Sprd Call/Put Strk Pr =		755	705
23-Dec-96	Execution Date	OEX	726.15	Call 2 Sig=	28.00	13MO
17-Jan-97	Expiration Date	NOPS=	4	Put 2 Sig=	21.00	13MO
20-Dec-96	Lst Month Expir Dte	NDTE=	25	L	COM/OP=	36.00
	Call Strike Price =	755	Jan-97		Call Mgn=	0.85
	Put Strike Price =	705	Jan-97		Put Mgn=	0.15
	Call Premium=	3.0000		1 ShC/ShP	Cltrl=	$50,000
	Put Premium=	6.1250		1	Mgn=	20.0%
	Tot Premium =	9.1250	Give Order to your Broker:		Margin =	$ 41,117
	Initial Credit =	$3,574	Sell Opn	4 Calls at SP =	755	Jan-97
	Ex Prft for +2Sig=	$3,574	Sell Opn	4 Puts at SP =	705	Jan-97
	Ex Prft for -2 Sig=	$3,574			Reserv	$8,884
	Actual Profit=					

OPEN NEW OEX Covered SHORT SPREAD				CovTwo Sigma Shrt Sprd Stgy		
25-Dec-96	Today's Date		OEX Sh Sprd Call/Put Strk Pr =		755	705
23-Dec-96	Execution Date	OEX	728.87	Call 2 Sig=	28.00	13 mo
17-Jan-97	Expiration Date	NOPS=	30	Put 2 Sig=	21.00	13 mo
20-Dec-96	Lst Month Expir Dte	NDTE=	25	L	COM/OP=	9.00
	ShrtCall Strike Price	755	Jan-97		Call Mgn=	-1.87
	ShrtPut Strike Price	705	Jan-97		Put Mgn=	2.87
	ShrtCall Premium=	3.7500		1 ShC/ShP	Capital	$50,000
	ShrtPut Premium=	5.7500		1	Margin =	$ 30,250
	LngCall Strike Price	760	Jan-97		Reserv=	$ 19,750
	LngPut Strike Price	700	Jan-97			
	LngCall Premium=	3.0000				
	LngPut Premium=	5.2500				
	Net Premium =	1.2500	Give Order to your Broker:			
	Initial Credit =	$2,670	Sell Opn	30 Calls at SP =	755	Jan-97
	Ex Prft for +2Sig=	($2,940)	Sell Opn	30 Puts at SP =	705	Jan-97
	Ex Prft for -2 Sig=	$2,670	Buy Opn	30 Calls at SP =	760	Jan-97
	Actual Profit=		Buy Opn	30 Puts at SP =	700	Jan-97

2. Enter the parameters for your new short spread or covered short spread in the spread sheet in the worksheet Trd_Frms which automatically computes the initial credit and margin required. Use the worksheet Da_quote to keep track of your short spread or covered short spread once opened. Cell K53 of that spread sheet keeps track of your unearned profit (URP) of four (4) short spreads and cell K54 keeps track of your URP for forty (40) covered short spreads. Should you have a different number than 4 or 40 then edit the number in cells H59 or H60 for the SS and CvSS, respectively.

3. Every day you should link the OEX value in cell B5 of the worksheet Da_quot to the OEX in both columns B of the spread sheets oex_qwkprft6 and oex_var so that as you enter your real time quotes from your Interquote portfolio to Da_quot, then the value of OEX in cells B5 and the values in oex_qwkprft6 and in oex_var are automatically updated. To do this linking copy cell B5 in the worksheet Da_quot, then EDIT/ PASTE SPECIAL/LINK into the B cells corresponding to today's date in the worksheets oex_qwkprft6 and oex_var. At the end of the day you must change the linking in those two cells (they are linked to the cell B5 in Da_Quot). Otherwise, the next day and all subsequent days will continue to be based on the same unchanging OEX value. To change the linking for the next day, take the linked cells in oex_qwkprft6 and in oex_var (with the closing OEX value for today), pull the right corner down into the next trading day. Then do two things: (1) enter today's closing price (by typing it) into the linked cell to make it a fixed number rather than linked, then (2) go to the next day's linked cell and edit the Da_Quot cell B6 to say B5 (due to a peculiarity of EXCEL) for OEX. During the trading day this linking will automatically update your market indicator charts so you can look at these charts and see what the OEX and the indicator curves look like as the day progresses.

4. At the end of the day you should also copy the premiums from Da_quot and paste them in the proper date of oex_var under columns J and K for the short Call and Put and under columns F and G for the long Call and Put (if you have a covered short spread).

5. If you have an open long Call or long Put, the premiums at the end of the day should be copied from Da_quot and pasted in columns I or J for the long Call or long Put of worksheet oex_qwkprft6.

6. Also at the end of each day you should increase the cell row number by one for each of the linked market indicators in Da_quot cells F47, F48, B49, and B53 for the WWI, Sto%K-%D, MAD9-4, and MAD4, respectively.

7. As the trading day approaches the end (just before 4 PM New York time), look at cell E55 to see if a "L Call" is signaled; look at cell D55 to see if a "L Call" is signaled, or look at cell F55 to see if a "L Put" is signaled. These signals will give you a prediction of whether the next trading day will be an up or down day. The Long Call in D55 or the long Put in F55 are composite signals and are the strongest. Many days these two indicators will be blank indicating neither a clear Long Call nor Long Put. The signal in B60 is based on the SPY compared with the SPX and is a short term indicator good for day trading as to whether a long Call or Put is signaled.

The best indicator to use for the Delta strategy is the indicator in cell B60 based on the SPY indicator. This often is a good indicator of a sell program (L Put) or a buy program (L Call). If it indicates L Call, then buy Calls at a strike price just above the market with a sell order at a delta of 1 more than received when bought; if the indicator signals L Put then buy Puts at a strike price just below the market with a sell order at a delta of 1 more than received when bought. The number of Calls or Puts depends on how much capital you are willing to put at risk. For example, in the beginning of the option month when the at-the-money premiums are high, you may want to buy 5 options; later during the option month when the at-the-money premiums have decayed to a low value, then you may want to buy 10 options. I recommend you risk no more than 50% of your capital for a long position. The trading forms for opening a long Call or long Put are in the work sheet Trd_Frms of the OEXTRD6.XLS workbook; use EDIT/GOTO to find the form you want. The form names are: Open New Short Spread, Open New Covered Short Spread, Open Long Call, Open Long Put, Close Long Call, Close Long Put. Enter the strike price and premium in the proper boxes of the form and the initial credit will be computed for you.

8. Close your long Call or long Put when the premium increases to a value which gives you a profit you are happy with. In most markets, I would

recommend you place a sell order at the time you place the buy order in order to profit from a rise during the day when you may not be watching the market. For example, I often place a sell order at a premium 1 greater than the premium I paid for a position. Then when the position is opened (executed) this locks in a profit of $500 less commission for 5 long positions or $1,000 less commissions for 10 long positions. If you are convinced the market is in a trend in the direction of your long position (up for Calls or down for Puts), then you may want to ask for a higher premium increase. ***But don't be too greedy - take your profit and run!!!*** Don't hope for too much. The program traders will try to take it from you. Remember the signals the program traders use to buy or sell. They are the same ones we use in the OEXSTRG6™ trading system. If you watch closely the "L Call" and "L Put" cells in the Da_quot sheet and the market signal charts you can predict what the program traders are going to do and what you should do. The trading forms for closing a long Call or long Put are in the TRD_FRMS spread sheet, use EDIT/ GOTO to find the form. Enter the premium in the proper box of the form and the profit (or loss) will be computed for you. In long position trading the probability of a profit is about 70% and of a loss about 30%. If you use the rules I've given you, perhaps you can improve the percentages in your favor.

- I would recommend limiting your long trades to five or six per month. If you can make about $2,000 to $3,000 net after commission for these trades, then you are earning a return on capital at risk of about 8% per month, since the 5 long positions at the beginning of the option month require about $4,500 initial cost and the 10 long positions near the end of the option month require about the same.

THE OEXSTRG6.XLS WORKBOOK SHEETS

The sheets in the OEXSTRG6.XLS work book are summarized below starting from LEFT to RIGHT (across the bottom of workbook sheet indicators): Figure A.8

1.	C_Prm	chart: scatter diagram curve for estimating OEX Call premiums
2.	P_Prm	chart: scatter diagram curve for estimating OEX Put premiums
3.	Da_quot	sheet for entering portfolio quotes copied from Interquote
4.	LC_Prft	chart: sample to show how L Call profits during Oct 96
5.	oex_hi_lo	sheet for entering OEX daily high, low & close from Da_quot
6.	4yr_oex_mad9-4	chart: shows OEX & mov avg. difference or 9 & 4 days for 4yrs
7.	oexstrg6_prft	chart: shows sample long Position profits over 2 year period
8.	WWI_CHRT	chart: shows the 7 Day Welles-Wilder RSI and OEX
9.	mad9-4_chrt	chart: shows the 9 day - 9 day Mov. Avg Diff. & OEX
10.	oex_sto%k-%d_chrt	chart: shows OEX & stochastics %K-%D indicator
11.	oex_mad4	chart: shows OEX & 4 day moving average difference
12.	oex_qwkprft6	worksheet for computing signal indicators and long Positions
13.	oex_var	worksheet for mad4 computations, short spreads, and 2 sigmas
14.	oex_cumD	chart: shows OEX & monthly Cum Delta for last 2 years
15.	PrmDec_Lst7Da	chart: shows how C&P premiums decay at end of option month
16.	Lst_7Da	chart: shows how C&P premiums decay for 8 different months
17.	Prm_Chrt_Code	macro for generating scatter diagram charts
18.	P_atm_vlty	chart: shows how Put prms decay & volatility VIX.X
19.	7da_prm_decy	chart: shows how PATM &CATM decay during last 7 days
20.	CATM_PATM	sheet: CATM & PATM values for chart 22 above.
21.	MyFn_Code	macro for computing commissions
22.	Trd_Frms	sheet with trade forms for spreads and long positions
23.	Module1	visual basic code for entering quote in Da_quot worksheet

SUMMARY OF MAIN SPREAD SHEETS IN OEXSTRG6 WORKBOOK

1. Da_quot

This is the principal spread sheet of the OEXSTRG6.XLS workbook. You copy the portfolio quotation from Interquote on the WWW at address http://www.interquote.com/cgi-bin/qs The cost for subscribing to this real time service from Paragon Software of Wisconsin is $27/mo. You copy the page of quotations from the above cited WWW page and then click on the button **Entr Quote** and an EXCEL warning box will be displayed asking if you want to overwrite the data on the spread sheet, just click **OK,** and the latest quotation will be copied into the spread sheet. At the same time, the OEX value will be automatically transferred (by means of EXCEL linking) to the OEX value column in the line for today's date on the other two main spread sheets oex_qwkprft6 and oex_var. In addition, the four main charts WWI_CHRT, mad9-4_chrt, oex_sto%k-%d_chrt and oex_mad4 will also be automatically updated from the computations on these other two main spread sheets.

2. oex_var

This spread sheet is linked to Da_quot for updating the OEX during the trading day. This spread sheet also computes the market signal Mad4 (the 4 day moving average difference) in columns AD and AE. Columns E thru P are set up for either naked short spread or covered short spread trading. The strike prices are computed in the first row of the new option month in columns F and G for the long Call and Put (for covered short spreads) and columns J and K for the 2 sigma short Call and Put for either the naked short spread or the covered short spread. I advise using the naked short spread position if you have the minimum required capital of $50,000; if not, you will have to use the covered short spread. The long premiums are entered in columns H and I (for the covered short spread, CvSS) and the short premiums are entered in columns L and M for either the CvSS or the naked short spread (SS). The margin required for the covered short spread is computed in column O and the unearned profit (URP) is computed in column P. For the case of a naked short spread, the number of options is in column T and the short spread margin is computed in column U. The 2 sigma computations are in columns V thru Z. Use the EDIT/GOTO to find the cells where the Call and Put 2 sigmas are computed. The monthly maximum and minimum (MAX and MIN) values used in the 2 sigma computations are computed in columns Q and R. So this is a very busy spread sheet performing the many computations crucial to short spread option trading.

3. **oex_qwkprft6**

This spread sheet is linked to the Da_quot spread sheet for entering the OEX values during the trading day as you obtain real time quotes for your portfolio. This spread sheet computes the 9 day minus the 4 day moving average difference (Mad9-4) using columns D thru F; it computes the stochastics %K-%D (Sto%K-%D) indicator using columns AA thru AI, and computes the Welles-Wilder Relative Strength Indicator (WWI or RSI) using columns V thru Z. In addition, G thru U are dedicated to keeping track of long Calls and long Puts, the profit earned and also the cumulative profit for long Position trading. Cells E55 and F55 of the Da_quot spread sheet tell you when the four market signals are right for opening a long Call or long Put position and, once the positions are open, when they should be closed. At the end of the day, you must update the linking between worksheets Da_Quot cell and the next day's OEX cell in column B of oex_var worksheet and oex_qwkprft6 worksheet. Go to current day of OEX, click on lower right corner of cell, hold left mouse button down, and pull down to cover the next date. Now go back to original cell, and write in today's OEX value. Go to next day's cell, and change the cell number from 6 to 5 to restore OEX value instead of SPX value from Da_Quot sheet. Do this on both spread sheets oex_var and oex_qwkprft6. This action will automatically update the charts Mad4, Mad9-4, Sto%K-%D, and WWI. In worksheet Da_Quot the row number of the linked values in cells B49 (Mad9-4), B53 (Mad4), B55 (Midc) F48 (WWI), and F47 (StoK-D) should all be incremented by 1, to update the linkage for the next trading day. ***If you forget to update this linking, then your long position signals will not be correct in Da_Quote!***

4. **Trd_Frm**

This spread sheet has the eight trading forms you need for opening new positions and closing out long positions. These forms can be found by using EDIT/GOTO and selecting the form whose title indicates the trade you want to make (see below). You need to enter the premiums, the capital you have, and the number of positions you want to open. The trade forms then compute your initial credit and your profit when you close a long position. It is handy to print out these forms both to document your trade and also because the form includes the instructions to give your broker to open the position covered by the form. The forms include:

- Open New Short Spread
- Open New Covered Short Spread
- Open Call Covered Short Spread
- Open Put Covered Short Spread

- Open Long Put
- Close Long Put
- Open Long Call
- Close Long Call

HOW TO UPDATE SPREAD SHEETS & CHARTS FOR NEW OPTION MONTH

- **Da_quot**

Each time a new option month begins, the spread sheet Da_quot should be updated with the new portfolio valid for the new option month. The codes for each option price are stipulated by the Chicago Board of Exchange (CBOE) and are given in Figure 7.1 of Chapter 7. If the Call and/or Put strike prices are changed, it will be necessary to change the initial Call strike price in cell I9 and the initial Put strike price in cell J19 to agree with the strike price codes in column B of the same rows. The 2 sigma covered short spread (rows 39 and 40 for the Call and rows 41 and 42 for the Puts) must be included in the portfolio to correspond to the 2 sigma values computed in the Trd_Frm spread sheet for the OEX covered short spread. For example, if the short Call is 755 and the long Call is 760, then the codes for the OEX January covered Calls would be AK and AL in row 39 and 40; if the short Put is 705 and the long Put is 700, then the codes for OEX January covered Puts would be MA and MT. Also you should up date the codes for the IBM long Call close to the market, and the Microsoft long Call near the market and the 2 sigma Intel short spread Call and Put. If you are paper trading a long Call edit the values in cell H46.

Also the cells for the unearned profit (URP) computations, such as cells K53 and K54, should be edited so they show the actual initial credit received for the short spread and/or covered short spread. Any other of your open positions or paper trade positions you wish to keep track of during the trading day can be added or edited to fit your particular positions.

- **oex_var**

This spread sheet is updated at the beginning of a new option month by entering the premiums for the new covered short spread or naked short spread you may open. After March 97, you will have to add new dates in column A and extend the other columns down by covering, and pulling down from the bottom right corner to extend any equations contained in the columns.

- **oex_qwkprft6**

This spread sheet must be updated monthly for the market signal indicators computed on this worksheet. During the month if you open any long Call or long Put positions you can keep track of any open positions in columns G through U, but there are no specific updates required at the beginning of the new option month.

- **Trd_Frm**

If you open a new short spread or covered short spread at the beginning of the new option month, then enter the OEX, number of options, the Call and Put 2 sigmas for the coming month from the spread sheet oex_var, your capital, and the premiums for the Calls and Puts in the proper cells. Then the trade form will compute your initial credit and display the order you give to your broker to open the spread.

- **Update Procedure for All Charts**

All charts are updated using a similar procedure, but first you must update the spread sheets from which the charts are generated. Normally you will update the charts from the last expiration date to the next expiration date all at the same time. First select the chart you want to update. Then, in the chart, click on the line or column group that you want to update first. A lot of little boxes should appear on the line or columns to highlight it - if the wrong part of the chart has been highlighted, click again on the line you want. Repeat until the little boxes appear on the correct line. Observe the spread sheet from which the line or column group is derived by examining the long box with a formula in it that appears at the top of the chart when you single click on each line. Go to the spread sheet for that chart and write down the row number of the next expiration date. Go back to the chart and, in the long formula box for that line at the top of the chart, cover the old row number and edit in the new row number. When you do that for each line or group of columns in the chart, the chart is updated for the new expiration date. EXCEL 5 makes this chart update very easy, once you get used to the procedure. Repeat these steps for each chart in the workbook. Then you are finished with your monthly update task. **Note**: The scatter diagram charts are updated automatically when you enter new quotes in the Da_quot worksheet. You don't need to do anything to update these charts except to make sure the beginning Call strike price number in cell I9 corresponds to the strike price in cell B9; also make sure the beginning Put strike price number in cell J19 corresponds to the strike price in cell B19. Sometimes during the option month when there is a large change in OEX you will want to edit your Interquote portfolio to cover the range of strike prices from just in the money to well out of the money. In such cases you will also have to edit the numbers in cells I9 and J19.

APPENDIX B

OPTRADE5™
AN OEX TRADING SYSTEM
AVAILABLE FROM AUTHOR

I have developed an OEX trading system for Covered Short Spreads and Long Position (Calls and Puts) trading strategies called OpTrade5, plus a companion menu driven Windows program called Opstrgy2, to make it easy for the options trader to access the type of charts used as trading signals by the program traders in New York, which drive the market daily by dumping in or extracting billions of dollars causing the market to jump or drop. The program traders are particularly active during the last 15 to 20 minutes of the NY market session.

The OEX (S&P 100) index options are the best trading vehicles because of the large open interest and daily trading volume. Typically the open interest of the calls and puts together is over a million options and the daily volume is between 20% and 30% of the open interest or 200 to 300 thousand options. This large trading volume assures good liquidity, allowing you to change positions at will.

The principle market signal indicators used are:

1. The Stochastics %D minus %K (special moving average indicators) difference

2. The Difference between the 9 Day and 4 Day Moving Averages

3. The 7 day Welles-Wilder Indicator (WWI), which is a Relative Strength Indicator (RSI)

The charts showing these three market signal indicators are generated in the OEXSCHRT.XLS workbook, and are used for determining when to open a long Call or long Put, and when to close them with a profit. These charts are also used to determine when a threat to your covered short spread is real or when it is temporary and will disappear.

The WWI or RSI chart shows when the market is *overbought* or *oversold* and many of the program traders use this chart to decide when to close a long Call or Put. When the RSI is greater than 80%, then the market is overbought and ready for a drop: close your open long Call position; when the RSI is less than 20% the market is oversold and ready for a rise: close your open long Put position.

Both the Stochastics %D-%K and the 9 Day-4 Day moving average difference charts are used to determine when to open a Long Call or a Long Put Position. When the indicator switches from negative to positive, this is called a *golden cross* and is the signal for opening a Long Call; close the long Call when you are happy with the profit or when the RSI reaches the *overbought* area. When the indicator switches from negative to positive, this is called the *death cross* and is the signal for opening a Long Put; close the long Put when you are happy with the profit or when the RSI reaches the *oversold* area.

STOCHASTICS MARKET INDICATOR

An often used market timing signal is the stochastics market indicator which is used to indicate when to open a long Call or long Put. The stochastics market indicator is a rather complex set of algorithms that are implemented in columns J through Q of the spread sheet OEX_mkt_signal in the OEXSCHRT.XLS workbook. The STOD-K (difference between the Stochastics %D and %K parameters) is computed in column AC of the same spread sheet. This last column is used to generate the short term signal for long Calls and Puts shown in the Sto_KD_Del following chart (in the same workbook), Figure B.1:

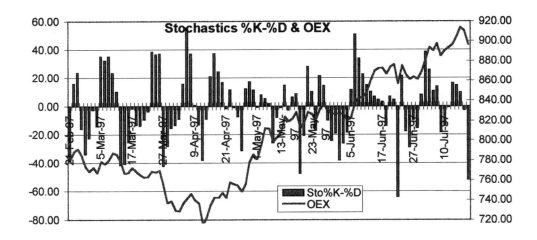

MOVING AVERAGE DIFFERENCE
MARKET INDICATOR

Another often used market timing signal is the moving average difference market indicator which is also used to indicate when to open a long Call or long Put. The moving average indicators use exponential moving averages algorithms and are computed in columns R through V of the spread sheet OEX_mkt_signal in the OEXSCHRT.XLS workbook. The MAD2-1 (difference between the 9 day and 4 day moving averages) is computed in column AB of the same spread sheet. This last column is used to generate the short term signal for long Calls and Puts shown in the MovAvg_Del_9-4 following chart (in the same workbook), Figure B.2:

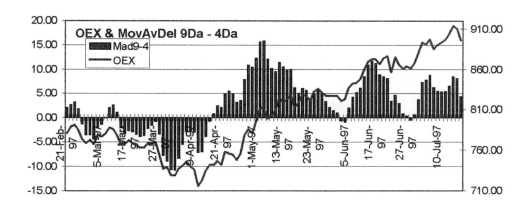

WELLES-WILDER (RSI) MARKET INDICATOR

Another often used market timing signal is the Welles-Wilder Relative Strength Indicator (called WWI or RSI) which is also used to indicate when to close a long Call or long Put. The RSI uses exponential moving averages of the ups and downs of the market to compute the RSI in columns D through H for the 14 day RSI and columns Y through AA for the 7 day RSI. The column H is used to generate the 6MoWWI chart and column AA is used to generate the RSI_ShrtTerm following chart (in the same workbook), Figure B.3:

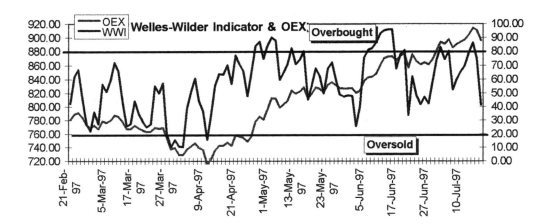

How do the Stochastics and Moving Average Market Timing Signals Compare? The stochastics indicator and moving average indicator charts shown above both try to tell you when to open a long Call or long Put position. The stochastics indicator changes direction more often, but when both agree, then that is a good time to open a long position. Both have *golden crosses* and *death crosses:*

- When the indicator switches from negative to positive you have the *golden cross*

- When the indicator switches from positive to negative you have the *death cross*

When do you use the Welles-Wilder Relative Strength Indicator (RSI) Signal? The RSI chart, also shown above, indicates when the market is in an overbought (RSI>80) or oversold region (RSI<20)and thus is ripe for a drop or a rise.

- When in the overbought area, this means the market is ready to drop, so if you have a long Call close it out; or if at the same time the stochastics or the moving average indicator signals a long Put, this would be a confirmation that the long Put strategy is ready for profit.

- When in the oversold area, this means the market is ready to jump, so if you have a long Put close it out; or if at the same time the stochastics or the moving average indicator signals a long Call, this would be a confirmation that the long Call strategy is ready for profit.

SUMMARY OF WORKBOOKS FOR OPTRADE5™

OPTRADE5 has three workbooks which are each described below:

1. OEXMKTV.XLS is the main workbook and the main spread sheet is OEXMKTV which is organized to trade covered short spreads and computes the short Call, long Call, short Put and long Put strike prices using Call and Put 2 sigmas which are also computed by this spread sheet. Enter daily the OEX price and the premiums for the covered short spread Calls and Puts.

2. OEXTRDFRM.XLS is used for keeping track of your trades. The user enters the number of options, strike prices for Long and Short Calls and Puts and the premiums for the Long and Short Calls on the spread sheet My_Trades. This spread sheet computes your initial credit, keeps track of you capital growth, and profit for each round trip trade.

3. OEXSCHRT.XLS has the main spread sheet called OEX_mkt_sig which computes all the parameters needed for the market signal charts including Mad4, Mad9-4, Stochastics %K-%D, and the Welles-Wilder relative strength indicator. This workbook also contains all these charts which are updated daily as you enter the OEX price for the day.

4. STOCHRT.XLS is a workbook for providing linking between the charts and spread sheet segments of OPTRADE5 and the companion menu driven OPSTRGY2 Windows program.

TRADING RULES FOR OPTRADE5™

The trading rules for the OPTRADE5™ trading system based on the 2 sigma short spread, the covered short spread and the long Call and Put position strategies are summarized below:

1. Open a covered short spread at the beginning of each option trading month. You open a new covered short spread, using OEXTRDFRM.XLS to compute the long and short Calls and Puts. Use the EDIT/GOTO to find the following Covered Short Spread form, Figure B.4:

2. Enter the parameters for your new covered short spread in the spread sheet OEXMKTV2 which automatically computes the initial credit and keeps track of your unearned profit (URP). You should enter daily the OEX and premiums for your short spread. My OPVAM algorithm estimates the premium values when you do not have them.

3. Examine the stochastics, moving average and RSI charts presented above to determine the market trends indicated by the charts.

Covered Short Spread		Covered Margin = 2*($2000+(5-PrmDel)*100*NOPS)					
24-Apr-96	Today's Date						
22-Apr-96	Execution Date	OEX =	621.25				
17-May-96	Expiration Date	NOPS=	35		Move Put dn by 5, Call dn for 2sig		
19-Apr-96	Lst Month Expir Dte	NDTE=	25	L		COM/OP=	17.00
	Long Call SP =	655				Call 2 Sig=	27.00
	Long Call Premium=	1.7500	-1			Put 2 Sig=	12.00
	Short Call SP =	650				Cmgn=	1.75
	Short Call Premium=	2.7500	1			Pmgn=	0.75
	Short Put SP =	610				Cltrl=	$35,000
	Short Put Premium=	6.5000	1			CovMgn=	0.06
	Long Put SP =	605				CovCltrl=	$32,000
	Long Put Premium=	5.5000	-1			Cap Mgn=	$13,000
	Initial Credit =	$6,405	Give Order to your Broker:				
For Jump:	Maximum Loss =	($11,095)	Buy Open	35	Calls at SP=	655	
For Drop:	Maximum Loss =	($11,095)	Sell Open	35	Calls at SP=	650	
	Ex Prft for +2Sig=	$6,405	Sell Open	35	Puts at SP =	610	
	Ex Prft for -2 Sig=	$6,405	Buy Open	35	Puts at SP =	605	

THE OEXSCHRT.XLS WORKBOOK

The sheets in the OEXSCHRT.XLS work book are summarized below starting from LEFT to RIGHT (across bottom of workbook sheet indicators), Figure B.5:

1. 6mWWI   chart: 14 day WWI
2. 6mSTOMAD   chart: shows OEX, stomad
3. Lng_MovAvg   chart: shows OEX & Long Moving Averages
4. RSI_6Mo   chart: shows OEX & RSI
5. Shrt_MovAvg   chart: shows short term moving averages
6. Stochastics_%D%K   chart: shows stochastics %D & %K lines
7. MovAvg_Del9-4   chart: shows OEX & mov avg difference or 9 & 4 days
8. Sto_KD_Del   chart: shows OEX & stochastics %D - %K bars
9. OEX_MKT_SIGNALS   spread sheet: computes all market signal indicators

THE OEXMKTV2.XLS WORKBOOK

The sheets in the OEXMKTV2.XLS work book are summarized below starting from LEFT to RIGHT (across bottom of workbook sheet indicators), Figure B.6:

1. 13mss   chart: shows the OEX & Short Spread Call & Put for last 13 mo.

2. 13mss   chart: shows the OEX & Short Spread Call & Put for last 4 mo

3. MAD30   chart: shows OEX & 30 day mov avg difference

4. Volatility   chart: shows daily Delta & Cumulative Delta for the OpMo

5. URPR   chart: shows Unearned Profit for the last 4 OpMo's

6. MoRet   chart: shows Unearned Profit for the last 4 OpMo's

7. Capital Growth   chart: shows Capital Growth using Covered Short Spreads

8. Return_AccumCapital   chart: shows Accum Capital & %Monthly Return

9. OEX_css_prftSum   spread sheet show monthly summary of profit since Jan 93

10. OEXMKTV   main spread sheet for entering daily data, links to chart SS

11. MACRO   visual basic macro that opens other workbooks, & comm f'n

THE OEXTRDFRM.XLS WORKBOOK

The sheets in the OEXTRDFRM.XLS work book are summarized below starting from LEFT to RIGHT (across bottom of workbook sheet indicators), Figure B.7:

1. Put_Prm_Chrt   chart: scatter diagram curve for estimating OEX Put premiums

2. PutPrm   spread sheet: enter Put premiums to generate Put_Prm_Chrt

3. Call_Prm_Chrt   chart: scatter diagram curve for estimating OEX Call premiums

4. PutPrm   spread sheet: enter Call premiums to generate
                           Call_Prm_Chrt
5. My_Trades   spread sheet: for logging your individual trades
6. OEXTRDFRM   spread sheet: with computing forms for opening Short
                           Spreads,
            Covered Short Spreads, Long Calls & Long Puts
                and for closing LngCalls & LngPuts

A monthly update of the spread sheets and charts is necessary using the EXCEL pull down feature that copies equations in the cells below and the chart line editing feature of EXCEL.

SUMMARY OF MAIN SPREAD SHEETS IN OEXMKTV2 WORKBOOK

1. OEXMKTV2.XLS The Spread Sheet OEXMKTV

This is the principal spread sheets of the OPTRADE5™ trading system and you must update it each trading day to enter the OEX market values and premiums for any covered short spread position you have. If you do not have the latest premium data, it is computed on your spread sheet using the OPVAM algorithm (parameters at top of spread sheet), or you can estimate it using the scatter charts. The most important function of this spread sheet is to keep track of any covered short spread you may have open and compute daily the unearned profit. At the beginning of each month it computes the initial credit and margin required for your covered short spreads. This spread sheet also computes the 13 month Call and Put 2 sigma values.

2. OEXTRDFRM.XLS The Spread Sheet OEXTRDFRM

This spread sheet has the six trading forms you need for opening new positions and closing out long positions. These forms can be found easily by using EDIT/GOTO and selecting the form you want to use. You need to enter the premiums, the capital you have, and the number of positions you want to open. The trade forms then compute your initial credit and your profit when you close a long position.

- **The Spread Sheet My_Trades**

This spread sheet allows you to enter the number and premiums for each trade you make. If you enter your initial capital, then it will compute your current capital based on the profit and losses of each trade. This is a very important spread sheet to keep track of your trades.

MONTHLY UPDATE OF THE TWO MAIN SPREAD SHEETS

OEXMKTV.XLS is the main workbook and the main spread sheet is OEXMKTV which is organized to trade covered short spreads and computes the short Call, long Call, short Put and long Put strike prices using Call and Put 2 sigmas which are also computed by this spread sheet. You enter daily the OEX price and the premiums for the covered short spread Calls and Puts. For the monthly update of OEXMKTV you should cover all the cells from column B through column AF, and pull down from the rightmost lower corner to the last date you wish to update and then all the equations will be extended, so when you enter the OEX value for each trading day the various computations will be made. The same procedure can be used for the OEXMKTV spread sheet in the OEXMKTV.XLS workbook with the caution that the equations under the OPVAM premium computations (columns M thru P) are different on expiration day from all other trading days. So copy the two rows the day before expiration and the expiration day for these 4 columns and paste at the day before and expiration day for the next expiration month. Also the equations under columns H through L are different on the first day after expiration from all other trading days, so copy the two rows on expiration day and the day after expiration day for these columns H through L and paste them on expiration day and the next trading day for the next option month. All other columns can be extended down by pulling down using the rightmost lower corner as described above.

OEXSCHRT.XLS has the main spread sheet called OEX_mkt_sig which computes all the parameters needed for the market signal charts including Mad4, Mad9-4, Stochastics %K-%D, and the Welles-Wilder relative strength indicator. This workbook also contains all these charts which are updated daily as you enter the OEX price for the day.

In the OEX_mkt_signals spread sheet, first update the dates by using a calendar to extend the computed dates in the spread sheet. Then cover all the cells from column B through column AF, and pull down from the rightmost lower corner to the last date you wish to update and then all the equations will be extended, so when you enter the OEX value for each trading day the various computations will be made.

UPDATE PROCEDURE FOR ALL CHARTS

All charts are updated using a similar procedure, but first you must update the spread sheets from which the charts are generated. Normally you will update the charts from the last expiration date to the next expiration date all at the same time. First select the chart you want to update. Then, in the chart, click on the line or column group that you want to update first. A lot of little boxes should appear on the line or columns to highlight it - if the wrong part of the chart has been highlighted, click again on the line you want. Repeat until the little boxes appear on the correct line. Observe the spread sheet from which the line or column group is derived by examining the long box with a formula in it that appears at the top of the chart when you single click on each line. Go to the spread sheet for that chart and write down the row number of the next expiration date (for OCT 97, ROW 85). Go back to the chart and, in the long formula box for that line at the top of the chart, cover the old row number and edit in the new row number. When you do that for each line or group of columns in the chart, the chart is updated for the new expiration date. EXCEL makes this chart update very easy, once you get used to the procedure. Repeat these steps for each chart in the workbook. Then you are finished with your monthly update task.

APPENDIX C

OEX: BASIC DESCRIPTION & LIST OF STOCKS

This description of the OEX and its components was found on the Internet by typing in the address for the Chicago Board of Exchange: http://www.cboe.com/   On about the third page of CBOE information, the S&P 100 data was located. The informative paragraphs below were located by clicking on OEX products: http://www.cboe.com/index/oex/oex.html The Internet pages include charts as well as text. Copies of the charts are at the end of this Appendix under "CBOE Internet Page Charts."
After the OEX write-up, the 100 stocks that make up the S&P 100 are listed. These were found on the Internet at http://www.cboe.com/products/cm/sp100c_w.html.

OEX BASIC REVIEW

OEX is the symbol for options on the S&P 100 Index. This is a capitalization- weighted index, covering a broad-range of industries.

Each index option contract represents 100 times the current value of the index. For example, when the index is 400, the dollar value of the index will equal $40,000....100 (the multiplier) times 400.

OEX option premiums are quoted in a manner identical to equity options, stated in points and fractions, the prices are multiplied by $100 to determine total cost. If the option price in the newspaper is 5, the premium is $500. Exercise, or strike prices, are set at five point intervals to bracket the current value of the S&P 100 Index.

OEX options are American Style. This means they can be exercised on any business day prior to expiration date. OEX options, available in each of the four nearby months, expire on a monthly basis. The expiration date is the Saturday following the third Friday of the expiration month. Settlement value is tied to the S&P 100 at expiration or to the value of the index when the option exercised. This value is calculated by Standard and Poor's. OEX options are cash-settled. This means that cash is delivered at settlement, not securities.

The index consists of 100 blue-chip stocks from diverse industry groups, and because of this it provides a measure of the overall market performance. Therefore, you can participate directly in the blue-chip market by using OEX options.

THE PUT/CALL RATIO

Sentiment indicators have long been a favorite technical analysis tool. Contrary indicators are those that mean the exact opposite of what they say. If such an indicator is registering a large percentage of bullish investors, the reading is considered bearish, given the assumption that most speculators are wrong most of the time. Prior to the introduction of listed options, odd-lot volume was a favorite contrary indicator. An odd lot is fewer than 100 shares of stock. Odd-lot buyers or sellers were generally considered to be at the bottom of the investment sophistication barrel, and thus were assumed likely to be making the wrong decision at key times in the market. The epitome of the odd-lot indicators was the number of odd-lot short sales. The arrival of listed options, along with an inflation rate that turned many odd lots into round lots, diminished the value of this indicator.

In recent years, the percentage of bullish investment advisors has become a popular sentiment indicator. Just as with individual investors, a relatively large number of bullish advisors is deemed to be bearish on Wall Street. Each week, investment advisors are polled in an effort to measure their bullishness, and the analyses are published frequently in various financial publications.

Buyers of options are generally considered speculators. Speculators are thought to be on the wrong side of the market most of the time, especially at market extremes. Logic would then suggest that an examination of the number of puts traded versus the number of calls might provide an ideal contrary sentiment indicator.

The CBOE publishes two put-call ratios. The S&P 100 Put-Call Ratio is calculated by dividing the number of puts traded on the popular OEX options during the analysis period by the number of calls traded. The CBOE Equity Put-Call Ratio makes the same calculation for puts and calls on individual stocks traded on the exchange. Some brokerage firms maintain their own put-call ratio calculations.

The CBOE ratios can be found each week in the "Market Laboratory" section of Barron's.

A put-call ratio of 125:100 for the S&P 100 (125 puts for every 100 calls), considered as a contrarian sentiment indicator, could be viewed as a bullish reading. It takes only a 60:100 ratio to reach a similar conclusion for the CBOE Equity Put-Call Ratio.

The difference reflects an opinion that index traders are somehow less vulnerable to "contrary indicator disease" than individual equity players. To reach contrarian bearish readings, the ratios must record a reading of 30:100 (30 puts for every 100 calls) for equity options and 75:100 for OEX options.

Figure 9-1 (see end of Appendix C "CBOE Internet page charts") shows the S&P 100 (OEX) Index graphed; it can be compared with both CBOE put-call ratios also in the figure. Some users prefer to plot a moving average to more clearly define the trend, thus helping filter out short-term "noise" that can be present in the numbers.

When using put-call ratios, it is important to remember that not all option activity reflects the trading of speculators. In fact, more than half the volume of trades comes from investment professionals and market makers. The percentage of public trades is a changing number, reflecting the overall condition of the market. It would seem logical that the value of examining put-call ratios would be greater during periods of high market interest by the public.

Remember also when viewing a put-call ratio that there is a direct, definable relative value between puts and calls. Traders on the floor of an exchange can "create" a put option by buying a call and selling the underlying stock short. They can create a call by buying a put and buying the stock. This process is known as conversion. They would choose to do this trade, or the reverse, if the prices for either option got out of line. This means that high call volume can generate high put volume and vice versa. While on the subject of volume, note that option volume is a moving target. A volume of 1,000 contracts does not necessarily mean there is a buyer or seller of that many options, although there might be. When an order reaches the floor of an exchange, the market maker can simply purchase the contracts for his or her own account. If the option is not desired, the trader can offset the new position by making a trade in the underlying security or another option. Offsetting a position with other option contracts pyramids the volume of such trading. With all these caveats in mind, the put-call ratio can provide valuable market insight. As with most technical indicators, though, successful use of the number is probably more of an art than a science.

OPTION PREMIUMS

The amount by which an option price exceeds its intrinsic value is called the premium. An option's intrinsic value is the difference between the current value of the stock and the strike price of the option. Premiums are the "product" of the options market. All of the fundamental, psychological, and mathematical factors in the market are incorporated in their value. Monitoring the level of premiums and their relationship is one of the simplest—and probably one of the most important ways option market information can be used to make stock decisions. If the strike price of the option is at or above the price of the stock (in the case of a call), or at or below the price of the stock (in the case of a put), the entire price of the option is premium. The level of premiums is an important consideration for option traders—and for stock traders. Traders in general want to be sellers when premiums are high, buyers when they are low. The problem is that what is relatively high or low is known for certain only after the fact. In other words, by looking at a chart of historical option premiums, the viewer can say what would have been the best approach for a trader to have taken. For example, if premiums had been declining, the trader should have been a seller, since the level obviously had been too high in the past.

OPTION PREMIUM INDICES

The CBOE calculates a dual index of option premiums. The index estimates the value of a theoretical call and put option on a stock of average market volatility selling at $100. The options have a strike price of $100 and expire in 180 days. Figure 9-2 (see end of Appendix C "CBOE Internet page charts") shows the put and call premium levels, according to the CBOE Put and Call Option Premium Indices, since the inception of listed option trading. As the chart shows, both put and call premium levels rise and fall together. This is due to the direct relationship between the two, and it reflects the fact that the most important factor in option pricing is the volatility assumption, which is the same for both contracts.

Of the two indices, put premium levels might be the most revealing and the easiest for investors to understand. A purchased put option represents the right, but not the obligation, to sell a stock at the strike price for a stated period of time. Puts are often used as insurance to protect a profit in the underlying stock. The seller of a put can be viewed as taking a position on risk equivalent to that of an insurance company. Just as in the more traditional forms of insurance, premium level is a key consideration. If insurance premiums turn out to have been too high, the insurance company will make a higher than expected profit. Higher profits attract other companies to the business and eventually lead to lower premiums. The same thing happens in the case of put options. Figure 9-3 (see end of Appendix C "CBOE Internet page charts") shows the level of option premiums in 1993.

As is the case with the put-call ratio, a chart on the level of option premiums provides valuable perspective. Traditionally, one can be found each week in "The Striking Price" column of Barron's. This chart shows the trend of premium levels over the last six months.

The long-term picture of premium levels suggests a cycle. In the insurance business, the premium cycle is an important consideration. The same might be true for the listed option business, although the history of the business is still too short to make such a statement with certainty. If so, the volatility cycle can provide additional insight into the underlying market. In addition, the long-term chart shows that the difference between put and call premium levels is not constant. The reason for this variance is the conversion process discussed previously. A put option can be converted into a call by simply buying the stock while holding the put. Actually, the process of conversion is one of the keys to efficient option pricing. The conversion process means that the long put, long stock position is equal in risk and return to a long call, long T-bill position. In order for this relationship to be true, the call option usually has a higher value than the put. This is true because under most conditions the dividend yield on the stock is lower than the T-bill yield. As short-term interest rates rise and fall, the spread between the value of the call and the put premium index changes. When the yield on T-bills rises, the value of the equity should decline, all other factors being the same. This tends to hold the put-call relationship steady.

Confidence Index: In actual practice, it has often been observed that at times both short-term yields and stock prices increase. This leads to an increase in the spread between bond and stock yields. Barron's publishes a number of yield spread indicators, the best known being the Confidence Index. The Confidence Index is calculated by dividing a high-grade bond index by an intermediate-grade index. Changes in the relationship are used to measure the confidence of investors. At some point it is assumed that investors will become overconfident. The CBOE Put and Call Option Premium Indices provide a simple way of calculating a yield spread. Since the results are based on a 180-day assumption, simply multiplying the spread by two gives an annualized spread. Figure 9-4 (see end of Appendix C "CBOE Internet page charts") shows how the relationship has changed in the past.

CBOE Market Volatility Index: In 1993, the Chicago Board Options Exchange introduced the CBOE Market Volatility Index. The CBOE Market Volatility Index, known by its ticker symbol VIX, measures the volatility of the U.S. equity market. It provides investors with up-to-the-minute market estimates of expected volatility by using real-time OEX index option bid/ask quotes.

The VIX is calculated by averaging S&P 100 Stock Index at-the-money put and call implied volatilities. The availability of the index enables investors to make more informed investment decisions. Figure 9-5 (see end of Appendix C "CBOE Internet page charts") presents the VIX history, consisting of daily minute-by-minute index values for the five-year period from January 4, 1988, through December 31, 1992. The chart also includes the S&P 100 OEX index for the same time period. Note that for the time period shown, all of the spikes in volatility accompanied market downturns and significant events that affected the market.

A study of Figure 9-5 (see end of Appendix C "CBOE Internet page charts") reveals a great deal about the relationship between the market and volatility. Note the tendency of the VIX to spike upward during periods of market decline. The high level of volatility at the beginning (left side) of the chart is a direct result of the October 1987 market decline, which is not shown. Volatility then declined steadily until late 1989. The spike in volatility at that time was the result of the sharp one-day market correction in October. Another sharp increase in volatility occurred in August and September 1990, the period during which Iraq invaded Kuwait. In January 1991, volatility rose sharply again, just before the initiative led by the United States known as Operation Desert Storm. The last peak in volatility displayed in the chart reflected the downturn in the market, occurring one month before the United States presidential election in November 1992.

The tendency of market volatility to expand during market downturns is clear from the illustration above. This tendency is the subject of numerous academic studies of the options market. Perhaps the best way to understand the relationship between volatility and market declines is to look at the options market from a "put" perspective.

A put is the option market equivalent of an insurance policy. An investor may purchase a put to insure a sale price for the underlying asset. The seller (writer) of a put may be viewed as the equivalent of an insurance underwriter. The put writer accepts a premium in return for accepting a risk, which in this case is ownership of the underlying asset. In the insurance business, premiums rise following significant negative events (such as a hurricane). In the options business, market volatility, the critical factor in determining put premium levels, increases in periods of market distress.

The same factor that leads to an increase in put premium levels, increased volatility, causes call option premiums to increase at the same time. Thus, put premium levels and call premium levels move together because they are both related to volatility. This relationship is critical to the option strategist. High call premiums during periods of market distress are the opposite of what most investors would expect.

A similar pattern would be observed if we looked at a chart of the implied volatility of an individual stock. The average investor has to search a little to find volatility numbers. Many online computer services compute an implied volatility for each underlying stock every day. The Daily Graphs Option Guide includes the historic volatility each week in its statistical section. Sooner or later the media will discover that implied volatility is an important statistic, and it will be included along with stock dividend and price earnings multiples in the daily stock quotations page. When looking at an implied volatility for a stock, remember that the number can vary from option to option within a family of options. It can also change for in-the-money or out-of-the-money types. For this reason, most services use a filtering process, or weight more heavily the more liquid at-the-money contracts. The most important consideration is that the service remain consistent in applying its rules. Remember also that as a stock's options become less liquid, the implied volatility becomes a volatile number. This would suggest that decisions based on implied volatility would be better for liquid issues than those less often traded.

LIST OF THE 100 STOCKS INCLUDED IN THE OEX INDEX
30 June 1997

Ticker Letters	Company Name	Shares	Price	Market Value	% of 100	CUSIP
ALT	Allegheny Teledyne Inc.	174.32	25.75	4488.74	0.16	17415100
AA	Aluminum Co. of America	173.403	73.625	12766.796	0.46	22249106
AEP	American Electric Power	187.435	40.75	7637.976	0.28	25537101
AXP	American Express	473.87	69.5	32933.965	1.2	25816109
AGC	American General	203.365	44.25	8998.901	0.33	26351106
AIG	American Int'l Group	469.532	135.375	63562.895	2.31	26874107
AIT	Ameritech	549.391	65.5	35985.111	1.31	30954101
AN	Amoco	497.255	89.375	44442.166	1.62	31905102
AMP	AMP Inc.	219.575	41.125	9030.022	0.33	31897101
T	AT&T Corp.	1620.284	36.875	59747.973	2.18	1957109
ARC	Atlantic Richfield	161.082	145.5	23437.431	0.85	48825103
AVP	Avon Products	132.843	63.75	8468.741	0.31	54303102
BHI	Baker Hughes	145.429	37.5	5453.588	0.2	57224107
BAC	BankAmerica Corp.	358.826	116.875	41937.789	1.53	66050105
BAX	Baxter International Inc.	272.932	52.75	14397.163	0.52	71813109
BEL	Bell Atlantic	437.769	70.	30643.83	1.12	77853109
BS	Bethlehem Steel	111.653	10.	1116.53	0.04	87509105
BDK	Black & Decker Corp.	94.26	34.75	3275.709	0.12	91797100
BA	Boeing Company	358.34	105.25	37715.285	1.37	97023105
BCC	Boise Cascade	48.472	38.	1841.936	0.07	97383103
BMY	Bristol-Myers Squibb	1001.588	73.375	73491.52	2.68	110122108
BC	Brunswick Corp.	98.419	30.5	3001.78	0.11	117043109
BNI	Burlington Northern Sant.	152.95283	83.	12695.016	0.46	12189T104
CEN	Ceridian Corp	80.366	36.75	2953.451	0.11	15677T106
CHA	Champion International	95.547	49.375	4717.633	0.17	158525105
C	Chrysler Corp.	702.581	31.75	22306.947	0.81	171196108
CI	CIGNA Corp.	75.181	173.75	13062.699	0.48	125509109
CSCO	Cisco Systems	657.416	67.75	44539.934	1.62	17275R102
CCI	Citicorp	463.217	114.375	52980.444	1.93	173034109
CGP	Coastal Corp.	105.24	50.125	5275.155	0.19	190441105
KO	Coca Cola Co.	2488.162	68.25	169817.057	6.18	191216100
CL	Colgate-Palmolive	293.778	62.	18214.236	0.66	194162103
COL	Columbia/HCA Healthcare	671.319	36.625	24587.058	0.9	197677107

CSC	Computer Sciences Corp.	76.491	77.375	5918.491	0.22	205363104
DAL	Delta Air Lines	73.141	93.75	6856.969	0.25	247361108
DEC	Digital Equipment	157.264	35.875	5641.846	0.21	253849103
DOW	Dow Chemical	242.993	83.375	20259.541	0.74	260543103
DD	Du Pont (EI)	562.977	108.875	61294.121	2.23	263534109
EK	Eastman Kodak	333.247	82.875	27617.845	1.01	277461109
ETR	Entergy Corp.	230.922	26.375	6090.568	0.22	29364G103
XON	Exxon Corp.	2483.562	59.25	147151.049	5.36	302290101
FDX	Federal Express	114.0	52.375	5974.678	0.22	313309106
FCN	First Chicago NBD Corp.	318.838	59.25	18891.152	0.69	31945A100
FLR	Fluor Corp	83.9	52.875	4437.376	0.16	343861100
F	Ford Motor	1185.475	37.5	44455.313	1.62	345370100
GD	General Dynamics	63.075	74.875	4722.741	0.17	369550108
GE	General Electric	3292.842	60.375	198805.336	7.24	369604103
GM	General Motors	755.968	57.25	43279.168	1.58	370442105
GWF	Great Western Financial	137.71	48.5	6678.935	0.24	391442100
HAL	Halliburton Co.	125.201	77.375	9687.427	0.35	406216101
HET	Harrah's Entertainment	102.901	18.625	1916.531	0.07	413619107
HRS	Harris Corp.	39.003	88.625	3456.641	0.13	413875105
HIG	Hartford Financial SvcG	117.451	78.	9161.178	0.33	416515104
HNZ	Heinz (HJ)	368.233	43.	15834.019	0.58	423074103
HWP	Hewlett-Packard	1014.123	51.5	52227.335	1.9	428236103
HM	Homestake Mining	146.672	13.875	2035.074	0.07	437614100
HON	Honeywell	126.755	72.75	9221.426	0.34	438506107
INTC	Intel Corp.	820.6	151.5	124320.9	4.53	458140100
IBM	International Bus Machi	1035.092	86.5	89535.458	3.26	459200101
IFF	International Flav/Frag	110.325	44.375	4895.672	0.18	459506101
IP	International Paper	300.156	48.	14407.488	0.52	460146103
JNJ	Johnson & Johnson	1331.719	59.875	79736.675	2.9	478160104
KM	K mar	484.361	14.	6781.054	0.25	482584109
LTD	Limited, The	271.062	20.25	5489.006	0.2	532716107
MKG	Mallinckrodt Group Inc.	73.965	37.375	2764.442	0.1	561232109
MAY	May Dept Stores	244.904	47.125	11541.101	0.42	577778103
MCD	McDonald's Corp.	697.713	50.25	35060.078	1.28	580135101
MCIC	MCI Communications	684.902	38.375	26283.114	0.96	552673105
MRK	Merck & Co.	1205.44	89.875	108338.92	3.94	589331107
MER	Merrill Lynch	164.698	106.	17457.988	0.64	590188108
MMM	.Minn Mining & Mfg.	417.993	91.75	38350.858	1.4	604059105

MOB	Mobil Corp.	393.964	139.875	55105.715	2.01	607059102
MTC	Monsanto Company	588.02	44.	25872.88	0.94	611662107
NSM	National Semiconductor	139.535	28.125	3924.422	0.14	637640103
NSC	Norfolk Southern Corp.	125.088	97.125	12149.172	0.44	655844108
NT	Northern Telecom	258.384	84.	21704.256	0.79	665815106
NYN	Nynex	439.989	53.75	23649.409	0.86	670768100
OXY	Occidental Petroleum	328.907	23.25	7647.088	0.28	674599105
ORCL	Oracle Corp.	676.	46.625	31518.5	1.15	68389X105
PEP	PepsiCo Inc.	553.55	36.75	57092.963	2.08	713448108
PNU	Pharmacia & Upjohn, Inc.	508.096	34.625	17592.824	0.64	716941109
PRD	Polaroid Corp.	45.447	51.	2317.797	0.08	731095105
RAL	Ralston-Ralston Purina G	106.32	85.25	9063.78	0.33	751277302
RTN	Raytheon Co.	236.036	47.75	11270.719	0.41	755111101
ROK	Rockwell International	218.968	64.5	4123.436	0.51	773903109
SLB	Schlumberger Ltd.	246.288	119.125	29339.058	1.07	806857108
S	Sears, Roebuck & Co.	391.521	49.125	19233.469	0.7	812387108
SO	Southern Co.	673.653	21.25	14315.126	0.52	842587107
TAN	Tandy Corp.	58.278	54.	3147.012	0.11	875382103
TEK	Tektronix Inc.	33.003	57.375	1893.547	0.07	879131100
TXN	Texas Instruments	190.412	89.875	17113.279	0.62	882508104
TOY	Toys R Us Hldg Cos	290.421	31.125	9039.354	0.33	892335100
UCM	Unicom Corp.	215.654	22.75	4906.129	0.18	904911104
UIS	Unisys Corp.	174.823	6.875	1201.908	0.04	909214108
UTX	United Technologies	237.347	80.375	19076.765	0.69	913017109
WMT	Wal-Mart Stores	2293.855	29.75	68242.186	2.48	931142103
DIS	Walt Disney Co.	675.099	81.875	55273.731	2.01	254687106
WY	Weyerhaeuser Corp.	198.311	49.875	9890.761	0.36	962166104
WMB	Williams Cos	156.983	44.125	6926.875	0.25	969457100
XRX	Xerox Corp.	324.562	67.75	21989.076	0.8	984121103
Total Market Value		2746724.219				

WHAT INDUSTRY GROUPS
ARE THE OEX COMPONENTS DRAWN FROM?

As of January 31, 1995 major industry sectors represented in the index, according to Standard and Poor's were as follows:

Consumer Goods (21.69%)

Electric Utilities (2.18%)

Energy (13.01%)

Financial (8.05%)

Health Care (9.51%)

High-Tech (23.26%)

Intermediate Goods (8.53%)

Transportation (1.31%)

Other (12.46%)

CBOE INTERNET PAGE CHARTS

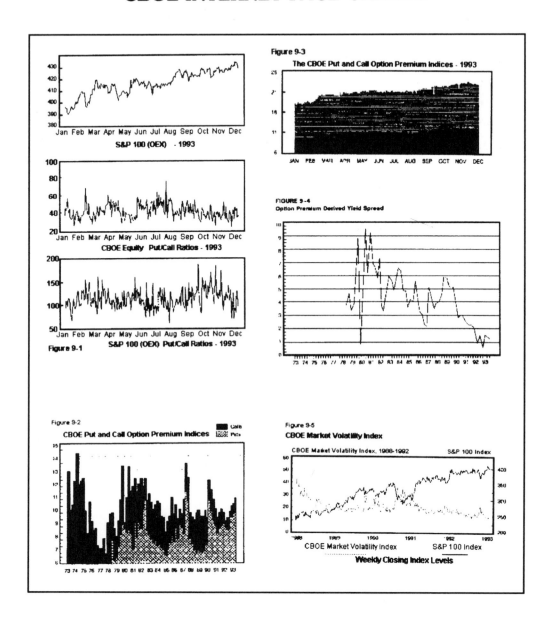

Figure 9-1

Figure 9-2

Figure 9-3

FIGURE 9-4

Figure 9-5

APPENDIX D

LIST OF INDEX OPTIONS TRADED IN THE U.S.

According to the "Directory of Exchange Listed Options," a booklet supplied by Benjamin and Jerold, Discount Option and Stock Brokerage, dated October 1996, the following are all the Index Options traded on the various exchanges in the United States and their symbols.

A = American Stock Exchange
C = Chicago Board Options Exchange
N = New York Stock Exchange
P = Pacific Stock Exchange
X = Philadelphia Stock Exchange

When placing an order, many brokers ask that you use these index option symbols followed by two letters to specify Call or Put, the month and strike price. These letter codes which are specified by the CBOE are detailed in Figure 7.1 of Chapter 7.

Euro means European style index options which can only be exercised on the last day of the option month. Amer means American style options which can be exercised at any time during the option month.

INDEX OPTIONS

Symbol	Name	Exchange
XAL	AMEX Airline Open/Euro Index	A
BTK	AMEX Biotech Open/Euro Index	A
XCI	AMEX Computer Tech Close/Amer	A
EUR	AMEX Eurotop 100 Open/Euro Index	A
HUI	AMEX Gold BUGS Open/Euro Index	A
HKO	AMEX Hong Kong Option Index Close/Euro	A
XII	AMEX Institutional Index Open/Euro	A
IIX	AMEX Inter@ctive Week Internet Open/Euro Index	A
JPN	AMEX Japan Open/Euro Index	A
XMI	AMEX Major Market Index Close/Euro	A

MXY	AMEX Mexico Open/Euro Index	A
CRX	AMEX Morgan Stanley Commodity Related Equity	A
CMR	AMEX Morgan Stanley Consumer Open/Euro Index	A
CYC	AMEX Morgan Stanley Cyclical Open/Euro Index	A
HMO	AMEX Morgan Stanley Healthcare Payor Open/Euro Index	A
RXP	AMEX Morgan Stanley Healthcare Product Open/Euro Index	A
RXH	AMEX Morgan Stanley Healthcare Provider Open/Euro Index	A
MSH	AMEX Morgan Stanley High-Tech 35 Open/Euro Index	A
XNG	AMEX Natural Gas Open/Euro Index	A
NWX	AMEX Networking Open/Euro Index	A
XTC	AMEX North Amer Telecom Euro/Open Index	A
XOI	AMEX Oil Close/Amer Index	A
DRG	AMEX Pharmaceutical Open/Euro Index	A
MID	AMEX S&P Midcap 400 Open/Euro Index	A
XBD	AMEX Securities Broker/Dealer Open/Euro Index	A
AUX	CBOE Automotive Index	C
BGX	CBOE Biotech Open/Euro Index	C
CWX	CBOE Comp Software Open/Euro	C
CXX/CWX	CBOE Comp Software Open/Euro	C
GAX	CBOE Gaming Open/Euro Index	C
GTX	CBOE Global Telecom Index	C
INX	CBOE Internet Index	C
ISX	CBOE Israel Index Open/Euro	C
LTX	CBOE Latin 15 Index	C
MEX	CBOE Mexico Index	C
MZX/MEX	CBOE Mexico Index	C
NIK	CBOE Nikkei 300 Index Cl/Euro	C
RIX	CBOE Reits Index	C
OEX	CBOE S&P 100 Close/Amer Index	C
OEZ/OEX	CBOE S&P 100 Close/Amer Index	C
CPS/SPX	CBOE S&P 500 Caps Euro Index	C
NSX/SPX	CBOE S&P 500 Close/Euro Index	C
SPQ/SPX	CBOE S&P 500 EOQ Close/Euro	C
SPB/SPX	CBOE S&P 500 Index	C
SPX	CBOE S&P 500 Open/Euro Index	C
NSZ/SPX	CBOE S&P 500 Open/Euro Index	C
SPZ/SPX	CBOE S&P 500 Open/Euro Index	C
SGX	CBOE S&P Barra Growth Open/Euro	C

SVX	CBOE S&P Barra Value Open/Euro	C
TXX	CBOE Technology Index (Open)	C
TCX	CBOE Telecom Open/Euro Index	C
EVX	Environment Sector Open/Euro	C
FSA/FSX	Ft-Se 100 Open/Euro Index	C
FSB/FSX	Ft-Se 100 Open/Euro Index	C
FSX	Ft-Se 100 Open/Euro Index	C
HCX	Healthcare Sector Open/Euro	C
IUX	Insurance Sector Open/Euro Index	C
NDX	NASDAQ - 100 Open/Euro Index	C
NCZ/NDX	NASDAQ - 100 Open/Euro Index	C
NDZ/NDX	NASDAQ - 100 Open/Euro Index	C
NYA	NYSE Composite Index	N
PLN	PHLX Airline Sector - Open/Euro	X
BKX	PHLX KBW Bank Sector - Open/Euro	X
FPP	PHLX Forest & Paper Sector - Open/Euro	X
XAU	PHLX Gold/Silver Sector - Close/Amer	X
XOC	PHLX National OTC Sector - Close/Euro	X
PNX	PHLX Phone Sector - Open/Amer	X
SOX	PHLX Semiconductor Sector - Open/Amer	X
HFX	PHLX SuperCap Sector - Open/Euro	X
TPX	PHLX U.S. TOP 100 Sector - Open/Euro	X
UTY	PHLX Utility Sector - Close/Euro	X
VLE	PHLX Value Line Composite Index - Close/Euro	X
PSE	PSE Technology Index (PSE Tech 100) Open/Euro	P
RUT	Russell 2000 Open/Euro Index	C
BIX	S&P Banks Sector Open/Euro Index	C
CEX	S&P Chemicals Sector Open/Euro	C
RLX	S&P Retail Sector Open/Euro	C
SML	S&P Small Cap 600	C
TRX	S&P Trans Open/Euro Index	C
WSX	PSE Small Cap Index Open/Euro	P

APPENDIX E

DISCOUNT BROKERS IN CHICAGO & LONDON AND INTERNET BROKERS

There are many discount brokers available, but I have good personal experience with those listed below and they do specialize in option trading. They will give you rapid and accurate confirmations by FAX or phone of any option trades you make with them. Also their commissions are very low. B & J will trade OEX options. Union Cal Ltd. will trade either SEI options or OEX options and have exceptionally low commissions.

Attn. Mr. Kopf   Mr. Duncan Dunn
Benjamin & Jerold Brokerage   Union CAL Limited
141 W. Jackson   39 Cornhill
Suite 3550   London EC 3V 3ND
Chicago, IL 60604   United Kingdom
FAX 312 554 0268   FAX: 44 171 522 3317

There are now many Brokers that trade using the Internet. You can find them by browsing the Net. I recommend the one below since they have been Barron's first choice for the last two years. I use their Internet site to obtain OEX Option Quotations (delayed 20 minutes) and almost real time intraday charts for OEX. You must register to access their Internet site, but once registered the access is free (no cost).

Lombard Brokerage, Inc
http://www.lombard.com/cgi-bin/PACenter/PAQuote

APPENDIX F

ORDERING EXCEL OPTION TRADING WORKBOOKS FROM THE AUTHOR

CAVEAT: It should be noted that all option trades, patterns, charts, systems, etc., discussed in the products offered by the author are not to be construed as specific advisory recommendations. Further note that no method of trading or investing is foolproof or without risk and difficulties, and past performance is no guarantee of future performance. All ideas and material presented are for the reader to consider and any trades made by the reader are strictly made by the decision of the reader at his or her own risk and are not to be construed as the responsibility of the Author nor of Windsor Books.

Please note that if you wish to purchase any of the items listed below, you should send an e-mail (my preference), letter, or FAX to the addresses listed below to the attention of the author. After purchase, if you need technical help or need answers to technical questions, you should address them to the author who will provide them from Spain. In no circumstance is Windsor Books responsible for the proper operation of the software or for any technical support. All proper operation and technical support will be provided by the author and if you are not satisfied with the product, the author offers you a money back guarantee.

If you are on the Internet you may be interested in the two EXCEL workbooks called OEXSTRG6.XLS (described in Appendix A) and SAMNMOD.XLS. These 2 workbooks and a 22 Page User's Manual are available for $195 on two 3.5" diskettes. This set of workbooks allows you to obtain real-time quotes from Interquote (a Wisconsin Software Co, about $27/mo, web address: http://www.interquote.com/cgi-bin/qs), to copy your portfolio quotes and enter them into the worksheet called Da_Quot of the OEXSTRG6 workbook by clicking on the Enter Data button that causes some Visual Basic code to be executed. The end result is that during the trading day the market indicators and computations of open Short Spreads, Covered Short Spreads, or Long Calls or Puts are automatically updated so you have instant information about the market and any open positions you have. The workbook called SAMNMOD includes some other unique market indicators (Oriental Candle stick indicator, Midi Indicator, and Samn Candle indicator), a market forecast and a Max-Min chart. All these charts are updated when the Real Time quote is entered into OEXSTRG6.XLS. This trading system is good for Intraday Trading using the Delta Strategy (described in Chapter 4) as well as naked short spreads and covered short spreads.

If you are trading SEI on the London market, I have 3 EXCEL workbooks available called FTSDATA1 (described in Chapter 8). The 3 workbooks are available on two 3.5" diskettes for $195 which includes a User's Manual. The main workbook FTSMKTV2.XLS includes work sheets for copying the LIFFE end of day SEI Option Premiums and the LIFFE all statistics which give the SEI Bid, Offer, Settle, High, and Low Premiums for each strike price as well as trading volume and open interest.

I have a set of 3 EXCEL5 workbooks called OPTRADE5 (described in Appendix B) which have the spread sheets and charts to do OEX short spread trading, covered short spread trading, and Long Call and Put trading. These workbooks contain charts with market signals to tell you when the market is trending up or down. This set of workbooks includes the Delta strategy for Long Calls and Puts including the charts that signal when to open a Call or Put and when to close them. These same charts also tell you when your short Call or Put position may be threatened. These 3 workbooks are available on two 3.5" diskettes for $195 including a 20 page User's Manual.

I have a WINDOWS computer program called OPSTRGY2 which I developed using Microsoft Visual Basic to be used as an add-on to the workbooks of OPTRADE5 and includes a special workbook called STOCHRT.XLS in order for OPTRADE5 to provide the linking to OPSTRGY2. You can use OPTRADE5 without OPSTRGY2, but the latter needs to access the charts and segments of spread sheets provided by OPTRADE5. The OPSTRGY2 Windows program has a main menu for opening the strategies described in the book including the naked short spreads, two sided covered short spreads, bear covered short spreads or bull covered short spreads or for changing a threatened short Call or Put. It also has menu items for opening Delta strategy Long Calls and Long Puts for those who want to do day trading and a Help menu for how to do the various tasks. This program comes on a 3.5" disk with user's manual for $95 when ordered as an add-on to OPTRADE5. When ordered later the price is $149, a bit more because of the extra handling and updating required.

I have a compiled version of a program written in MS QWICKBASIC for naked short spread trading for running on an IBM compatible PC. It is called OPTEVAL7 and is available on a 3.5" diskette with user's manual for $50 plus $5 for handling and shipping expenses.

I have a WINDOWS stand-alone (compiled) computer program called OPSTRGY1 which I developed using Microsoft Visual Basic. The program has a main menu for opening a naked short spread, changing a threatened short spread, and switching to a Combo spread during strong up or down markets. This program comes on a 3.5" disk with user's manual for $95 + $5 shipping and handling.

All of these computer software tools require an IBM compatible PC with 386 or better processor with at least 8 MB RAM. The EXCEL spread sheets require EXCEL 5 or better with WINDOWS 3.1 or better (I use them with WINDOWS 95 & OFFICE 95 which I strongly recommend).

I also have available a Monthly Newsletter and compilation of past Newsletters in a soft back book summarized below:

- Newsletter Subscription Price $120 per year: Air Mailed the Saturday after Option expiration

- Newsletter: $120 per year: E-mailed within 2 hours after option expiration, including the charts as an attachment to the e-mail. (If you don't know how to load chart attachments to your files, ask your Internet Server's technical advisor.)

- Newsletter sent by FAX (2 hrs. after the 3rd Fri. Expiration) $240 / year

- Two Soft back Books at $40 each plus $5 postage: *Compilation of Jon Schiller's Options Trading Newsletters: (1) March 93 to June 95 and (2) July 95 to Jan 98*

One gracious reader said about the newsletter compilations: "I have really been enjoying reading your compilation of letters, 1993-95. Looking beyond the nuts and bolts of the research and techniques, I've found something that really interests me. That is, the evolution of strategies you have produced in response to the non-static character of the market. I enjoy seeing your mind at work. Moreover, I appreciate the fact that you have a hard-earned, well grounded education in the cognitive skills of careful, meaningful research toward narrowly focused ends. I am trying to differentiate here between what you do and what virtually the entire pack of "famous gurus" and "well known traders" do. As I see it, they are individually almost incapable of clear, fruitful research. The results produced by the "pack," as I'm sure you know, is largely junk which is not viable for trading. In short, I really applaud your mind and your work."

If you want any of the items I referred to above just send a personal check to Jon Schiller at the address below and they will be airmailed to you by the author from Spain.

Jon Schiller
Marcos de Obregón 6-2C
29016 Málaga
ESPAÑA (SPAIN)
FAX 34 95 221 77 10
E-MAIL jonsch@vnet.es
Website: http://www.vnet.es/~jonsch/